# Shakespeare and YouTube

## RELATED TITLES

*Shakespeare's Theatres and the Effects of Performance*, edited
by Farah Karim-Cooper and Tiffany Stern
*Nine Lives of William Shakespeare*, Graham Holderness
*Shakespeare for Young People: Productions, Versions and
Adaptations*, Abigail Rokison
*Emotional Excess on the Shakespearean Stage: Passion's
Slaves*, Bridget Escolme

# Shakespeare and YouTube

# New Media Forms of the Bard

*Stephen O'Neill*

B L O O M S B U R Y

LONDON • NEW DELHI • NEW YORK • SYDNEY

**Bloomsbury Methuen Drama**

An imprint of Bloomsbury Publishing Plc

50 Bedford Square     1385 Broadway
London     New York
WC1B 3DP     NY 10018
UK     USA

**www.bloomsbury.com**

**Bloomsbury is a registered trade mark of Bloomsbury Publishing Plc**

First published 2014

**British Library Cataloguing-in-Publication Data**
A catalogue record for this book is available from the British Library.

ISBN: HB: 978-1-4411-2092-2
ePDF: 978-1-4725-0028-1
ePub: 978-1-4725-0028-1

**Library of Congress Cataloging-in-Publication Data**
A catalog record for this book is available from the Library of Congress.

Typeset by Fakenham Prepress Solutions, Fakenham, Norfolk NR21 8NN
Printed and bound in Great Britain

*In memory of my parents, Vera and Heuston*

# CONTENTS

# ACKNOWLEDGEMENTS

I have incurred many debts in the writing of this book, which was completed during a university sabbatical that freed me from teaching duties. I would especially like to thank Professor Philip Nolan (President, NUI Maynooth) and Professor Chris Morash, School of English, for granting the research leave. My sincere thanks to Margaret Bartley and Emily Hockley at Arden Shakespeare for their extraordinary patience and encouragement throughout. Thanks to Ronnie Hanna and Dominic West of Fakenham Prepress Solutions for their diligence and efficiency. The anonymous reader for the press provided insightful and generous feedback. For the initial interest in the project, thanks to David Avital and also to Mark Thornton Burnett for strongly supporting it in its earliest form.

The ideas and arguments in this book have long been in gestation and were first aired as conference and seminar papers at the European Shakespeare Research Association in Pisa (2009) and Weimar (2010), and the European Society for the Study of English conference in Turin (2010). I would like to thank the seminar participants whose responses, questions and observations helped me to reflect on arguments and develop new directions. Especial thanks to Maurizio Calbi, Laura Campillo Arnaiz, Tom Cartelli, Mariacristina Cavecchi, Anna-Maria Cimitile, Janet Clare, Douglas Lanier, Alessandra Marino, Ángel-Luis Pujante and Mariangela Tempera; and to Sharee Deckard for inviting me to give a paper as part of the Research Seminar of the School of English, Film and Drama, University College Dublin (2012). An earlier version of Chapter 2 appeared in the special issue of *Anglistica*, 'Shakespeare in Media: Old and New'; my thanks to the editors, Katherine

Rowe and Anna-Maria Cimitile for their helpful suggestions. An earlier version of Chapter 4 is forthcoming in the special issue of *The Shakespeare International Yearbook* (Ashgate, 2014) on 'Digital Shakespeares', edited by Hugh Craig and Brett D. Hirsch. The book also took shape through teaching: particular thanks are due to the students in my elective seminar on 'Contemporary Shakespeare', who responded to YouTube Shakespeare with a genuine enthusiasm that enabled me to look at material anew; to Liam O'Dowd for his earlier work on the YouTube channel; and to students in the elective on 'Shakespeare, Feminism and Popular Culture', who found more examples of Ophelia than one pair of eyes could ever have spotted. Claire McAvinia provided much needed advice from a teaching and learning perspective and my thanks to her for inviting me to contribute to the Teaching Showcase at NUI Maynooth.

Colleagues and friends have continued to offer encouragement, support and practical advice. Warm thanks to Maurizio Calbi, Padraig Kirwan, Catherine Leen and Moynagh Sullivan, who each took time to carefully read earlier drafts and provide extensive feedback, and to Kylie Jarrett for not only indulging my questions about new media, but also pointing me in adroit directions. Needless to say, I take responsibility for any errors that may have occurred. Colleagues in the Department of English and the Iontas Building more generally have been supportive, often ensuring that it lives up to its name ('wonder'): to Moynagh Sullivan, in the office next door, for her support and good humour; and to Amanda Bent, Conrad Brunstrom, Denis Condon, Ide Corley (and to her son, Daire, for identifying a track in a video), Tracy Flaherty, Oona Frawley, Sonia Howell, Declan Kavanagh, Margaret Kelleher, Jeneen Naji, Tom O'Connor, Catherine O'Leary, Maggie O'Neill and Stephanie Rains warm thanks are also due. Family have proved a source of continued support: my thanks to my siblings, Eamonn, Brian, Peter, Helen and the extended network of O'Neills for always putting things in perspective. Friends, too, have provided support: to Susan Cahill, Justin Dolan, James Foster, Gwen Horan, Aoife Leahy, Jane McGann (R.I.P.), Gillian O'Brien, Shaun Regan, Margaret Robson and Andrew Whelan warm thanks. I would also like to use this opportunity to thank the collegial network of Shakespeare and early modern scholars that has formed through the Irish Renaissance Seminar, in particular Victoria Brownlee, Mark Thornton Burnett, Daniel Carey, Danielle Clarke, Derek Dunne, Anne Fogarty, Jane Grogan, Andrew King, Edel Lamb, Patrick Lonergan, Naomi McAreavey, Adrian Streete and Ramona Wray. And to the convivial atmosphere of the Shakespeare Association of America Conference (Toronto, 2013) and to Christy Desmet, Kyle Diroberto, Kirk Hendershott-Kraetzer, Grace Ioppolo, Jessica McCall, Jennifer Roberts-Smith and Geoff Way, who made the seminar on Social Media Shakespeare convened by Maurizio Calbi and myself such a pleasure.

Finally, my sincere gratitude to the hundreds of YouTubers, without whose creative projects this book would never have come to fruition. The enthusiasm with which individuals responded to my email requests to cite their videos reminded me just how much Shakespeare and YouTube have become prized dimensions not just of amateur culture but perhaps of people's everyday lives too.

*Stephen O'Neill, Dublin, 2013*

# ABBREVIATIONS AND ONLINE RESOURCES

## A note on the text

All Shakespeare quotations are from the Arden Shakespeare, Third series (General Editors: Richard Proudfoot, Ann Thompson, David Scott-Kastan and H. R Woudhuysen) and, where not yet available, from the Second series.

## Abbreviations

**DHQ**   Digital Humanities Quarterly

**ELH**   English Literary History

**IPEDR** International Proceedings of Economics Development and Research

**JeDEM** Journal of eDemocracy and Open Government

**MLQ**   Modern Language Quarterly

**NWSA**  National Women's Studies Association Journal

**PMLA**  Publications of the Modern Language Association

**RSC**   Royal Shakespeare Company

**SQ**    Shakespeare Quarterly

SS     Shakespeare Survey

SSt     Shakespeare Studies

TWC     Transformative Works and Culture

# Online resources

Videos are identified by title, upload date and view count. Unless otherwise stated, urls are provided in the notes. All of the videos discussed in the book are arranged in playlists on the YouTube channel http://www.youtube.com/user/Shakespeareonutube

# Introduction: Interpreting YouTube Shakespeare

*The web of our life is of a mingled yarn, good and ill together.*

SHAKESPEARE, *ALL'S WELL THAT ENDS WELL* (IV.3.68)[1]

YouTube hardly requires any introduction. As the dominant video-sharing platform within the contemporary networked mediascape – reportedly attracting more than 1 billion views per month – using YouTube has become part of everyday activity and carries considerable cultural currency.[2] Some of these terms might also be applied, with varying degrees of emphasis, to Shakespeare, that most recognizable and accommodating cultural entity. Yet YouTube's surface associations with the instant gratification of the gag or the recorded prank may appear to put it at odds with Shakespeare, at least when the playwright is conceived in literary terms, or as a token of high culture. Searching Shakespeare on YouTube is something of a niche activity, while noticing the latest YouTube meme or trending video is not. Where the latter activities are habitual to YouTube culture, the former evokes a discrete subject category. As such, the scholarly pursuit of this niche might appear a self-validating enterprise, that familiar scenario of the Shakespearean finding new sites of Shakespeare's construction particularly compelling, because by affirming the vitality of Shakespeare, they also affirm the critic's interests.[3] For all that, seismic shifts are afoot. As YouTube becomes a habitual element of the Shakespeare classroom, as Shakespeare theatres recognize YouTube's value as a promotional space, as cultural institutions like the Folger Shakespeare Library and Shakespeare Birthplace Trust use YouTube to disseminate their activities to the wider public, as actors upload their show reels, as Shakespeare texts are mashed with a pop music video or adapted into a meme, and as the easily embedded YouTube video is shared across media, a study melding YouTube and Shakespeare looks a less specialized and less quirky combination than we may first think. Indeed, as a dynamic hermeneutic field, the transmedia Shakespeare of YouTube marks a fascinating point of intersection for concepts such as high and popular culture. It may even prove a significant location for constructing them.

YouTube is a space where anyone with access to a computer and an Internet connection can share their response to Shakespeare, participating in the social network. Users access a vast repository of Shakespeare material, while at the same time contributing new forms of do-it-yourself Shakespeare. A search under Shakespeare generally returns over 1 million results.[4] Within these results, we can determine what plays prove most recurrent: 'Shakespeare, Romeo and Juliet' generates over 86,000 results, making it by far the most cited play on YouTube. *Hamlet* comes second, with over 68,000 results. *Othello* accounts for some 25,000 videos. YouTube thus affirms the cultural and curricular prominence of certain Shakespearean texts over others (for instance, *Timon of Athens*, the late tragedy co-authored with Thomas Middleton, generates a comparatively low 603 results, though this most likely reflects the absence of a major film adaptation of the play). As these figures attest, the small screens of YouTube grant access to an accidental archive of Shakespeareana, to user-generated Shakespeares and to such genres as the video mashup (combining one or more audio tracks with moving images, sometimes with ironic effect), the vlog (or video diary) and the fan-made movie trailer. YouTube is now one of the dominant media through which Shakespeare is iterated, produced and received in the twenty-first century. As such, it invites a thorough investigation into the culture of online video creation, and its effect on Shakespeare's meanings and cultural value is timely.[5]

Irreverent or simplistic, celebratory or parodic, the YouTube Shakespeare video is many things and stretches the already pliable Bard in new directions. For instance, *Dr Seuss vs Shakespeare: Epic Rap Battles of History* #12 (uploaded 17 August 2011) currently ranks the highest Shakespeare view count, with over 55 million views.[6] The video reworks the format of the now defunct MTV series *Celebrity Deathmatch*, one episode of which pitted the Bard against rapper Busta Rhymes to determine the title of world's best poet.[7] Alongside the schlock associations of Seuss Shakespeare, there are also the rare finds, including Sarah Bernhardt in the silent film *L'Duel Hamlet* (1900), believed to mark *Hamlet*'s filmic debut.[8] YouTube also functions as a discovery space for inventive projects such as *Chicken Shop Shakespeare*.[9] Showcasing emerging talent, these vignettes produce a deliberately contemporary location of Shakespeare. YouTube videos can be inventive, as in Rebecca Mellor's *Ophelia RM10* (discussed in Chapter 2), and challenging, as in *Othello blacking up* (discussed in Chapter 3), which provide us with a surprising and satisfying new media edification of Shakespeare. Indeed, YouTube Shakespeareans instance the vitality and interpretative openness of Shakespeare. There is value for students of Shakespeare, since what emerges is a sense of Shakespeare as a body of knowledge that is shifting, incomplete and thus awaiting new interventions. In this way, YouTube Shakespeare not only has much to offer as archive, as a platform for vernacular expression, as a space to participate in what Shakespeare means. YouTube also has implications for scholars. It can become a space where Shakespeareans disseminate and share their work or where different roles – of

YouTuber, fan and creator – might be assumed, thus enabling scholars to bridge the gap between popular culture and Shakespeare's more institutional markings.

## YouTube Shakespeare in/as new media

YouTube is a far more complex medium than many descriptions of the video-streaming platform characterize it as. Recent work in media studies has importantly deepened our knowledge and understanding about the dynamic surrounding YouTube. Scholars have considered YouTube's commercial imperatives and their bearing on notions of community. [10] They have also explored YouTube's invitation to 'Broadcast Yourself' and its implications for individual agency within mass media.[11] Genres of YouTube video have been identified and interpreted as cultural texts.[12] Building on such work, this book seeks to initiate a productive dialogue between new media theory and the field of Shakespeare studies. The interplay between these subject areas and approaches gives rise to a host of questions, questions that reach to the shifting cultural significance of Shakespeare, to the affordances of the YouTube platform – and to its predations.

Several terms have already been introduced which require further elaboration, as they form the book's conceptual categories. Before turning to these, it might be helpful to pause on 'Shakespeare'. As a signifier, Shakespeare is heterogeneous and is understood throughout this study as an increasingly unbounded category, one extending beyond the corpus of the texts or the work to encompass a range of media forms and cultural stratifications (high, mass, popular). My focus on Shakespeare contributes to established notions of Shakespeare's exemplarity, which have all too often depended on a separation of Shakespearean texts from their early modern peers.[13] Yet, as a user-curated archive, YouTube affirms Shakespeare's prominence and reminds us that, as nurtured through popular culture, academic research and teaching, the Bard's profile is largely inescapable.

The circulation of Shakespeare across mass media has been interestingly theorized as 'post-hermeneutic'. While this categorization is helpful, on some levels it also has certain limitations. Namely, reworkings of the Bard are interpreted as a kind of schlock or regarded as reflecting the 'eternal sameness' of the culture industry and the depthless culture of postmodernity.[14] Other commentators have formulated Shakespeare's mass media presence in terms of popular culture.[15] In both instances, however, the relation between, on the one hand, Shakespeare as an aggregate of texts by a historical figure, and, on the other, Shakespeare as an aggregate of adaptations, citations, allusions, uses, transpositions, appropriations, revisions – or any of the available metaphors to describe Shakespeare's 'appropriability' – can be productively conceptualized as mutable and dialogic.[16] In negotiating these interrelated Shakespeares, it is as important to 'challenge the idea that Shakespeare must always already be co-opted by the dominant culture' as it is to 'caution against the easy assumption that Shakespeare can set us free'.[17] Moreover, the issue of Shakespeare's appropriability poses questions of Shakespeare 'proper', challenging the presumed stability of the Shakespearean text that in turn functions as the measure for those subsequent iterations. As Margaret Kidnie observes of contemporary Shakespeare performance and adaptations, 'the site of adaptation keeps getting entangled in the work's ongoing development'.[18] In this respect, any conclusive comprehension of the texts is 'indefinitely postponed by each act of interpretation'.[19] This is the logic of haunting in which the text returns, often in surprising ways and in ways we cannot yet conceive.[20] YouTube Shakespeare videos are adaptations, in the etymology of that word as in 'to fit'.[21] In making and then uploading their productions, YouTubers accommodate Shakespeare to YouTubers and to its culture. At stake are various forms of recontextualization or transposition; videos involve performance and citation too.

The 'Shakespeare' within YouTube Shakespeare is an open, dynamic process, in which the authority of the Shakespearean work is simultaneously invoked and constructed, renewed and dispersed.

To consider YouTube Shakespeare is also to address the vocabularies of media studies. 'Affordances' has a specific resonance within the field, denoting the material, physical attributes of a given object and the actions that those attributes facilitate: 'the affordances of any given object make certain actions possible, exclude others and structure the interaction between actor and object'.[22] To address YouTube's affordances is to consider how the design of the interface facilitates certain uses (easy uploading, viewing, commenting, connecting through channel subscriptions), shapes user experience (the click through to more videos and the attention economy of the site) and also imposes certain limits on use (unlike a personalized web page, for instance, each YouTube channel has a uniform look). We can look not only at affordance, but affordability. For YouTube entails questions about access to technology, the leisure time involved in video production, as well as the concern that media corporations will exploit the labour of tubers.[23]

Interpreting YouTube's affordances raises the question of medium specificity – a useful concept for alerting us to the platform's formal properties, but one that can also imply a degree of medium-essentialism, where a set of attributes come to denote certain effects (it is like *this*, so it must result in *that*).[24] YouTube is a medium because, like other forms of communication, it mediates older media (television, film). Moreover, in the defining double logic of the process known as remediation, held by Jay Bolter and Richard Grusin to be characteristic of all media, the online viewing platform simultaneously erases and also proliferates or 'hybridizes' earlier forms and practices into something novel or unprecedented.[25] For Shakespeare, this means that YouTube does not so much replace earlier media such as film and theatre, as sustain them in new guises. In this respect, as much as YouTube

Shakespeare suggests contemporaneity, a Shakespeare of and for now, it also has the potential to foster historical consciousness via its repository of Shakespearean materials. As the concept of remediation reminds us, a medium always has a history – it cannot 'do its cultural work in isolation from other media, any more than it works in isolation from other social and economic forces'.[26] As such, if we insist too strongly on medium specificity, we risk overlooking the extent to which YouTube, like any other media, 'does not pre-exist its mediation' but 'is itself constructed – co-ordinated, organized and integrated – in mediation, in mass movement', and through the medium of the computer (or tablet or smart phone).[27] After all, YouTube is contiguous with (new) media and other Web 2.0 technologies such as Twitter, Facebook and Flickr. Therefore, this book deploys the terms 'platform' and 'platform-specificity' in order to convey the distinctive features of YouTube's interface.[28]

Even as one recognizes the particular attributes of the YouTube platform, it is nonetheless important to address the focus this book grants to YouTube, as well as to reflect on the terms of the subtitle, 'New Media Forms of the Bard'. In other words, why YouTube and why new media? YouTube emerged in 2006, so it already has a history and in that sense is not new. Yet, as with other Web 2.0 technologies, 'a rhetoric of newness' is still associated with it.[29] YouTube is new media in that it instantiates several changes in media (from production and distribution to use and storage) and contains interrelated attributes, such as the hyperlinked digital object, mass connectivity and social networking, each of which is enabled by a 'technicist logic of computation'.[30] In many ways, these attributes define our contemporary media use and interactions. In the more exuberant accounts of networked culture as posited by theories of media convergence and spreadability, new media involves possibilities for the media consumer to become an active participant and to intervene in the flow of mass media.[31] For this reason, it is worth considering what media theorist Henry Jenkins describes as convergence culture. This describes a set of inter-sections between old and new media and, most importantly for Jenkins, between 'the power of the media producer and the power of the media consumer'.[32] Yet, in this paradigm, there is no Samson and Goliath battle between a disenfranchised media user or impassive spectator and established big media players. Rather, the media consumer is an active participant who seeks out new content, repurposes old and forges new connections with other media users. 'Convergence occurs within the brains of individual users and through their social interactions with others'.[33] For Michael Wesch, among the earliest critics to analyse YouTube and explore what he calls its anthropology, the platform transforms the humble webcam or mobile camera: 'anyone with a webcam now has a stronger voice and presence'.[34] YouTube becomes an empowering technology for democratic expression.

There has been much debate within media studies regarding the conceptual usefulness and limitations of the collective designation 'new media'. It has been critiqued for imposing linearity on media history, with 'old' media giving way to the 'new' in a narrative of 'technological progressivism'.[35] It can imply that as users, our interaction and entanglement with technologies is a completely new phenomenon, thus eliding the extent to which we, as humans, were always already techno-logical. Or, as Sarah Kember and Joanna Zylinska argue, this profound sense of evolutionary development through media might also suggest that, today, human life itself 'becomes' through media.[36] As a conceptual category, I would argue that *new* media already presupposes a relation to, rather than the erasure of, the past and earlier media, while at the same time recognizing that there is something novel about our contem-porary media arrangements. In reading YouTube Shakespeare through the theory of remediation, this book identifies a continuum between past and present media. As such, it argues that YouTube is not after Shakespeare film or theatre, but coincides with these media and, through its distribution function, may even sustain or disperse them. The novelty of these current arrangements resides in what Mark Hansen calls the advance of 'many-to-many connectivity'. '[W]hat is mediated by Web 2.0', he explains, 'is less the content that users upload than the sheer connectivity, the simple capacity to reach myriad like-minded users.'[37]

In relation to Shakespeare, Hansen's formulation may seem familiar, recalling Terence Hawkes' argument, made over a decade ago, that citations and quotations of Shakespeare no longer possess any intrinsic value themselves, but have instead become ciphers: 'Shakespeare doesn't mean: *we* mean *by* Shakespeare.'[38] In relation to YouTube, Hansen's argument about the newness of new media, namely, that 'the transmission of media ... itself mediates the situation of the user in the regime of networked computation', suggests that a YouTube video (or the post on Facebook) is a cipher for connectivity and networking, for rendering a digital presence, because to be absent from this terrain is tantamount to entropy.[39] In our current media culture, to be online is to be alive. At the same time, however, if we interpret life and mediation as co-constitutive, to echo Kember and Zylinska, we can begin to appreciate the various pleasures – of connectivity, browsing, expression and social networking – that new media signals.[40]

Another implication of this argument, however, is that mediation becomes an end in itself. Here, the YouTube Shakespeare video becomes merely the vehicle enabling connectivity, in which citations appear as if on a continuous loop and where the centrifugal force of the Shakespearean text cannot be located. Again, for Shakespeare studies, these are familiar patterns, in light of the aforementioned theories regarding 'post-hermeneutic' Shakespeare. Offering us more and more videos, YouTube Shakespeare suggests such loop effects, a potential sameness within plenitude. Yet, those vehicles for connectivity nonetheless have a ground: responses to Shakespeare on YouTube variously suggest an intervention in or contribution to meaning, perhaps as an attempt either to stave off or to compensate for the homogenizing effects of mass culture.

A wider implication in the term new media is a sense of loss. Embodied communication and personalized expression give way to a 'standardized technicity'.[41] The computer algorithm replaces our capacity for decision-making, though as users we also contribute to the efficiency of the algorithm by feeding such metadata as titles and tags into it, thus augmenting its authority.[42] As Hansen observes, 'to the extent that each new medium operates by exteriorizing some function of human cognition and memory, it involves both gain and loss'.[43] That he makes this point in relation to Plato's discussion of the medium of writing as a pharmakon ('at once the poison and the antidote, a threat to memory and its extension') might remind us of the long history of anxieties about technologies of representation and the suturing of human agency with machines, anxieties that have often been played out in the popular press and popular culture.[44] For the so-called 'Generation M' or 'Gen V' (as YouTube's marketers prefer), the use of media has arguably become so habitual that there is very little consciousness about how individual agency is being outsourced to technologies.[45] YouTube instances the predations associated with new media more generally, from mediated expression and the production of identity as simulacrum, to the externalization of personal and cultural memory onto an online platform and into a YouTube playlist. To consider YouTube Shakespeare as new media is to bring such effects into critical focus and to partake in what has been called a 'recombinant new media literacy'. This is vital because such literacy 'actively pays attention to how our sense of subjectivity, individually and collectively, changes through our (inter)relationship with technology'.[46]

In part, then, the focus of this book on YouTube permits a case study of the challenges and affordances of new media as they pertain to Shakespeare's contemporary reception. Moreover, because of YouTube's cultural visibility, it marks the default place from which to initiate an investigation into Shakespeare online video. YouTube is the dominant video-sharing site within the contemporary mediascape. More precisely, and despite YouTube's global pretensions, it is a predominantly Western mediascape.[47] Since it has created a horizon of expectation regarding how a video-sharing platform should look and operate, YouTube attains a high visibility over comparable sites.[48] The site has become the 'go to' space for video-sharing and is integral to the transfer of content from one platform to another.[49] Admittedly, my focus on a particular platform runs counter to the transmedia nature of contemporary online participation and expression, since users navigate and connect across a range of platforms. Yet, for both pragmatic reasons and because of YouTube's prominence, the book focuses its object of analysis on YouTube Shakespeare rather than range across a vast media terrain.

The emphasis on YouTube is also about recognizing that for Shakespeare studies this platform carries especially attractive properties. One of these has already been mentioned: YouTube's function as an accidental archive. The archive is accidental because there is no centrally controlled curatorship, but rather a system of user-generated titles and tags. Like other Shakespeareans, my initial interest and first use of YouTube occurred in a teaching context, as I sought out instructive clips to incorporate into presentations. My earliest searches involved using YouTube as archive. I assumed, unconsciously, that YouTube was the natural place to go to in order to seek out a performance or film clip. To use the site in this way is to avail of the convenience of the YouTube video as hyperlinked digital object, which can be easily embedded into PowerPoint, or shared via a virtual learning platform. It also involves participating in the culture of spreadable media. As I elaborate in Chapter 5, YouTube signals intriguing opportunities both for teaching and learning, enabling students to deepen their knowledge about the multi-directional nature of Shakespeare. By extending their use of YouTube beyond the illustrative clip for class, scholars can also benefit from the archive. At the same time, however, we must confront the challenges posed by inconsistent collation and annotation, as well as more complex, ethical questions regarding our use of the labour that enables the content in the first instance.[50]

# Broadcast yourBard: YouTube's dual culture

YouTube as archive, YouTube as spreadable or embeddable Shakespeare, YouTube as learning resource: these are just some of the reasons why YouTube Shakespeare should matter to anyone interested in Shakespeare's reception and why a critical analysis of the subject is important. YouTube Shakespeare is of further value to the field because as a platform for user-generated content, it provides access to vernacular productions. YouTube's tag line invitation to 'Broadcast Yourself' announces the site's dependence on users not to only share but also to create content. It instances the language and logic of participatory culture, in which individuals enter media production that was typically – though not universally – the preserve of commercial producers. YouTube allows everyone to perform their own 'bardic function', as John Hartley puts it, here invoking the Celtic bard as a singular teller of stories in order to capture the turn towards open, democratic and diffuse media production associated with Web 2.0.[51] YouTube offers new media forms of the Bard and a range of partici-pative responses – the user as creator-viewer, who not only browses through content but also generates and comments upon it. Put another way, if other media presume minimum participation, new media constitute additional layers of inter-vention.[52] As such, YouTube has patron-like qualities, which provide both the technology for the distribution of vernacular content, as well as a social space, which encourages people towards online expression.[53]

For Shakespeare studies, the logic of participation and vernacular creativity means access to a range of responses to the texts, thus allowing us to build on existing knowledge about the rich history of amateur Shakespeare performance.[54] Participation through YouTube is similar to pop culture citations and uses of Shakespeare, affording forms of response outside of institutions like universities and theatres that shape what Shakespeare means in culture more generally.[55] The culture of YouTube and Web 2.0 also signals new iterations of the Bard, however, that bring their own aesthetics – and indeed politics – to the texts. These genres suggest a bricolage of texts, of which Shakespeare might be only one referent among many. Of course, this is not an entirely new approach to the plays or their contexts: Shakespeare and early modern dramatists have long been viewed as bricoleurs who put together 'things already produced (even used) and circulating in culture', thus lending their plays a rich intertextuality.[56] If we read across genres and historically, the analogy can be pressed a little further: just as Renaissance dramatists, YouTubers also engage in a creative imitation of their predecessors and peers.

In interpreting YouTube as a patron, or a catalytic platform that enables users to upload and share content, it is crucial that we acknowledge the commercial and corporate imperatives that shape the site's structures and uses. YouTube is 'both industry and user-driven'.[57] As much as YouTube presents itself as a community-based network that encourages self-expression, the site's function as a user-generated technology is enabled by its political economy (as evidenced by its dependence on advertising, promotion of industry content and commercial partnerships).[58] Thus, even though YouTube Shakespeare affords insight into what a version of Shakespeare that is by and for the people might look like, the intersection of user-generated content with commercially produced content means that such popular iterations are already inscribed by the market, by the flow of capital.[59] The coincidence of industry and vernacular content entails more complex relations too. For instance, it can often be the case that commercially produced content (as in the Shakespeare film) is subject to user appropriation (as in the fan-made trailer). In this case, the fan paratext has its own internal formal properties and its own effects that may involve a distancing from the industry text. Yet, in ways similar to the sharing of a movie trailer via YouTube, the fan-produced videos become indirect, free promos for the film, potentially enhancing its cultural capital and creating new audiences. While these arrangements are not especially new – Shakespeare has long been absorbed into mass media and has proved a pliable commodity within globalization – the coincidence of YouTube's corporate and participatory logic suggests that we regard vernacular Shakespeare production as an affordance of mass media and even inseparable from its operations. YouTube may be a patron of a do-it-yourself Shakespeare. However, the trade-off is an implicit acquiescence to YouTube branding and to the broader commodification of individual expression. This is the flip side of participatory culture, which tends to be elided by convergence theory.[60]

The intersection of disparate content is just one way in which YouTube culture impacts on Shakespeare's meaning and poses challenges to the scholarly analysis of the texts. Indeed, for some critics the Internet anxiously represents the wisdom of crowds, which undermines both professionalization and specialisms.[61] When combined with the dilutive properties of YouTube clip culture, such as the tendency towards synecdoche, 'highlighting' and distracted viewing, Shakespeare's transposition into a visual medium like YouTube can be easily framed as a narrative of loss, which reflects broader debates about the relation of digital to print culture.[62] At stake here are issues about the hyper-attention or the attention deficit associated with the Internet. The live, embodied performance, Shakespearean language and a sense too of reading a play in full are just some of the things that might be lost via YouTube Shakespeare. Where a video involves the diminution of language, or its effacement altogether, YouTube may be part of and even accelerate what Douglas Lanier calls 'post-textual Shakespeare'. This phenomenon is already familiar to us on account of Shakespeare films from the 1990s and has more recently been amplified by the mediatization of our culture, in which the 'horizon of recognition' for Shakespeare is decidedly visual: more images, fewer words, words, words.[63] We might well question the claim that Shakespeare's post-textual presences constitute a 'paradigm shift' – after all,

Shakespeare in performance has never been simply about the words. That said, visual, cinematic and other treatments of Shakespeare 'without words' prompt reflection (Is it really Shakespeare?) and encourage us to question our cultural and disciplinary investments in an 'essential' or 'authentic' (textual) Shakespeare.[64] It should be noted too that YouTube is not entirely post-textual. While analyses of user behaviour of the interface have suggested that text goes unnoticed, videos frequently incorporate text – in Chapter 4, I examine the interplay of text and image in those videos that respond to the *Sonnets*. YouTube videos also elicit textual commentary through viewer posts, thus realizing a cacophony of feedback – positive, critical, sometimes hateful – a 'mass hermeneutics'.[65] Furthermore, as Christy Desmet has persuasively suggested, YouTube Shakespeare productions enact focused performance, spotlighting specific aspects of the text in a process that is quite often 'thoroughly rhetorical, a matter of textual give-and-take rather than a wholesale usurpation of the Bard's words and authority'.[66]

This book argues that YouTube Shakespeare videos are cultural texts in themselves. Moreover, if we leave aside any sense that they are substitutions for the act of reading a play and recognize the pleasures of viewing a YouTube video *and also* of reading Shakespeare, or seeing a play in performance, we can begin to recognize them as forms of creativity and as Shakespeare interpretation, even criticism. It is a commonplace to observe that the value of Shakespeare's latest media form resides in its contribution to the text's field of meaning. In a teaching context, the value of Shakespeare adaptations becomes entwined with their capacity to enable a return to the text itself.[67] To which one might reply, why not simply begin with the text? As two critics on Shakespeare and film claim, 'to teach Shakespeare today, we must teach today's Shakespeare – as refigured through the distorting lens of the movie camera'.[68] Within this claim for a pedagogy focused on contemporary reimaginings of Shakespeare is a slightly defeatist logic. The film is envisaged as 'distorting'

– presumably a recognition of transposing the play to that medium – when it might be more usefully considered as quite simply different, neither the thing itself nor pretending to be such, but a medium that generates interesting comparisons with Shakespearean media (drama and verse) and genres (comedy, tragedy, history), while at the same time unsettling their perceived stability. 'When Shakespeare is reinvented in other media,' as Anna Maria Cimitile and Katherine Rowe remind us, 'it meets other complex textualities and forms. The encounter produces what we should learn to treat no longer as an "adapted" Shakespeare but Shakespeare in/as the present–past of new media.'[69] YouTube Shakespeare involves the kind of conjuncture of present and past, old and new media, envisaged here. However, recognizing the aesthetics of the YouTube video may require a conceptual readjustment, so that we accord less primacy to language as an expressive idiom and think instead of a competitive dynamic between different media and registers (text, image, word, sound).[70] Quite simply, YouTube Shakespeare is Shakespeare through different media.

# YouTube Shakespeare and presentism

A search on YouTube reveals Shakespeare as a network of connections between disparate digital objects. Even as these items spread to other media, they are nonetheless identifiable as YouTube videos. In this regard, YouTube Shakespeare invites interpretation as an aggregate of Shakespeare 'in/as the present–past', the platform enabling us to pursue the rhizomatic nature of contemporary iterations of Shakespeare.[71] While attending to the fragmentary nature of online Shakespeare, this book is also concerned with examining the genres and forms within the broad categories of the 'YouTube video', or 'YouTube Shakespeare'. Consequently, my purpose is to consider the mutations of Shakespeare's cultural capital as constructed via YouTube and I aim to explore the ways in which individual iterations are possibly part of more discernible trends. Accordingly, the arguments in this book operate in tandem with the methodological premise of critical presentism as it has evolved in Shakespeare studies.

Presentism begins with the recognition that the time of the text is out of joint with the present of the critic.[72] As a mode of critical inquiry, explains Terence Hawkes, it 'deliberately begins with the material present and allows that to set its interrogative agenda', although, as he concedes, 'perhaps this simply makes overt what covertly happened anyway'.[73] There are correspondences between this theory and the praxis of tubers, who often quite knowingly and deliberately style Shakespeare after the fashions of their own time and for whom the point of access into the Shakespearean text is decidedly presentist. In valuing the site of reception and interpretation over the context of the writing itself, presentism reads Shakespeare as spectral, the thing that 'never was and can never be lived in the originary or modified form of presence'.[74] As such, it 'relinquishes the fantasy of recovering the text's previous historical reality', Ewan Fernie argues, 'in favour of embracing its true historicity as a changing being in time'.[75] If historicist criticism appears to erase the location of the critic and of the interpretative act, only for these to emerge through the proxy of the author, then critical presentism boldly engages the 'now' of our readings.[76] In fact, there is an attractive logic to the presentist claim that the present matters more than history. There is a tremendous risk, too, however, since this perspective might be said to represent something of an erosion of our ethical responsibilities to the past, especially in terms of past traumas. For all that, presentism need not be antithetical to history; it is concerned, explicitly so, with pursuing the relationship between the historical text and the present (a concern it partly inherits from cultural materialism). Presentists are 'aware of historical difference but aware as well of the approachable but real epistemological barrier between ourselves and the past'.[77] Crucially, presentism is also concerned with the *presence* of the critic in making Shakespeare present. As Fernie puts it, foregrounding 'the presence of the text in the present ... involves a recognition of being in the presence of the text: *of being required to respond, to being responsible*'.[78]

In this formulation, we have moved from presentism as an unapologetic reading of Shakespeare as our contemporary – to evoke that formative presentist interpretation by Jan Kott – towards a sense of the aesthetic and of the text's irreducibility to history.[79] Presentism's interest in the affectivity of the text, and thus the efficacy of art, runs contrary to established understandings about the commodification of art, or the aestheticization of commodities under postmodernism and within mass culture. To the extent that postmodernism defines the present moment, associated with the loss of an aura, presentism seems to suggest a partial rediscovery. Consider, for instance, Fernie's insistence that 'It is time ... to recover the creativity and agency that blaze in the Shakespearean text as the promise of human possibility.'[80] For his part, Cary DiPietro wonders if presentism offers the 'potential to liberate the aesthetic in mass culture society as a potential site of critical or counter-cultural Utopian desire'.[81] If presentist criticism risks overplaying Shakespeare's singularity, its interpretative emphasis on the present and the call for 'a reinvestment in the aesthetic' provides for a reading of YouTube Shakespeare as a site of productive tension between the homogenizing effects of mass culture and new forms of individual vernacular expression.[82] By reading presently, we can examine YouTube productions not only as enactments of Shakespeare's mediation through the cultural present, but as indices of how Shakespeare's alterity is negotiated.

# YouTube Shakespeare and the ethics of selection

In selecting Shakespeare videos from across YouTube, this book involves the production of a subject category, 'YouTube Shakespeare'. However, this move is not intended to place online interpretations into a single, homogeneous category. Instead, I hope to comment on the interrelated processes of search and selection, and the patterns that might become noticeable to an individual user viewing from any one location. Selection invariably entails subjective choices and while the book does undertake sampling of videos and draws on the findings of data mining undertaken by social science researchers, its approach reflects a humanities research perspective. To those ends, Chapter 1 elaborates on the relation between serendipitous search, the YouTube algorithm and IP addressee(s). Furthermore, a set of external criteria for inclusion has not been imposed on videos, even though I have sought to represent different YouTube genres, and also Shakespeare texts and genres. In this regard, the book is a product of its object of analysis, since all of the videos on YouTube are, in theory at least, of equal value. Videos with view counts into the tens of thousands are discussed alongside those that have fewer than ten. The value of a YouTube Shakespeare video cannot be determined by a pre-set of preferences. That said, evaluations of Shakespeare adaptations tend to work from traditional 'preconceptions about "what Shakespeare intended"', especially since culturally ingrained notions of the singular literary genius prove recurrent.[83] If YouTube Shakespeare videos and comments quite frequently valorize the author, they also invite other determinants of value that extend beyond Shakespeare, such as the accomplishment of a given mashup, the currency of the movie star who is the subject of a fan trailer, the interchange between visual and textual registers that a video achieves. Once again, the aesthetic evaluations implied here carry their own subjective dimensions. Indeed, the videos that feature in this book are a consequence of the pleasures of browsing referred to earlier and each of them reflects the challenges of identifying patterns amidst YouTube's unbounded content.

As well as raising methodological issues, it is important that this work should focus on the ethics behind the selection of specific vernacular productions. In uploading a video, creators and/or users enter into an agreement with YouTube to publish that content.[84] The result is that material is immediately placed in the public domain. However, the Internet occasions complex negotiations between public and private spaces, negotiations that pose ethical dilemmas for research.[85] Tubers may make certain assumptions regarding the relative privacy of their video. For instance, the simple reality of a video being openly available on YouTube may belie more discrete intentions, with videos intended for a finite community, or regarded as circulating among 'videos of affiliation'.[86] Similarly, YouTube subscribers tend to use online aliases, but nonetheless an individual may be identifiable in a video. There are issues, too, where content is produced by, or features, minors. Furthermore, YouTube is an ephemeral archive: videos can be removed from the site, either for infringing copyright or simply because a creator elects to delete a video from their account. This reminds one that YouTubers may not necessarily be interested in preserving their work, or at least in doing so publicly. Equally, one needs to be conscious that the academic study of videos enacts a form of institutionalization, as materials from vernacular culture are drawn into the orbit of Shakespeare studies and into an academic discourse that online creation and viewing may, in part, be about avoiding in the first place. This is problematic, since one of the potential attractions of YouTube Shakespeare for its creators and users is that the site offers an alternative entry point into Shakespeare apart from academic discourse.

These are complex issues to which one response is to anonymize videos altogether (removing titles, usernames and even video URLs).[87] However, omitting the provenance of one's object of study is antithetical to academic scholarship and its protocols of bibliographic citation. It also deprives tubers of credit for their work. The omission of video metadata also presents obstacles for future research. One of the key advantages of YouTube is that it uses a system of embedded codes – the capacity to share these is not simply convenient, but offers intriguing possibilities for the kinds of scholarship we undertake. With these factors in mind, it has been decided to provide metadata for videos throughout. Importantly, permission has been sought from content uploaders to discuss their videos as part of an academic study.[88]

The chapters that follow elaborate on the objectives of this study to examine the genres of YouTube Shakespeare and to assess what implications the platform has for Shakespeare's meanings. Chapter 1 examines the YouTube interface, taking the reader through a phenomenological overview of a single search page for *As You Like It* to consider specificities of use and the attention economy of the information age, interrelations between commercially produced and vernacular content, as well as the potential motivations behind the bardic function. The snapshot of search results discloses key genres of YouTube Shakespeare such as the fan trailer, the performance and the iconic speech. It also urges us to recognize YouTube as a site of contradictions and paradoxes, especially in terms of the serendipity of search versus the algorithmic shaping of results, a tension that illustrates the extent to which the 'technical infrastructure of media is no longer homologous with its surface appearance'.[89] The implications of this discrepancy between interface and machine are pursued with reference to YouTube's global pretensions and the role of regionalized search and computer IP addresses, which limit YouTube's capacity to provide us with a transnational Shakespeare.

Focusing on *Hamlet*, Chapter 2 continues the book's interest in YouTube as the site for new media genres of Shakespeare. 'To be or not to be' is examined as an exemplary text of YouTube's self-generated Shakespeares, where it is frequently remediated as the vlog or video diary. I trace the recycling of the play's signature speech as fascinating spaces where tubers negotiate originality, derivation and the consequences of their own mediation (as with the succession of *Hamlet* videos, they seem to ask 'Are we humans also imitations?'). Questions of subjectivity and agency are further pursued through a detailed discussion of Ophelia, whose image floats among the currents of YouTube, both as motif and as metaphor in videos. As with the soliloquy, Ophelia's iconicity is recycled. However, unlike the 'To be or not to be' videos, it is predominantly young women that respond to Ophelia, in ways that suggest a negoti-ation of inherited constructions of gender identity, as well as a frustration with representations of women in dominant culture. The chapter also considers the issue of copyright as it emerges through the case of disputed ownership over an Ophelia film.

If, as I have being suggesting, YouTube Shakespeare offers a certain vitality to our field – even in relation to such estab-lished motifs as Hamlet and Ophelia – then Shakespeare studies has in turn a critical role to play in analysing this site of Shakespeare reception. We need to scrutinize an all too easy correlation between the volume of videos available and a meaningful heterogeneity and diversity. Chapters 3 and 4 take up this challenge with reference to race and sexuality respectively. How race is iterated within YouTube Shakespeare and to what extent racial diversity flows out of online participatory culture are among the guiding questions of Chapter 3. Drawing upon Lisa Nakamura's work about racialized aesthetics online and self-representations as raced, as well as debates regarding colour-blind casting, the chapter explores how race emerges in Shakespeare performance on YouTube. I consider the video performances by Marcus Sykes entitled *Shakespeare in the Ghetto*, attending to viewer posts as an important dimension of the reception context – the mass hermeneutics referred to earlier – that afford insight into how a performer's race emerges as semiotically (ir)relevant and, more problematically, disclose the nexus of aliases, viewer-as-critic and racism-as-performance that mark online dialogue. The limits as well as the possibilities of YouTube's online community emerge here. The chapter turns to blackface and other racialized signifiers as deployed in responses to *Othello* (a text never far from the politics of racialized representations). Here, as in the uses of *Romeo and Juliet* that I analyse, Shakespeare emerges as a metalanguage of race in contemporary iterations, yet one that does not necessarily prove adequate for contemporary racial politics. As users and viewers of YouTube Shakespeare, I argue, we have a responsibility to critically engage race and its challenging and unpredictable consequences.

Chapter 4 reaffirms the need for a critical alertness, this time in relation to the *Sonnets*. This chapter shows how the medium of the sonnet is being adapted to YouTube's visual culture, with kinetic typography suggesting some dynamic ways of thinking about textuality that have pedagogical appeal. It is also concerned with examining how the sonnets addressed to the young man are reconfigured on YouTube: three sets of samples are examined and these cases are discussed in terms of a queer erasure or the effacement of the male object of address. Old interpretative blind spots about Shakespeare texts can re-emerge through new platforms. In noting a potential disconnect between vernacular Shakespeare productions and Shakespearean criticism, I argue that the latter has a role to play in promoting more progressive forms of online video creation on YouTube and in interpreting such activities as contributions to the hermeneutics of the *Sonnets*.

The final chapter discusses YouTube and its Shakespeare video as a learning resource, a concern throughout the book. Teachers in the field are already encouraging new forms of response and engagement with Shakespeare through the platform – as evidenced by the wealth of videos associated with a classroom assignment – or using its archive. Mapping YouTube Shakespeare onto wider issues about the affordances and limitations of e-learning, the chapter argues that the platform presents important opportunities for students, from fostering independent learning and staking a claim to the kind of Shakespeare that emerges in their classroom to the development of digital literacy. To this end, the chapter includes detailed suggestions for assignments using YouTube. There are opportunities for teachers and researchers too. For Shakespeare studies to realize these opportunities will require not only an active engagement with the platform, but a willingness to move beyond text-based pedagogy.

YouTube Shakespeare does not just mark an efficient and convenient distribution of Shakespearean texts. It is not simply the archive we increasingly go to, or where the continuum of past–present Shakespeare unfolds. Nor is it a seemingly endless succession of vernacular-generated performance, response and interpretation. It is all of these things. Interpreting YouTube Shakespeare as amorphous and mutable, this book seeks to assess its media effects, its hermeneutics and its ideological limits. To enter YouTube Shakespeare is to encounter the circular logic of contemporary Shakespeare, where the dispersal of the texts across media, and the loss of the aura associated with the Bard, ultimately feeds into and propels the extraordinarily accommodating phenomenon we call Shakespeare. Within these loop effects and the move from one video to another, we may experience Shakespeare as repetition, and at the same time encounter innovative forms of media creation, which speak to Shakespeare's present vitality.

# 1

# Searchable Shakespeares: Attention, Genres and Value on YouTube

*We must take database watching seriously, not just dismiss it as 'consuming video clips'.*

GEERT LOVINK[1]

*What the search engine reveals through its list of returns increasingly becomes equivalent to what we can know.*

KEN HILLIS, MICHAEL PETIT AND KYLIE JARRETT[2]

*After watching all these videos, I now want to read Shakespeare ... Any suggestions?*

POST ON THE GEEKY BLONDE'S *TWELFTH NIGHT*[3]

YouTube presents us with the exciting prospect of Shakespeare in multiples. There are thousands of videos, making up thousands upon thousands of hours of Shakespeare text, image and sound. The copiousness of content on YouTube is a function of the site's interrelated dimensions as distribution

channel, social network and accidental archive. These create
the mix of commercial and non-commercial media, which as
users of YouTube we have become so accustomed to. As a
video enters YouTube's databank, it is not subject to a prior
set of aesthetic determinants. Nor does YouTube assume any
editorial oversight in relation to content uploaded to the site,
apart from the requirement that users agree to its terms and
conditions.[4] As digital objects, all videos are equal: this is
the YouTube logic of cultural relativism. Value is determined
by user search and crucially by the algorithm, which maps
and refines use patterns to arrive at the most relevant search
results. Within the culture of video-share, then, more traditional determinants of value based on distinctions between
high and popular culture come under pressure. The logic of
cultural relativism also applies to YouTube's search function,
at least on a superficial level. In searching for any item, we
simply input or paste text into the blank white rectangular
dialogue box at the top of the screen and then sift through the
results that are returned. However, coupled with an automatic
and unreflective use of the site as an archive, the ubiquity of
the search function potentially blinds us to the computerized
search working behind the interface and to the production of
knowledge that is occurring.

As noted in the second epigraph, search assumes an
epistemological standing, a development that has significant
implications.[5] Value becomes a matter of what attention the
user pays to the information or knowledge he/ she is presented
with. In the information overload of the Internet, attention is
the new economy. We can decide to direct our attention in
certain ways – towards the video thumbnail that catches our
eye as we scan across the interface. However, the interface
not only places demands on our attention, it also shapes
what we notice. While YouTube is serendipitous – part of the
pleasure of the site comes from the element of surprise derived
from happening upon a video through surfing – it is also a
controlled-search experience, where relevance is determined
algorithmically and where search preferences are increasingly

personalized (as evidenced by the 'Recommended for you' feature).[6]

In moving from a sense of the plenitude within YouTube Shakespeare towards terms like relevance and determinism, the objective of these opening remarks is not to posit a version of the YouTube algorithm as a sinister form of artificial intelligence (the 'Halgorithm', if you will). After all, YouTube's content comes from its users who, in addition to uploading videos, provide YouTube's information management system with semantic units (video title, description, tags, comments and so on), which it then processes algorithmically.[7] Rather, my purpose is to open up a set of questions and contradictions about YouTube, which have a bearing on the Shakespeares we find there, the forms they take and their different locations. When we look closely at YouTube, it presents a set of oppositions, which blend into continuums. These include: copiousness and limitation; chaos and control; humans and machines (or users and the algorithm); the serendipity of video surfing and algorithmic sorting; professional and amateur; consumer and producer; traditional and new media; high and popular expressive forms; global and local.

By exploring these contradictions, this chapter aims to deepen our understanding about the kinds of Shakespeare that YouTube's culture of video-share occasions. Why do YouTubers engage with Shakespeare and how do we determine what constitutes participation? To what extent does the choice of content within YouTube Shakespeare realize a transnational Shakespeare? Close attention is paid here (and developed over subsequent chapters) to the key genres through which responses to Shakespeare occur. Some genres such as the meme are characteristic of YouTube and Internet culture. Others such as 'vids' or fan-made music videos, are associated with earlier forms of amateur culture, but are afforded greater visibility on YouTube. Yet more genres come to the platform via Shakespeare's citational status, as in the example of the iconic speech.

This chapter inevitably prioritizes some videos over others in discussing these genres and, as with any act of selection, the analysis carries its own value judgements. Recent critical work on Shakespeare adaptations and popular culture provides a useful interpretative framework for approaching the range of Shakespeare content on YouTube. I am thinking here of the move from an evaluative model based on faithfulness to the Shakespearean urtext towards an increasing recognition that those texts that variously cite, adapt, remake or repurpose Shakespeare are themselves cultural objects, with their own set of generic protocols.[8] In other words, the orientation is Shakespeare-eccentric rather than Shakespeare-centric. This formulation provides for a productive dialectic between those texts that seem to take us away from Shakespeare and those that draw us back towards an enigmatic Shakespearean 'centre'.[9] What follows is the consequence of ranging across the unwieldy terrain of YouTube Shakespeare. The chapter seeks to complement the eccentricities and distractions of that terrain with a desire to uncover patterns of Shakespeare's meaning in that setting.

# 'Load more suggestions': Search as You/Tube like it

YouTube culture brings its own specificities of use, engagement and response to Shakespeare. In pursuing these specificities, I want to take an example of a search category and consider the results of a single search page. By attending closely to a search page, we can begin to consider the key terms or vocabularies of YouTube culture (such as tubing, user-generated content, user-circulated content, watch-page) and to reflect critically on the features and protocols of the browser, its 'platform-specificity' and their implications.[10] A search performed on 'Shakespeare, "As You Like It"' (with the search filter set on Relevance, geographic location to Worldwide, and language as English) returns 'About 10,200 results'.[11] As viewed on a desktop computer, the search page displays 20 results per page and the search is indicative of YouTube's mixed content. Of the first 20 videos, 17 come from traditional media (10 from theatre, 6 from film and television, 1 from music), reflecting YouTube's status as a platform where existing media are re-presented or remediated.[12] The videos include trailers and excerpts from an RSC production currently in the repertory; a clip from a reading of 'All the World's a Stage' for a BBC documentary; the BBC *Animated Tales* series; the full *As You Like It* (1936), starring Laurence Olivier; and a full stage production from Bangor University. We have to scroll down to the ninth video – a slide-show video of a Japanese production starring Hiroki Narimiya – before we find a video that can be classified as user-generated content, a term that has gained currency within analyses of YouTube and Internet culture.

User-generated or user-created content refers to amateur media production as distinct from commercial or professionally produced content, although it often borrows from the latter through processes of creative redaction and repurposing.[13] At work here is the practice of 'tubing', that is the 'act of participating and contributing material with which others will interact'.[14] Within YouTube studies, there has been a tendency to valorize user-generated video because it satisfies a version of YouTube as a community of grassroots users somehow at a remove from the operations of large-scale media. As Jean Burgess and Joshua Green argue, however, 'it is not helpful to draw sharp distinctions between professional and amateur production, or between commercial and community practices'. Rather, they read YouTube as a 'continuum of cultural participation', a model that 'requires us to understand all those who upload, view, comment on, or create content for YouTube, whether they be businesses, organizations, or private individuals, as *participants*'.[15] The results for *As You Like It* reveal the blurring of boundaries between professional content and the activities of non-commercial users: of the six videos from film and television, for example, the *Animated Tales As You Like It* and *Shakespeare's As You Like It – Helen Mirren* have been uploaded by individual users rather than the original producer and copyright holder (the BBC). They constitute user-copied content, where users upload and share found content from existing media, often infringing copyright in the process.[16]

These examples illustrate the importance of noting the basic elements of videos. Details such as the title and username constitute video metadata, which enable us to determine the type of content we are dealing with and its provenance.[17] YouTube imbues disparate content with uniformity – each video is presented on the search page with a thumbnail, hyperlink title, upload date and view count. Nonetheless, we should attend to a video's aesthetic, or how it is 'calling out to the viewer a specific set of rhetorical or semantic referents'.[18] In some instances, these are easily identifiable but in others it is necessary to look at the upload context. Thus, to return to the example of the Japanese production of *As You Like It*, the video can be interpreted as a fan homage to actor Hiroki Narimiya on the basis that he features significantly among the other videos in the uploader's channel. Each subscriber to YouTube has a channel or page, which afford some insight into a user's activities, including what videos have been uploaded and favoured, the organization of video into playlists and the production of a community through subscriptions to other channels.

The YouTube interface is dynamic and cluttered. At the same time, however, because the site is familiar, the experience of using it can be one of immediacy, with little or no awareness of its medium. Drawing on Bolter and Grusin's theory of remediation, however, YouTube can also be regarded as a hypermedia environment. First, in remediating older technologies of representation (such as television, theatre and film), YouTube simultaneously absorbs these different forms and also marks their presence, thus 'maintaining a sense of multiplicity and hypermediacy'.[19] Second, the relation between the user and the interface fosters medium-consciousness: 'the user as a subject is constantly present, clicking on buttons, choosing menu items', a level of interaction that interrupts the 'transparency of the technology'.[20] YouTube involves a number of specific features, which shape viewing experience and use. While there are visual constants to the YouTube search page (including the YouTube logo, the search dialogue box, upload button, the Filter menu, the organization into thematic categories and the advert that appears to the right of the search results), its appearance also depends on whether or not a user is logged in. For the non-subscriber, there are highlighted icons and links ('Popular on YouTube'), subject categories (Music, Sports, Gaming) and a 'Sign in' icon that invites the user to subscribe. As a YouTube subscriber, the initial search page will also display Channel features on the left-hand side of the screen. These include links to 'Watch Later', 'Watch History' and 'Playlists', and a list of Channel subscriptions, with feeds indicating new videos that have been posted. As a YouTube subscriber, the user is afforded an added menu of viewing options, thus enabling enhanced interactivity.

Human–computer interfaces, Lev Manovich reminds us, operate according to a selection logic, whereby the user 'navigates through a branching structure consisting of pre-defined objects'.[21] Thus, although users are presented with a menu of viewing options, their choices are pre-programmed by the conventions of the YouTube interface.[22] In one sense, the vertical arrangement of videos implies a ranking of material in descending order. YouTube also deploys various strategies such as 'Featured Videos' and 'Promoted Videos' that are designed to optimize the viewing of certain videos.[23] However, each video is a hyperlinked digital object; accordingly, 'despite the rating systems, each media object on YouTube has equal weight'.[24] To borrow Manovich's terms, YouTube is a 'flat surface where individual texts are placed in no particular order' but instead are part of a branching structure, where one object leads to another.[25] As a result, the viewing experience becomes a type of 'spatial wandering' in which there is a lessening or perhaps even an erosion of temporal consciousness as we move from one video to another and another.[26] We are 'playing the medium, rather than watching it'; the effect 'is a partial – and somewhat unfocused – consumption'.[27]

This is to arrive at the consuming pleasures of YouTube – 'the YouTube sublime' – or the element of surprise involved in browsing its vast archive.[28] As with online life more generally, YouTube involves a new attention economy where the sheer quantity of information available leads to incomplete viewing and reduced concentration.[29] The average time for a single YouTube session has been variously placed at between 15 and 28 minutes.[30] In the information age, as Richard Lanham has argued, it is not information itself that holds intrinsic value, but rather the attention that it commands: 'In an information economy, the real scarce commodity will always be human attention.'[31] YouTube certainly presents viewers with a breadth of content and is structured in such a way as to prompt click-throughs to new videos.

YouTube's attention economy shapes the kinds of user-generated content found on the site, where properties such as brevity, accessibility, humour, spectacle and self-referentiality prove recurrent.[32] This development risks a self-perpetuating sameness and accounts for YouTube's association with 'numbing entertainment' and acritical consumption.[33] Geert Lovink formulates this as the numbing nexus of 'Boredom-Surprise-Boredom' that leads to 'digital disillusionment'.[34] Nonetheless, he argues that 'we must take database-watching seriously, not just dismiss it as "consuming video clips"'.[35] While the predatory effects of online surfing certainly require ongoing critical appraisal, it is equally important to note how users adapt their mode of participation to the platform, in the process demonstrating 'site-specific competencies' that often signal significant levels of critical digital literacy (a point I examine in Chapter 5 with regard to YouTube Shakespeare as a learning resource).[36] Lanham is especially interesting here. While his concern with the new economics of attention implies a critique of Internet culture and its corrosive effect on traditional modes of information retrieval or aesthetic appreciation, he is in fact interested in digital productions as highly competitive fields of expression where text, image and sound interact in intriguing ways that call upon us to attend to their style, indeed to relish it.

This model of the attention-savvy user involves considerable demands, envisioning as it does a viewer that sifts through the abundant flow of information with curiosity and openness. Such an ideal viewer might combat what has been regarded as the circularity many YouTube users experience as they move from euphoria (at the unanticipated discovery within 'its referential expanse') to entropy (the 'ennui of repetition', leading to a sense of a void) and back again.[37] In highlighting the affordances of the digital as well as the possibilities of an active viewer, Lanham's model remains valuable. It is borne out by the so-called 'long tail effect', in which the digital, with its vast storage capacities and easy distribution, has created new degrees of popularity based on niche markets and interests. In this scenario, users 'wander further from the beaten path', in the process discovering that their tastes are more complex than the dictates of a 'hit-driven culture'.[38] As such, assessments of YouTube as an entertainment site, or as a kind of 'postmodern TV of distraction' providing 'an endless chain of immediate but forgettable gratification', must be balanced with a recognition that there are many different types of video, audiences and patterns of attention.[39]

As the YouTube browser currently functions, however, it is only possible to watch one video at a time, even if the eye wanders across to other available choices.[40] Selecting a video on the initial search page creates a 'watch page', which is itself replaced when another video is selected.[41] The platform's protocols thus have important implications for Shakespeare, with the flow of videos shaping what kind of Shakespeare we notice and experience. On the one hand, the scale of the YouTube archive suggests a potentially endless depth of multimedia Shakespearean texts, thus disclosing a deep reception context and an infinite 'long tail' into niche content. On the other hand, the interface's distractions, combined with a tendency among users to view fragments rather than complete narratives, mean that YouTube Shakespeare risks becoming diffuse, even bewildering.

The *As You Like It* search page instances these contrasting reverberations on Shakespeare's meaning. As a user selects particular functions on the hypermedia platform, he/she elects to follow certain branches: YouTube is Shakespeare as *You* like it. These selections may lead him/her further into iterations of this particular Shakespearean text. However, other videos may prove alluring, leading the user away from Shakespeare altogether. At issue here is the interface's shaping power on viewer behaviour and use. After all, interfaces present a structuring of knowledge and a representation of the world. They are enabled by algorithms, which 'prove that something is happening behind and beyond the visible'.[42] Through IP address(es), the YouTube algorithm identifies the individual self that undertakes a search and makes selections. Our user's search is also Shakespeare as the Tube constructs it.

Continuing a phenomenological account of YouTube search, let us imagine that our viewer selects the second video on the initial search page, *Shakespeare, 'As You Like It', Act 2, Scene 7, Jaques: 'All the world's a stage'* (uploaded 17 May 2011; 16,684 views), thus opening up a new watch page.[43] The accompanying description provides the context for the reading by actor Larry Lamb, filmed as a promotion for a BBC competition, *Off by Heart Shakespeare*, aimed at 13–15-year-olds. Consequently, the Suggestions menu on the right of the watch page features some of the other videos filmed as part of the competition as well as other items which, through their hyperlinked titles, allow a user to pursue yet more performances of Jacques' speech (II.7.140–68). Available videos include user-copied content in the form of a clip from TV's *Morgan Freeman – Seven Ages of Man* (uploaded 13 January 2010; 30,895 views).[44] There is also user-generated content such as *As You Like It: 'All the World's a Stage' by Dex Curi* (uploaded 31 December 2009; 6,526 views).[45] The video takes the form of a slide-show, a common genre of YouTube amateur culture, which in this instance combines audio or voice-over by the uploader himself with a series of images that visualize – and literalize – Jaques' melancholic reflections. The speech has also received the corporate treatment, as in the advert for the social networking space Google+.[46] The imprimatur of Shakespeare, or perhaps, more precisely, the voice of actor Benedict Cumberbatch, is co-opted in the interests of Google's vision of the digital as the space where we lease out our memories.

These are just some of over 1,400 videos featuring Jaques' speech that we could potentially click through.[47] As an aggregate, these can be categorized as a genre themselves: the iconic Shakespearean speech. This is neither a new phenomenon, nor is it exclusive to YouTube. Rather, the iconic speech or the extracted quotation is part of a long tradition through which Shakespeare emerges 'as inspirational sound bite, aphoristic, provocative, disseminated, and scattered far from its source'.[48] As grafted onto Jaques' catalogue of human life, the theatrum mundi trope was already a cliché to the play's first audiences only to subsequently become as indicatively Shakespearean as 'To be or not to be', 'Tomorrow, and tomorrow, and tomorrow' or 'Friends, Romans, countrymen'. Operating synecdochically for Shakespeare's literary genius and universalism, these speeches come to YouTube pre-loaded with meaning. Similar to such iconic Shakespearean scenes as Hamlet looking at Yorick's skull or the balcony scene of *Romeo and Juliet*, these set pieces constitute 'powerful memorial centres in popular culture … with each repetition encapsulating for their audiences the "essence" of Shakespeare'.[49] Relatedly, they underwrite the curriculur centrality which certain Shakespeare plays enjoy over others. At the same time, the iconic speech may reflect Shakespeare's 'post-hermeneutic' status in popular culture, where citations of the texts float freely from the anchoring authority of the Shakespearean text.[50]

Yet, the practice of quotation is sufficiently broad to suggest that we are dealing with something approaching a

continuum between these two positions. Hamlet's soliloquy
is the most frequently cited on YouTube, with over 33,700
search results; Macbeth's speech produces some 3,240 results
and Brutus' 2,570.[51] If YouTube is facilitating anything new
here, it is predominantly at the level of distribution, participation and connectivity. The platform enables the mass
circulation of these quotes on a scale hitherto impossible. The
effect is also viral: YouTube perpetuates the concept of the
exemplary Shakespearean speech, reaffirming the iconicity of
certain lines. Video compilations such as *Quotes by William
Shakespeare* (uploaded 10 September 2012; 1,197 views)
suggest a correlation with the early modern tradition of the
commonplace book and its databank of sententiae available
for the reader's use.[52] Furthermore, while the practice of
selective quotation entails forms of loss – the dramatic context
of a speech or a more general neglect of other plays owing to
their comparative unfamiliarity – the relational organization
of videos on YouTube puts these iconic speeches into contact
with their texts. The 'Seven Ages of Man' videos may instance
the phenomenon of the 'disembodied quotation', but they also
connect with other *As You Like It* videos, allowing the speech
to be understood as a constituent part of an expansive multimedia corpus.[53] As such, the iconic speech video is a form of
meta-Shakespeare and part of a larger web of related videos
that entail at least the potential for a diachronic perspective.

Just three selections or click-throughs have been made from
the original search page and we can apprehend the range of
choices within 'As You Like It'. A user might be inclined to
scroll down to *Star Wars As You Like It Shakespeare Project*
(uploaded 5 April 2013; 83 views), the thirteenth video on
the search page.[54] As this video has its origins in a school-
based assignment, the Suggestions menu features videos that
similarly modernize Shakespeare via popular culture texts like
*Star Wars*. The video's inclusion of light sabre effects – used
here to dramatize the wrestling match between Orlando and
Charles in Act 2, Scene 1 of the play – connects to other
*Star Wars* and light sabre parody videos.[55] Once again, the

paradoxical features of search and selection on YouTube are evident. While a user exercises choice through selection and may undertake focused viewing as close attention is paid to a single video, selection is also being determined by the available menu of options on the YouTube interface and by its busy attention economy. Thus, within YouTube's architecture resides both a useful aggregation of content through hyper-linked titles and, by virtue of the copiousness of that content, also an innate capacity for distraction.

# The bardic function, or why upload Shakespeare?

Overviewing a single search also provides insight into the potential reasons why Shakespeare content appears on YouTube and the different genres that users draw upon. With videos posted by professional organizations like the RSC and the Globe (accounting for 6 of the 10 theatre-related videos in the sample search), the reasons for uploading to YouTube are readily apparent since, as with other social media, the platform provides a convenient promotional space that appeals to a key demographic.[56] Social media has become a way for these cultural institutions not only to engage with audiences – videos from both the RSC and the Globe feature vox pops from audience members – but also to construct and disseminate their own cultural value, and indeed Shakespeare's too.[57]

For user-circulated and user-generated content, the motivating factors behind Shakespeare production and posting are more varied. On the surface, amateur or vernacular Shakespeare videos reflect both the prominence of the Bard within education and also the use of YouTube and social media as learning resources. As an accessible approach to the text, teachers are encouraging their students to create perfor-mances and adaptations and then share them on YouTube.

These developments explain the emergence of the genre of the 'classroom-inspired performance video'.[58] At the same time, however, YouTube Shakespeare videos do not neatly coalesce around educational or school culture; rather, they intersect with youth or teen culture and their interests. For aspiring and working actors, the YouTube video proves a convenient way of sharing their show reel and, as integrated into other social media platforms, is an effective way to get noticed. For students of film, Shakespeare provides a deep repository of narratives, plots and tropes to be variously emulated, adapted or altered.

Shakespeare comes to YouTube as a well-established trans-media text that is ripe for re-use in vernacular culture, as the example of the renowned quote mentioned above demon-strates. However, in hypothesizing about the motivating factors at work in YouTube Shakespeare, it is important that we move from a Shakespeare-centric viewpoint, which privileges the texts and their cultural cachet, towards a deeper consideration of YouTube as a site of participatory culture and social networking. The YouTube strapline 'Broadcast Yourself' exemplifies the logic of participatory culture: by way of contrast with 'older notions of passive media specta-torship', media consumers are understood to have greater opportunities to intervene in media production that was typically – though not universally – the preserve of commercial and professional producers.[59] The term participatory culture has been associated with fan culture, in particular Henry Jenkins' concept of fans as 'textual poachers' who actively 'participate in the creation and circulation of new content'.[60] In this respect, participatory culture is not a consequence of YouTube. The forms it takes on the platform, from the vlog to the fan video, have antecedents in pre-digital video technol-ogies, just as YouTube Shakespeare videos are preceded by a rich and long history of amateur performance and creative response.[61] However, YouTube signals a new phase of participatory culture through its provision of a 'distribution channel', where a range of vernacular productions can be shared and engaged with.[62] Furthermore, YouTube creates an enabling environment where media consumers habitually conceive of themselves as media producers. As such, it fosters new types of 'vernacular creativity', which act as a ground for social networking and community.[63] In accounting for the proliferation of do-it-yourself Shakespeare on YouTube, participatory culture is therefore an important explanatory reference point – such content reflects the shifting relationship between individual users and the larger mediascape.

That relationship has attracted different degrees of emphasis. For John Hartley, 'YouTube allows everyone to perform their own "bardic function"'.[64] In a Shakespearean context, this is a resonant phrase. However, Hartley is using the bard of Celtic tradition as a metaphor to express what he sees as the fundamental transition from a centralized form of communal storytelling to one that is more democratic and polyphonic. The idea of online participation as a form of storytelling, with users making their own content rather than receiving it from traditional broadcast media, corresponds well with YouTube's image as a popular platform for 'ordinary people', as evidenced by its now iconic videos of everyday life.[65] The idea of the 'bardic function' also provides an attractive way of thinking about YouTube Shakespeare. In turning to a Shakespearean text, character or motif, YouTubers are engaging in forms of storytelling and creative production. Their activities reflect an interest in producing their own take on the Bard, as in the example of The Geeky Blonde discussed below, and in ways that involve both a distancing from, as well as a dialogue with, a more institutional, professional, or otherwise culturally valorized Shakespeare. As much as it instances Shakespeare's cultural valency, a YouTube Shakespeare video also reflects a personal investment in the texts. Through participatory culture, a variety of roles variously associated with the reception of Shakespeare, such as performer, producer, auteur, editor and translator, are available for vernacular or amateur appropriation. While this availability is contingent on material factors, including access to computer technologies, an Internet

connection, leisure time and media literacy, in theory participatory culture fosters a situation where these different forms
of response to Shakespeare are possible and can be shared
with similarly interested users. YouTube's existing archive
of amateur performances and creative responses authorizes
ongoing vernacular production in that setting.

YouTube Shakespeare videos suggest a productive attitude
to the texts as open to further interpretation, especially where
they transpose the Shakespearean text to new contexts or
combine it with other media. However, while these videos
ultimately contribute to Shakespeare's citational availability, they can also have an attenuated relationship to
the Shakespearean text. For example, a remix video of a
Shakespeare film might be more concerned with a particular
actor than with Shakespeare. Similarly, a Shakespeare video
made with movie-generator software such as Xtranormal or
iClone may be addressed primarily to other users of these
programmes and just happen to draw on a Shakespearean
quote. The participatory culture of YouTube Shakespeare thus
marks Shakespeare's interaction with an array of media texts
and online cultures. It also encompasses different levels of user
participation. Content production provides an overt manifest-
ation of participatory culture and 'all users are addressed
as potential content providers'; however, production is only
one among a range of contributory possibilities available
on YouTube, which include video commenting, 'favour-
iting', and channel building.[66] Undertaking one or more
of these 'practices of audiencehood' involves contributing
to YouTube's interpretative community.[67] These practices
entail 'the evaluation, appraisal, critique, and recirculation
of material'.[68] Accordingly, we should broaden our understanding of 'what constitutes meaningful participation', so that
it does not privilege 'active' user-production vis-à-vis 'passive'
consumption, but rather considers production and response as
interrelated and dialectical components of YouTube.[69]

Interpreting online video productions as bardic activities
allows us to contemplate the possibilities of individual agency

within mass media. At the same time, however, liberating narratives about 'grassroots' or bottom-up media participation require scrutiny. Hartley's model of participatory culture problematically assumes that everyone has access to online technologies and that individuals possess the leisure time to engage in these new forms of storytelling. It also fails to consider that seemingly individualized media interventions can have generic properties and become repetitions of familiar themes. The notion of the 'bardic function' comes under further pressure in light of YouTube's proprietorial assertions over content.[70] We may all exercise the 'bardic function', but we do so on YouTube's terms. YouTube Shakespeare is no different to other forms of content on the site. User-created content coexists, cheek-by-jowl, with the commercially produced content. YouTube Shakespeare is also imbricated by the logic of the market, often overtly so through adverts that appear on the interface, or through image-overlay advertising.[71]

The proximity of YouTube culture and commerce is playfully explored in the film short *Shakespeare with Fries* (uploaded 1 April 2010; 38,819 views), where a struggling theatre company finds itself forced to integrate product placements into its performances.[72] The actors' performances are overlaid with placards for the fictitious 'Booth Burger' ('To Booth or not to Booth?'; 'Two burgers both alike in quality'). As one viewer comments, 'from the first add running at the bottom of the screen, to the ads becoming more popular than the content', the film is a commentary on YouTube as the cultural equivalent to fast food. Shakespeare's dual identity as a cultural classic and an advertising slogan suggests that the current state of all cultural expression is a dependence on the flow of global capital.[73] The film may exhibit some nostalgia for a putatively authentic type of art – it ends with the demise of the sponsorship deal – but the irony of placing on YouTube a film that critiques a situation in which art condescends to the marketplace is not lost on viewers: 'Funny that you post this on YouTube which has now been taken over by huge companies. SEND THIS TO THE BOARD OF YOUTUBE!'

The concern in *Shakespeare without Fries* – that amateur or vernacular production is on the wane, or that it is being compromised by an ever increasingly commercialized world – may have a broader resonance for YouTube Shakespeare. For instance, Christy Desmet has suggested that user-produced content is attritional, and is being sidelined by commercial and professional content producers.[74] The 'As You Like It' search page supports this point, with user-generated content accounting for only 15 per cent of the first 20 videos. YouTube's development of Auto Generated Channels has further implications for the relative prominence of user-generated content. Created where the algorithm detects popular topics – a channel for 'William Shakespeare' is an example – these channels tend to feature professionally and commercially produced content.[75] They reflect YouTube's efforts to organize and curate videos. However, there is a real risk here that these channels will ultimately feature sponsored-only content. In the case of the Shakespeare page, this might mean that the featured content comes exclusively from a commercial entity. These are legitimate concerns, because they speak to YouTube's vitality – its community of users – and their capacity to make and share their own content, often in ways involving critical distance from mass media. The business logic of YouTube is such that the activities of its non-commercial users are exploited for their monetary potential: as an industry observer puts it, 'Many of the things that YouTube users regularly do – start their experience at the home page, search for a video, visit a channel, watch a movie trailer or a music video – translate into appropriate advertising opportunities.'[76] At stake, therefore, in claims regarding the attrition of user-generated productions is a wider suspicion about new media whereby, in ways similar to Frederic Jameson's understanding of the fate of creative expression within postmodernism, sites like YouTube appear less like platforms for the dissemination of the latest vernacular creations than convenient spaces where advertisers avail of eye-catching content to draw in consumers.[77]

We need to remain alert to the far-reaching implications of YouTube's corporate logic. Equally, however, it is important to scrutinize a potential nostalgia for the early days of the site, one that posits a notion of authentic vernacular production as somehow apart from consumer culture. It is the very nature of the site that disparate types of video circulate simultaneously. Many YouTubers have successfully monetized their content in ways that redefine their status as amateur producers. Furthermore, the provision of a free (at least for now), accessible vernacular broadcasting platform is contingent on the commercial viability of YouTube itself and the continuing capacity of the site to attract advertisers and commercial partners.[78] The consequences of YouTube's corporate underpinnings, never far from view in its trademarked tag line, might be the necessary trade-off we make for a free, fully functioning user-generated technology.

# What's in a meme?: From *Harlem Shake[speare]* to *Downfall*

Recognizing the compromises implicit in our engagement with YouTube culture might further an appreciation of its affordances and effects, among them the genres of online Shakespeare video. The analysis of vernacular participation becomes an especially important activity because it documents content that is not only ephemeral but may also turn out to be the condition of a particular cultural moment. Studies of YouTube have already performed this type of archival and curatorial function, identifying certain videos such as *LonelyGirl* and *Chocolate Rain* as exemplary of Internet culture more generally.[79] As work on YouTube Shakespeare evolves, we may begin to see similar identifications. Indeed, by highlighting and selecting material, the current discussion contributes to the creation of a canon of Shakespeare videos. The 'As You Like It' search has already revealed some of the genres of YouTube Shakespeare (the slide-show, the classroom-inspired performance, the iconic speech) but what is the relation between the dominant modes of YouTube culture and the kinds of vernacular Shakespeare that occur in this setting? The meme offers an interesting case study here, exemplifying the language and logic of YouTube.

Borrowed from the field of genetics, the concept of the meme was first employed by Richard Dawkins as an analogy for cultural transmission. As applied to Internet culture, it captures the gene-like propagation of an image and its rapid dispersal.[80] Typically, memes exhibit three properties: they involve humour, they are readily understandable and they are easily replicable. These characteristics account for the popularity and 'spreadability' of memes across participatory culture.[81] Memes instance YouTube's distribution power, as well as its association with social connectivity and community. For instance, the *Gangnam Style* phenomenon, the music video by South Korean pop star PSY, which prompted thousands of copies, has become synonymous with YouTube. Even where memes spread to other platforms and social media such as Twitter or Facebook, they contribute towards YouTube's cultural currency. Memes are also used in the service of the YouTube brand, with the site arrogating disparate content and packaging it as a YouTube phenomenon, as in *Rewind YouTube Style 2012*.[82] There may be no Shakespeare memes within this retrospective and there is no Shakespeare video to rival *Gangnam Style*; nonetheless, as an available template repeated across YouTube, Shakespeare acquires meme-like properties. More intriguingly, Shakespeare has been explicitly incorporated into two YouTube memes, *Harlem Shake* and *Downfall*.

Since the first *Harlem Shake* in February 2013 when Australian teenagers posted a video of themselves dancing to a track by Baauer, there have been over 100,000 imitations (including one in an episode of *The Simpsons*).[83] Generally lasting no more than 30 seconds, the videos take the same simple structure: a shot of a group in a state of staged calmness, with one member dancing in a variety of settings (including an office, a park, a bus, a classroom), is followed by a frenetic group dance or 'shake'. The short length and the addictive beat of the track account for the popularity of the videos but there are other factors at work too. The videos involve a liberating dance movement and frequently some element of bodily display and undress, all of which suggest an alluring carnival attitude that provides a temporary disruption of otherwise formal settings.

An initial search under 'Harlem Shakespeare' returns some 927 results. However, not all of the videos included in this search figure contain a Shakespearean context. This is because several YouTubers have used 'Shakespeare' in the title of their videos, even though they have no Shakespeare connection other than allowing for a word play on 'shake'.[84] Such uses imply a decidedly postmodern citational form, in which Shakespeare becomes an empty signifier. Yet, in several instances, the Harlem Shakespeare videos do indeed have something to say about Shakespeare. The earliest use of Shakespeare in conjunction with 'Harlem Shake' is *The Harlem Shake (Romeo + Juliet)*, uploaded on 14 February 2013 (827 views), where the meme is integrated into the fan-made music video.[85] Baauer's track is set to the ballroom scene from Luhrmann's *Romeo+Juliet*. However, the two predominant contexts for the fusion of Shakespeare and the meme are classrooms or a school setting (accounting for 28 videos) and theatres (21 videos).

In the first category, performances take place in the classroom, sometimes featuring a teacher as in *Harlem Shakespeare* (uploaded 26 February 2013; 2,992 views), which introduces its use of the meme with a title sequence: 'Harlem Shakespeare: When AP English class meets Hamlet and memes'.[86] The classroom versions tend to be much more conservative than others available on YouTube, most likely a result of their institutional setting and the age of the participants. The video begins with the class quietly reading, and then dancing. Apart from one Viking helmet – presumably a comic signal to the play's Danish setting – the costumes offer no visual cues to the play. The meme is applied to the Shakespearean context more extensively in *Harlem Shake Julius Caesar Version* (uploaded 15 March 2013; 320 views). As the class read quietly, one student, dressed in a toga and wearing a gold paper crown, dances. As the hypnotic beat of Baauer's track begins, there is a jump cut to the group, now all wearing togas, attacking the Caesar figure. Other videos develop the meme as part of a theatrical performance. *Harlem Shakespeare* (uploaded 1 April 2013; 266 views) is set on a stage and frames the dance with a close-up of a Shakespeare figure writing at a desk. The video then cuts to students performing in Shakespearean costumes, with post-edit titles indicating the various groupings from the plays (Romeo and Juliet, the fairies and Nick Bottom, Rosencrantz and Guildenstern, Julius Caesar and Brutus) that are represented. In other school-based theatrical performances, the meme is used as part of a promotional trailer, as in *The Tempest Harlem Shake* (uploaded 26 March 2013; 281 views), or is even integrated into a performance, with the clip subsequently shared on YouTube, as in the performance of *A Midsummer Night's Dream* (uploaded 9 March 2013; 742 views).

What do these various 'memeings' of Shakespeare reveal? In relation to the classroom and school-based videos, they reflect the latest mode through which school goers approach Shakespeare. The meme is to a current cohort of students what rap or hip hop was to an earlier one. Rather than merely providing an entertaining class activity, the videos reflect the use of experiential learning, as in the example of *Julius Caesar* above, where the *Harlem Shake* is used to represent the action of the play. In relation to theatre, the meme not only has a demonstrative promotional function, but as integrated into a performance can operate on a deeper level. Its inclusion in a *Midsummer Night's Dream* production may serve to draw out the pleasures and unruly dimensions of the forest, as well as complementing the festive comedy of the play more generally. In a classroom, the temporary abandonment provided by the meme, and its containment by an institutionalized setting, mirrors the dynamic of Shakespeare's play, where the freedoms and misrule afforded by the faery world are closed off with the return of the young courtly lovers to the relative order and decorum of Athens. The combination of *Harlem Shake* and Shakespearean comedy suggests further analogies between the two, encouraging us to see them as mutual spaces for entertainment, laughter and pleasure. As such, the meme is not just a gimmick, but can contribute to how a performance achieves meaning or enable students to find an entry-point into the play. The creators are exploiting the meme's instantaneity and cool cachet. In the process, we can see how Shakespeare's meaning is invariably filtered through and contingent on the present, on the specificities of a time, place and their cultural dominants.

Memes are indicative of YouTube's temporal immediacy. They can quickly go viral, yet their lifespan can be short lived as they are displaced by the next trend. At the same time, given the site's status as an archive, it is also possible to revisit earlier memes, even though their moment has passed. The *Downfall* meme is a case in point. Beginning in 2007, it seemed to have reached its apotheosis in late 2009 and early 2010, though derivations continue to be shared.[87] It is something of a YouTube classic. Adapting the German film *Der Untergang* (2004) that focuses on the last days of Hitler's regime, the meme involves the insertion of new subtitles into scenes.[88] This is usually with comic effect, as in *Hitler gets banned from Xbox Live* (uploaded 7 June 2007; 8,006,793 views).[89] Videos can be satirical too, especially where they target politicians. *Downfall* has given rise to 'meta-memes' or videos that advert their status as memes, as in *Hitler Hates "Hitler Gets Banned" Parody Videos*.[90] As well as its satirical properties, the meme's appeal has been framed in terms of the dissonance it creates between intensely dramatic scenes and the comical or incongruous text within the subtitles.[91]

Shakespeare gets the *Downfall* treatment in 5 videos. Well-established aspects of Shakespeare's image in popular culture are exploited to comic ends. For instance, the authorship controversy provides the impetus for *Hitler Reacts to Discovering Marlowe was really Shakespeare* (uploaded 30 November 2011; 94 views).[92] The long history of students' aversion to Shakespeare is tackled in *Hitler Learns That He Will Be Learning about Shakespeare in School* (uploaded 30 April 2011; 191 views).[93] Similarly, recognizing that Shakespeare can be off-putting, the educational video *Romeo and Juliet: Brief and Naughty* (uploaded 19 February 2010; 10,738 views) prefaces its plot outline with the *Downfall* meme, with the revelation that 'the friar never told Romeo that Juliet was still alive' synced with Hitler's outburst.[94] The dominant tone here is irony, and both the figure of Hitler and the conventions of Shakespearean tragedy are played for laughs. However, the *Downfall* treatment becomes disquieting and problematic when, as in *Hitler Reads Shakespeare* (uploaded 29 March 2011; 2,568 views), it is applied to Shylock's monologue from Act 3, Scene 1.[95]

The selection of this particular speech, in which Shylock's expression of vengeance moves into an impassioned reflection on perceptions of 'a Jew' (lines 48–66) brings the video into the charged hermeneutic field that is Shakespeare's *Merchant of Venice*. In turn, the video brings into focus the politics of the *Downfall* meme itself: at what point 'does featuring the image of Hitler go too far?'[96] The question might be answered with Adorno's observation that in a world where holocaust remains a possibility, 'lighthearted art is no longer conceivable'.[97] Relatedly, the figure of Hitler as a visual constant that can be comically replicated signals a postmodern vacuity, and even an erasure of history. The syncing of Shylock's words with the image of Hitler railing against his peers is potentially inflammatory and doubly offensive to Jewish identity, involving as it does the combination of the Nazi dictator with a representation of 'a Jew' that is itself problematic. The comments on the video afford some insight into its reception, with one viewer referring to Shakespeare as 'an early anti-Semite'.[98] At stake, here, is the representation of Shylock and also the politics of Shakespeare's play.

Shylock has been described as 'an empty signifier that has been subsequently invested with historical and cultural meaning'.[99] Yet this description overlooks the signifying powers of the text and its representations. On these, some critics are unequivocal: 'it would have been better for the last four centuries of the Jewish people had Shakespeare never written this play'.[100] In a post-Holocaust context, Shylock instantiates what Rob Conkie calls 'aftershocks' in the way that Shakespeare's texts so often 'provide an earthquake-like impact, the vibrations of which continue to echo throughout history'.[101] Mindful of the play's acute reverberations for modern audiences, some directors have sought to forge a 'sympathetic portrait' of Shylock, often through the excision of those lines that reflect the 'unacceptable "attitudes of the time"'.[102] For instance, playwright Arnold Wesker criticized David Thacker's 1993 RSC production for altering the text and erasing those aspects that, to Wesker, evidenced the play's work in the transmission of anti-Semitism.[103] In his own rewriting of the play, Wesker confronts the problematic sentiment of Shylock's 'Hath not a Jew eyes', remarking: 'Jews do not want apologies to be made for their humanity ... Their humanity is their right.'[104] Responses to Wesker's Shylock suggested that it succeeded in showing the character 'from inside the ghetto, inside the man, inside the experience of being an alien'.[105] However, as Barbara Hodgdon asks, 'And Shakespeare's play does not?'[106]

Arguments that Shakespeare's play discloses the workings of stereotypes by building into the audience's experience of the drama 'a critical distance on the phenomenon of anti-Semitisim' run into difficulties with the ending, Shylock's forced conversion to Christianity.[107] Our culture has secured for Shakespeare a positive portrayal of Shylock largely by bifurcating the 'Hath not a Jew' speech from the play. Provocatively, the *Downfall* Shylock provides a visual reminder of that separation. By transposing into the Hitler meme a speech that has sometimes been regarded as affording empathy to the otherwise maligned Jew, sometimes seen as indicative of the play's offensiveness, the video draws a correlation between the violence of Nazism and the prejudice that undergirds cultural representations like *The Merchant of Venice*. The *Downfall* Shylock suggests the challenges of this play, and asks us to confront its 'aftershocks'.

# Vidding, paratexts and parodies

Another indicative YouTube Shakespeare genre is the fan-made music video, part of a practice known as 'vidding', where clips from TV and movies are set to music. Among the Shakespearean iterations of this genre, *Romeo and Juliet* stands out, most likely as a consequence of the play's appeal to youth culture and the success of Luhrmann's 1996 film.[108] The subsequent incorporation of the film into school and college curricula as a key text to teach Shakespeare also explains its popularity in the early years of YouTube, as students responded anew through classroom-inspired projects and through forms of vernacular expression.

Of YouTube fan responses to Luhrmann's film, *Romeo and Juliet (Sacrifice)* has the highest view count (uploaded 23 September 2007; 8,453,667 views).[109] Applying the logic of remix, the YouTuber combines visuals from the film with the song 'Sacrifice' by Russian band tATu to produce a fan-made music video.[110] The accompanying description provides some insight into the motivations behind the production: 'Back in 1996, the remake of Romeo and Juliet was my obsession ... mainly because of Leonardo DiCaprio! After hours of editing and making 10 different versions, here is a music video I have made in honor of this wonderful film.' Fan culture – in this instance surrounding the then 21-year-old Leonardo DiCaprio – accounts for the video's relation to Shakespeare. That relation can also be understood as paratextual. As Jonathan Gray argues, fan-made trailers, TV spoilers and other texts of fandom are paratexts. Elaborating on Gerard Genette's sense of paratexts as those properties that prepare us for entry into texts, Gray reads fan vids as critical objects through which a reader frames their relation to a text, creates an interpretative community and thus shapes the meanings and reception of the text.[111] At the same time, fan-created trailers often echo industry-created paratexts, retaining the aesthetic and editing of the official trailer, a tendency that might lead us to regard them as free promotion tools for a particular film or TV series.

However, as Matt Hills argues, fans are already situated within consumer culture; the difficulty is that much academic work on fandom continues to assign value to fan practices on the basis of their anti-consumerist stance, or in such terms that posits a false binary of the 'good fan' and the 'bad consumer'.[112] Fans undertake close readings, and their paratexts not only entail a level of commentary, but can also be understood as annotations or traces of the fan's responsiveness to the text.[113] As such, they should not be regarded as consumptive derivations of the commercial content that they cite. While *Romeo and Juliet (Sacrifice)* is ostensibly about DiCaprio, the video is also an indicator of the fan's responsiveness to the film. It constitutes a form of remembrance, or a reactivation of the initial pleasure of viewing the Luhrmann film (and its Hollywood star).

The video presents an interesting example of how a high view count does not always guarantee video quality. The impressive view count is most likely a result of DiCaprio, supported by the iconic status of Luhrmann's film, rather than the quality of the remix. While the song choice works particularly well with the movie, the editing undertaken is minimal. By contrast, *Paire (Peter and Claire) – Romeo and Juliet trailer* (uploaded 9 October 2007) has a lower view count (8,449), but provides a far more accomplished remix. The title alludes to two characters, Claire Bensen (played by Hayden Panettiere) and Peter Petrelli (played by Milo Ventimiglia), from the science-fiction drama *Heroes*.[114] The video is reflective of how cult TV fandom involves an 'emotional investment' in a TV series, amplifying or reimagining couplings that are not pursued in the original plot, or that perhaps are not sanctioned by it.[115] Deftly mixing *Heroes* with Luhrmann's film, the video is especially effective where it substitutes dialogue between Peter and Claire with the voices of DiCaprio and Claire Danes. Shakespeare's 'classic love story of Romeo and Juliet' (as the description below the video puts it) is invoked as the exemplar of *amor vincit omnia*, with the star-crossed lovers at once valorizing and giving way to the fan pairing of Peter and Claire.

In these videos, the point of connection to Shakespeare is mediated. Viewed from the perspective of fandom and vidding, Shakespeare is not top ranking in terms of a hierarchy of cultural value. Within YouTube culture, Shakespearean texts are one among a diffuse set of cultural references to be remixed. In the *Heroes* video, Romeo and Juliet ultimately play a supporting role, which serves the video's celebration of the Peter and Claire coupling. This illustrates the broader paradoxical effect that vernacular productions can have on Shakespeare. On the one hand, the texts continue to circulate or resonate within popular culture through their paratexts, thus sustaining meaning in the broadest sense. On the other hand, they do so in a way that is both fragmentary and dilutive. While recognizing that YouTube Shakespeare videos result in a reduced Shakespeare, or that videos frequently involve a derivative familiarity with a text rather than a full knowledge of it, I would caution against interpreting this situation negatively, since to do so would be to rely on an overly dichotomous sense of the relationship between popular iterations of Shakespeare and a putatively stable body of original texts. Videos can more usefully be understood as paratextual contributions and interventions, which have a rhizomatic relation to Shakespeare, at once contributing to the circulation of his works, while also occupying other lines of flight.[116]

Videos can have an attenuated relationship to the Shakespearean text, becoming 'texts in and of their own right'; equally, they can involve a return to the urtext and even spotlight an interpretation of it.[117] To take the example of a more recent Shakespeare film, the trailer for *Coriolanus* (2011), directed by Ralph Fiennes, is available on YouTube as official content posted by Lionsgate.[118] There is also user-circulated material and, as with other Shakespeare films, Fiennes' film has inspired fan-made trailers and music videos. Indeed, as the first filmic adaptation of *Coriolanus* and, in the assessment of Peter Holland, likely to 'be the most watched version of the play for a long time to come', it will be interesting to see what other kinds of video response it generates.[119] The official trailer does its work of promoting the film and preparing an audience. Distilling the film's modern-day militaristic aesthetic – while filmed in Serbia, the action is set in an unspecified military state – the trailer is largely expository. It establishes the relation of the protagonist, the Roman general Caius Martius Coriolanus (played by Fiennes), to his *agon*, the Volscian general Aufidius (Gerard Butler), and the subsequent reversal which occurs as enmity gives way to a new but volatile proximity in their mutual animus toward Rome.[120] Themes of betrayal and vengeance are foregrounded, with the latter dramatically outlined through a close-up of Coriolanus' sword and shots of bloodied faces. The trailer markets violence as part of this film's offering, with Shakespearean verse incorporated as soundbites, so as not to disrupt explosive images.[121]

Fan-created responses augment the film's visual orientation through selection and editing, but they also constitute inter-pretative acts. *Coriolanus Trailer – Nothing Else Matters* (uploaded 18 December 2012; 2,350 views) foregrounds the centrality of the Coriolanus–Aufidius relationship and retains the official trailer's inclusion of short excerpts of verse.[122] It also captures, and arguably dwells upon, the video-game quality to the violence in Fiennes' film. Yet the choice of score here, 'Nothing Else Matters' by Scala and Kolacny Brothers, brings an elegiac quality to these images that is not conveyed by the official paratext. By contrast, *Coriolanus music video* (uploaded 24 July 2012; 221 views) amplifies the film's battle scene between Coriolanus and Aufidius, mashing it with the track 'Mutter' by German band Rammstein.[123] The angry lyrics and the heavy-metal beat of the track complement the selected images from the film to recreate the trailer as a music video. When we appreciate that the lyrics are addressed to a maternal figure from the perspective of a child, then their association with Coriolanus, whose relation to his own mother person-alizes and deepens his tragic suffering at the hands of Rome, becomes more intriguing still. Fiennes' film is a complex text. It is at its most effective where it uses Shakespeare's play to explore the interrelations of warfare, political leadership and the media.[124] It also undertakes a character study, drawing out the anxieties about emasculation that lurk within Coriolanus' distinctly masculine code of *virtus* by pursuing the suggestion in the play of a homoerotic dimension to the proximity between Coriolanus and Aufidius. The casting of Vanessa Redgrave as Volumnia serves to enrich the intensity of that role, which in Shakespeare's play brings considerable power and privilege to the maternal, while also locating it as the fatal source of the son's sense of valour and thus of his manhood.[125] However, while conveying the intricacies of the maternal-filial bond, the star turn of Fiennes in the title role means that the tragic pathos of the warrior remains the focus and with it the masculine code of honour. *Coriolanus music video* poses further questions as to the gender politics of the Coriolanus story. By combining the battle scene with the track 'Mutter', with its figurative treatment of a child railing against its unknown maternal figure, the video positions the Coriolanus story as patriarchal wish-fulfilment, in which the threat of the feminine and the maternal are erased. However, the politics of this particular *Coriolanus* video may be an unintended consequence of fan activity: the user's channel suggests that the response to Fiennes' film is part of a wider interest and enjoyment in music video creation, rather than a concern with Shakespeare per se.

# The fan performance

Yet, as I have been arguing, even where fan videos appear to have a tangential concern with Shakespeare, or quote Shakespeare texts and film as they would other popular culture elements, they nonetheless contribute towards the meaning of Shakespeare. Other YouTube videos reveal a level of Shakespeare fandom, in that they focus their attention on the texts or some proxy for the author. Considering that the phenomenon of Shakespeare sampled and enmeshed within popular culture is now held to be the normative condition of the Bard as he is consumed in global culture, it is these videos rather than mashups that might strike us as the truly radical texts. Whereas the channel for the creator of *Coriolanus music video* reveals a minimal interest in Shakespeare, the series of one-woman performances by The Geeky Blonde indicate a sustained emphasis on things Shakespearean and a construction of online community through the plays.[126]

The Geeky Blonde evidences a dynamic and evolving vernacular Shakespeare production on YouTube. The first video in the series, *The Merchant of Venice*, was posted in April 2011, and the most recent is *Romeo and Juliet*, posted in February 2013. While moving across Shakespearean genres, with comedy (*The Merchant of Venice*, *A Midsummer Night's Dream*, *Twelfth Night*), tragedy (*Hamlet*, *Macbeth*, *Romeo and Juliet*) and romance (*Cymbeline*, *The Winter's Tale*), the videos are nonetheless consistent in terms of their overall approach and aesthetic, although some developments are evident when more recent videos are compared with earlier ones. Her productions are noteworthy not only because they each involve one-person performances of the major – and indeed minor – parts by the creator, but also because they range beyond Shakespeare's most prominent plays.[127] With the shortest of the videos lasting 10 minutes, they also challenge YouTube's reduced attention economy. There is a striking variety to The Geeky Blonde's performances, with characters differentiated through vocal modulation, facial and other non-verbal expressions, an extensive wardrobe (especially of hats) and well-paced editing.

With the exception of the first video, each production features 'Sockspeare', a Shakespeare sock-puppet, and the shared conceit throughout the series is that The Geeky Blonde has been tricked by this proxy for the Bard to undertake solo-performances of the plays. As part of the conceit, The Geeky Blonde is given, or finds, a copy of the Shakespearean text. The device is sent up, as in the preamble to the *Macbeth* (uploaded 31 October 2012; 2,867 views) performance, where The Geeky Blonde berates the puppet for suggesting the Scottish play, calling him 'an anthropomorphic codpiece'.[128] The inclusion of the sock puppet establishes the tone of the performances, which tend towards parody, irony and the incongruous. It might denote a *Sesame Street* Shakespeare, but precedents for reincarnating the Bard indicate that seemingly juvenile absurdities often carry deeper effects.[129] There may also be echoes of the Reduced Shakespeare Company, as well as more recent pop culture treatments of Shakespeare available on YouTube such as *Sassy Gay Friend* (their *Hamlet* is included in Geeky Blonde's channel as a favourite video), although Geeky Blonde's performances incorporate a greater degree of Shakespearean verse than either of these texts.

The productions support the argument for regarding parody as the predominant mode of YouTube Shakespeare, in the tradition of such classic parodies as Tom Stoppard's *Fifteen Minute Hamlet* and *Rosencrantz and Guildenstern are Dead*.[130] The Geeky Blonde videos share certain attributes with these Shakespeare parodies: anachronisms and plot absurdities are foregrounded, aspects of the text are amplified with ridiculous effects, and an incongruous style is chosen. While recognizing such patterns to Shakespeare parody, we must be careful to avoid totalizing assessments of YouTube Shakespeare. The Geeky Blonde's videos engage in parody, but do so from the perspective of a fan concerned with addressing troubling and implausible aspects of Shakespearean texts.

Significantly, her productions entail a meta-commentary on the text and performance that reflect on the distance between the Shakespearean texts and contemporary culture in terms of attitudes to gender and sexuality. In *Cymbeline* (uploaded 1 October 2011; 1,547 views), for example, the exposition is interrupted by the persona of The Geeky Blonde, who notes of the play's Queen, 'just pause here – everyone calls her the Queen, a brilliantly dehumanizing technique since she is essentially the villain'.[131] In the *Hamlet* production (uploaded 27 May 2012; 4,085 views), what seems like an earnest rendition of the first soliloquy, 'O that this too too sallied flesh would melt' (I.2.129) breaks off into a comically mundane expression of Oedipal frustrations: 'Oh, my mother has so much sex.'[132] Hamlet's latent desire for his mother is coupled with recurring comic allusions to a homoerotic subtext – of the first appearance of the ghost, Marcellus says to Horatio 'that's really going to upset your boyfriend', and after the death of Hamlet, The Geeky Blond interjects with 'Hamatio forever.' The comedies provide further scope for mocking such proximities between men – indeed Shakespeare texts are construed as forms of Slash fiction (the classic example in fan culture is the imagined pairing of Kirk and Spock from *Star Trek*).[133] In The Geeky Blonde's *Merchant of Venice* (uploaded 3 April 2011; 821 views), for instance, Antonio jealously contemplates destroying the marriage of Bassanio and Portia.[134] *Twelfth Night* (uploaded 2 January 2013; 1,859 views) similarly provides for a comic sense of suppressed male–male relations: a title head for the character Antonio reads, 'Sebastian's (cuddle) buddy (seriously read the play and pay attention to this pair)'.[135]

The use of the parodic mode here to disclose subtexts prompts a broader consideration of the effect and politics of parody. Simon Dentith defines parody as 'any cultural practice which provides a relatively polemical allusive imitation of another cultural production or practice'.[136] His qualifying terms are deliberate here, with the polemical characterized as 'relatively' in order to allow for the degrees of critique that the hypertext (or the text doing the parodying) performs on the hypotext (the text being parodied). The qualifications also steer a line between the influential theorizations of parody as offered by Frederic Jameson on the one hand and Linda Hutcheon on the other.[137] In Jameson's formulation, meaningful forms of allusiveness and imitation once associated with parody have, in the contemporary 'cultural dominant' of postmodernism, given way to pastiche, or parody 'amputated of the satiric impulse'.[138] At work here is Jameson's broader argument about postmodernism as the cultural logic of late capitalism, a logic which sees aesthetic production as inseparable from commodity production, where the collapse of modernist distinctions between high and popular culture signal 'a new kind of flatness or depthlessness', as exemplified in Andy Warhol's art, or postmodern architecture.[139] For Hutcheon, however, postmodern productions – and she too takes the example of architecture – do not involve the meaningless recycling of existing or dead styles. Rather, they involve 'imitation characterized by ironic inversion' or 'repetition with critical distance', at once exploiting the cultural significance of the older style, while also pointing to its distance from the contemporary world.[140] Hutcheon reminds us of the dual and paradoxical possibilities inherent within parody, that is its deferential and critical registers, as captured in the prefix 'para', as 'close to' and yet 'counter' to the original.[141] Thus, instead of interpreting parody as *either* depthless *or* critically efficacious, we might note that it can have a range of effects – it can be 'more or less playful, critical, ironic, or empty' – depending on the specific dimensions of its use.[142]

The Geeky Blonde videos reveal these various forms parody takes. They exploit what is already comic in Shakespeare's plot (as in the interchange in *Twelfth Night* between Orsino and Viola disguised as the boy Cesario), but they do so with a critical edge. The performances allude to the trans-vestism of Shakespearean theatre, as The Geeky Blonde cross-dresses and plays both female and male roles. They also involve a critique of the one-directional nature of female impersonation in Shakespeare.[143] Thus in *A Midsummer Night's Dream* (uploaded 3 August 2012; 1,881 views), Peter Quince complains to his fellow players about the gender restrictions imposed on casting Thisbe: 'because of some stupid laws, women aren't allowed to act yet … you think I want some scrawny chicken boy playing the part of my tragic heroine?'[144] This is just one of the ways that The Geeky Blonde's performances suggest the generic and ideological limitations of Shakespearean comedy.[145] Elsewhere, by making explicit what is often implied or contained within the plot, The Geeky Blonde highlights the distance and conservatism of Shakespearean drama in terms of its attitude to same-sex relations. As such, she achieves the kind of critical distance Hutcheon identifies as the hallmark of parody. In another sense, however, playing homoeroticism for laughs might not be the most productive way to unsettle heteronormativity and its cultural expressions.

The treatment of Shakespearean verse is also revealing in terms of the status of the videos as Shakespeare parodies. Each features culturally familiar nuggets of quotes, such as Lady Macbeth's 'Out, out damned spot! Out, I say!'(V.1.33), or Malvolio's 'Some are born great' (III.2.39–43), as well ones comparatively less familiar, such as Iachimo's 'Let me my service tender on your lips' (I.6.140) to Imogen from *Cymbeline*. As the series has developed, the proportion of Shakespeare lines has increased: the most recent video of *Romeo and Juliet* includes over four lines from Mercutio's Queen Mab speech (I.4.53–94), to which Polonius, making a cameo, replies 'This is too long.' Through such intertextual cues, The Geeky Blonde self-referentially addresses the supplementing of verse with a colloquial idiom, thus pushing at the constraints of her condensed Shakespeare. What the videos are doing in these moments is establishing a set of protocols for their reception, and constructing a Shakespeare that is funny, concise and accessible to an audience. Crucial to this process is the persona of the 'Geeky Blonde', with its gesture towards two recognizable types of femininity within contemporary (teen) culture. In *A Midsummer Night's Dream*, Helena's unrequited love for Lysander is summed up by her claim, 'My life is a Taylor Swift song.' In *Hamlet*, Ophelia listens to Justin Bieber's track 'Baby' in order to avoid hearing her father's advice. 'I'm ADDICTED to these bad boys. This counts as revision right?' posts one viewer.[146] As another viewer comments, 'After watching all these videos, I now want to read Shakespeare.'[147] By drawing Shakespeare within the orbit of popular and, more specifically, teen culture, and peppering the exposition of plot with contemporary allusions, The Geeky Blonde makes Shakespeare seem less intimidating and pretentious.

The pop music references not only suggest that teenage girls constitute the target audience for the video, but also signal The Geeky Blonde's interest in sending up the traditional patriarchal Bard. Her act of parody might be interpreted as 'an empowering, even subversive, act of transgression', one that disrupts boundaries between high and popular culture.[148] At the same time, however, because parody presumes an audience 'with enough knowledge of the parodied texts to understand its references', it can reinstate those boundaries and appear 'culturally elitist in itself'.[149] Some of these terms are applicable to The Geeky Blonde series, in which the self-styled 'geek' assumes the role of interpreter, not only mediating the texts to her YouTube audience, but also determining which ones to perform. This is especially evident in her vlog-style video *I Fell for Hamlet* (uploaded 16 September 2012; 1,175 views), which parodies Michelle Ray's novel *Falling for Hamlet*.[150] Of further significance is the inclusion in each video of a copy of the play being performed, a signifier of textual authority from which the ensuing performance is derived. A potential effect is the production of a hierarchy of knowledge between the creator and the audience, a hierarchy that risks invoking an inflexible idea of the Shakespeare text, situating it in opposition to popular culture.

Yet, for the parody to work, and the gags to be effective, The Geeky Blonde's audience needs to appreciate both Shakespeare and popular culture. The videos rely on both of these vocabu-laries. The pop culture references, while self-evident and more accessible than Shakespeare, are carefully matched to the Shakespearean context, so they only really work where the viewer appreciates how they relate back to the play. A familiarity with plot and character is therefore necessary – the cuts are so quick and the parts sometimes subtly differentiated that the performances would not make much sense otherwise. Fast-paced and ironic, current and accessible, ultimately The Geeky Blonde offers an unashamedly pop culture Shakespeare. Yet, in placing demands on the viewer, referring back to the text, or inserting an additional Shakespeare intertext into a performance, her series suggests a more literary, canonical Shakespeare in contradistinction to its 'Sockspeare'. There are glimpses too of earnest performance, especially in those moments where Shakespearean verse is allowed to be heard or where the quick edits give way to a close-up of a character. Within this condensed Shakespeare, it is as if a fuller account of the plays is awaiting iteration.

# Mr Shakespeare reads

The Geeky Blonde's Shakespeare reflects a wider tension regarding what Shakespeare means and how the plays are experienced in contemporary popular culture. The unease that sometimes attaches to the imbrication of Shakespeare in popular culture is bound up with a nostalgia for the lost aura of the Shakespearean text, as if to say that pop culture operates on a destructive logic that ultimately kills a putative textual origin (seeing the movie replaces reading or seeing the play, or watching a video clip replaces the movie). Critics writing on Shakespeare and film have noted that nostalgia is a recurring trope of filmic adaptations of the plays.[151] It can take different forms, as in a visual cue to an older medium. Invoking a surrogate or proxy for the author constitutes another form of symbolic compensation for a lost aura. YouTube contains several Shakespeare surrogates. These invocations of the author represent one of the more curious aspects of pop culture responses. They also controvert one of the central tenets of literary theory: that the meaning of a text is not reducible to its author's life, experiences or attitudes. However, on some level, they reflect a desire to connect the individual literary imagination to the works. The mythic quality accorded to Shakespearean authorship in popular culture reflects a return to a Romantic period conception of the individual artist and his creative genius, one that is taken up by pop culture as an 'alternative to the dehumanizing effects of mass production and the profit-driven imperatives of advanced capitalism'.[152] YouTubers have taken to performing in the likeness of Shakespeare, quite literally enacting the 'bardic function', dovetailing their own creative intervention into mass media with the iconic image of Shakespeare or with a Shakespearean alias.

The channel billyharper11 features 4 videos, each of which involves the user dressed as Shakespeare and lip-syncing to well-known tracks by Vanilla Ice, Snoop Dog and Barry White. In *Shakespeare does Barry White* (uploaded 28 August 2007; 1,032 views), we see Shakespeare, dressed in a doublet, and sporting large earphones, lip sync to 'Can't Get Enough of Your Love' while on a public bus in an American city.[153] A similarly playful investment in the human face behind the texts – or at least a simulacrum of the author drawn from popular culture representations – is offered in *Mr Shakespeare Reads*.[154] By adding the visual gimmick of Shakespearean disguise and hairstyle, these videos develop the established genre of the vernacular Shakespeare performance. What we have is an embodied performance of the Droeshout image from the First Folio, a curious animation of an authorial and textual corpus. Through the paratexts that accompany the videos, such as the channel description ('William Shakespeare reads "The Complete Works of Me". Sonnets, speeches, and prose, in full Elizabethan regalia') and the description below each video ('William Shakespeare reading from ...'), we are encouraged to view the performances as the Bard taking up YouTube's invitation to 'Broadcast Yourself'. Holding his book, with a copy of the Folio image on the front, Shakespeare reads a sonnet, occasionally looking to the camera. It is no accident that thus far the series has focused on the *Sonnets*, for it is these texts that have proved most accommodating to the idea of the singular author as literary genius.

*Mr Shakespeare Reads* may signify little beyond the obvious visual gag. In part, the undertaking may be about acquiring the username 'Mr Shakespeare Reads' on YouTube and being the first to do so. Yet, as visual registers of the mythic author, the videos posit a Stratfordian Shakespeare, thus indirectly engaging with the authorship controversy, itself a space where the primacy of individual genius finds ongoing expression in the popular imagination.[155] The videos are contiguous with a theme-park Shakespeare, or those street performers who don Shakespeare disguises for the entertainment of visitors to Stratford-upon-Avon and other locations of the Shakespeare industry.[156] As in those instances, the simulacrum of 'the man himself' in *Mr Shakespeare Reads* reflects a desire for a grounding authenticity, which permits the illusion of unmediated access to the texts.

That desire is comically sent up in *Shakespeare Reborn*, a series of sketches that parody educational documentaries, especially their use of the expert talking to camera.[157] In the final sketch (uploaded 6 July 2012; 26 views), a Shakespeare doll talks from behind *The Complete Works*, expressing some bemusement about 'his' posthumous achievement.[158] The camera angle serves to minimize the doll in relation to the book, perhaps conveying how the work ultimately subsumes the writer, a phenomenon that has been traced back to the First Folio itself.[159] *Shakespeare Reborn* pushes the idea of the author to an absurdity, and its use of a Shakespeare doll (sold in tourist shops, galleries and online) enacts a distinctly postmodern sense of the author as fetishized commodity. This is taken a step further in *7 Ages of Man.wmv* (uploaded 16

February 2010; 4,884 views), a video that, when first opened, looks to be a simple still of the Chandos portrait combined with audio of the 'Seven Ages of Man' speech.[160] However, when we hit play, Shakespeare's eyes and mouth move, in sync with the audio. What we have in this Shakespeare cyborg is no more than the product of computer software, of a YouTuber's deft use of movie-generator software. Yet, there is also a sense here of the uncanny and of quotation as itself ghostly and disconcerting – the 'return of the expressed', to borrow Marjorie Garber's adroit phrasing. [161] The video captures the state of Shakespeare in contemporary culture – as always already remediated through technologies of representation.

# Is YouTube Shakespeare global Shakespeare?

Refracted in these YouTube videos are some of the wider issues marking contemporary popular culture's relation to Shakespeare. However, in exploring YouTube as one of the spaces where that relation occurs, we need to address how contemporary culture is being understood, especially in the context of the increasingly globalized sphere of cultural production. As Burgess and Green note, 'YouTube is "global" in the sense that the Internet is – it is accessible from (almost) anywhere in the world.' They also point out that it is '*globalizing* in that it allows virtual border-crossings between the geographical location of producers, distributors and consumers'.[162] Shakespeare is also understood as global to the extent that the transnational travels of Shakespearean texts and adaptations seem unremarkable. At the same time, we have become attentive to the specific localities of contributions to the ever accommodating, expanding reach of the Bard.[163] Sonia Massai has sought to complicate the relation of these global and local Shakespeares.[164] Others have argued for continuing reflection about our use of these terms. Mark

Houlahan wonders whether critics sometimes take 'the global to be the multinational and the corporate, blandly disseminating sameness through the world, and the local to be the heroic, small scale attempts to sustain ... difference'.[165] Shakespeare may have become a global icon, but the operations of his cultural capital remain contingent on the local field of reception. For instance, within Shakespeare studies itself, differential values have applied to Anglophone and non-Anglophone materials, perhaps as a function of 'Anglophone cultural globalization' more generally.[166] However, Mark Thornton Burnett's recent work on non-Anglophone Shakespeare films has importantly broadened understandings about Shakespeare and world cinema.[167] In relation to YouTube, the plenitude of the platform should signal access to vernacular Shakespeare productions from across the globe. For instance, the evolving 'Global Shakespeares' database has a YouTube channel that might draw users to the database and its video-archive of world performances.[168] However, despite these developments and YouTube's own self-image as a global network, factors such as the site's search function and the user's IP address(es) limit the possibility of experiencing truly transnational content.[169] As one critic puts it, 'assertions about the YouTube utopia breaking down geography are overstated'.[170]

As I have been arguing, the protocols of the site have implications for the kinds of Shakespeare that a user encounters there. YouTube content is a product of its users and in certain respects is subject to the wisdom of crowds. The search function may appear to require no further thought, but each search presumes a set of hidden arrangements regarding geographic location and language. Search defaults to the location of the user's IP address and to the primary language of that location. There is an option enabling users to select the language in which they want to view the interface. A user can also change YouTube's location by selecting one of the 57 countries or regions listed. The United States is not an option on this location menu, since it constitutes the unnamed home of the site and its presumptive 'Worldwide' default setting.

This raises the issue of YouTube's contributory role in the Americanization of global culture. YouTube is keen to position itself as global, stating '70 per cent of YouTube traffic comes from outside the US'.[171] Yet, localization or regionalized search, as well as the role of IP addresses in pinpointing a user's search location, complicate claims about YouTube's global reach.[172] As Burgess and Green argue, 'Localization ... may have the effect of filtering out non-US and non-English speaking content for US viewers, and make it decreasingly unnecessary for Western, English-speaking users to encounter cultural difference in their experience of the website.'[173] Sampling of YouTube content suggests that approximately '15 per cent of the videos were in any language other than English'.[174] The case study of the *As You Like It* search bears out perceptions as to the Anglophonic predominance of content on YouTube: 14 of the 20 items on the first search page are from the US or UK; one is Japanese; and the others are unspecified.

The risk here is that a user might be inclined to accept these results – admittedly only a snapshot – as requiring no critical reflection, since they are after all determined by algorithmic relevance. As discussed earlier, recent critical work on algorithms has sought to examine why they are 'being looked to as a credible knowledge logic' and to address the implications of this self-affirming perception for epistemology.[175] The Google algorithm is the most obvious example here, having assumed a symbolic role as a producer of 'how we come to know' and relatedly 'what we *can* know'.[176] There are instructive parallels for YouTube, not simply because it is owned by Google and is integrated into its algorithm, but also because search results on YouTube similarly come to be regarded as objective truths.

The objectivity and validity of search results is only intensified through the operation of 'personalization algorithms', which map and predict a user's searches to form an aggregate of pre-stated preferences that tell the user what they mean and what they want.[177] The personalization of search is evident through the predictive search (as a user begins to type in a search) and also the videos that appear alongside a search with the message 'Recommended for you'. By viewing the site from an IP address in Ireland, for example, results are localized and weighted in favour of Anglophone content, even when the search filter is set to 'Worldwide'. A consequence of this arrangement for YouTube Shakespeare is that while a search appears to offer a genuinely diverse global picture, in reality the displayed results involve a certain complexion of the global. Moreover, since algorithms need users and their searches, it is also the case that, as searchers, we are becoming habituated to a kind of search parochialism.[178]

For all of its apparent newness, then, YouTube Shakespeare may involve a structural privileging of Anglophone content and, by extension, a positioning of the English language as a world language through which other cultures are filtered or made comprehensible. This has a bearing on understandings of YouTube's clip culture that generates an archive of Shakespeare materials. The accidental nature of that archive has already been recognized. It might now be necessary to recognize its potential to create a cultural memory of Shakespeare that is skewed towards the English-language centres of Shakespeare's performance and adaptation histories. As such, we may need to consider complementing our use of YouTube as a Shakespeare archive with curated sites like the 'Global Shakespeares' performance archive or the international database of Shakespeare on film and TV.[179] Rather than a blind acceptance of a first set of results, purposeful and active searching becomes crucial. After all, our searches as users are always legible to algorithms and are fed back into their computational provision of knowledge: 'Algorithms are made and remade in every instance of their use because every click, every query, changes the tool incrementally.'[180] In this regard, users play a role in determining what matters in the new knowledge economy.

However, while Anglophone Shakespeare film is well represented in the archive, indeed repetitively so, it would be misguided to dismiss YouTube Shakespeare as purely Anglophone, or as an Americanized Shakespeare. The filmography of Shakespeare and world cinema compiled by Mark Burnett provides a useful case study for exploring the global potentiality of YouTube Shakespeare. By analysing films from Latin America, China, India and several European locations, Burnett's work importantly reorients understandings of Shakespeare from the traditional 'US–UK axis'.[181] The filmography includes 75 titles. By undertaking a search of each title on YouTube, I was able to determine that 56 of the films are available on the site as official trailers or excerpted clips.[182] In the case of 8 of the titles, the entire film is available, though it is sometimes divided into parts. On the one hand, the availability of non-Anglophone Shakespeare films suggests the depth of YouTube's archive, which the language used in searching and the genericism of the search function itself may obscure.[183] YouTube is a potential discovery space for filmic adaptations of Shakespeare outside of an established canon – consider the example of *Gedebe*, a Malaysian film adaptation of *Julius Caesar*, which is available in full and with English subtitles.[184] On the other hand, YouTube instances and accentuates the differential value that has attached to Anglophone and non-Anglophone Shakespeare films. For example, the Mexican film *Amar te Duele* is available in full, but this adaptation of *Romeo and Juliet* does not have the recursive frequency on YouTube that Luhrmann's film enjoys. Furthermore, non-Anglophone films do not generate anything approaching the culture of vernacular remix and amateur performance associated with their Anglophone peers.[185]

Of course, this differential value extends beyond the particularities of YouTube's search function to encompass the fortunes of a particular film, as well as the vicissitudes of the global cinematic marketplace.[186] Just as some Anglophone Shakespeare films have greater appeal than others, so it is the case with non-Anglophone ones. The relative profile of Shakespeare films 'suggests fundamental variations in the universal cultural imprimatur with which Shakespeare is invariably associated'.[187] While the concept of the global may privilege certain perspectives at the expense of others, or lead to certain films being prized over others, we need to avoid positing too stark a binary of Anglophone/non-Anglophone Shakespeare films. To do so is to obscure the inter-citational dimensions of these films. For instance, *Chicken Rice War*, Chee Kong Cheah's adaptation of *Romeo and Juliet*, ironically references *Shakespeare in Love* and Luhrmann's *Romeo + Juliet*.[188] Michael Almereyda's *Hamlet* may make much of its Manhattan location, but its cultural referents are thoroughly intercultural, encompassing a Vietnamese Buhddist monk as well as Irish subtexts.[189] The Tibetan Hamlet film, *Prince of the Himalayas*, contains a visual cue to Julie Taymor's *Titus*, referencing that film's treatment of Lavinia in its own treatment of Ophelia's drowning.[190] Additionally, too stark a distinction obscures the workings of 'transnationalizing strategies' where, as in other Asian Shakespeare films such as *The Banquet*, film-makers endeavour to appeal to an international as well as local constituency.[191]

YouTube signals opportunities to pursue such connections further, with the playlist function within a channel allowing for compilations of Shakespeare and film organized thematically or by play title rather than by geographic or national designations. Yet the availability of these films raises issues regarding copyright infringement, as well as the exploitation of the costs and labour that have been incurred in their making. This is a problem for all commercial content producers, but it becomes especially acute in relation to independent film-makers working from small budgets. We need to acknowledge the evolving culture of openly available content – sometimes posted without permission of the copyright holder, sometimes made available by the studio or director – and its bearing on which examples of Shakespeare and world cinema get noticed (and by implication get watched, analysed and taught) over others. YouTube's embedded codes make it extremely easy to share content across platforms, which suggests that even those films available as clips or trailers can be showcased for teaching or research purposes. Teachers and researchers can thus play a role in bringing these films to the attention of the field and creating new audiences for them, yet they also have a responsibility to use the available content within the terms of fair use.

Sometimes used to emphasize the constituent elements within the global, sometimes invoked as an idealized alternative to the forces of globalization, localization has become an attractive concept in Shakespeare studies. There is something desirable in a future imagined for Shakespeare studies, where 'qualifying adjectives as Asian, European, African or even global' are no longer necessary, not least in its positing of a diffuse, dispersed Shakespearean 'home' and the disruption of a normative centre.[192] Yet there is a risk too that by dropping such culturally specific designations, we lose sight of the different histories of Shakespeare's global reception and, more worryingly, allow new forms of cultural imperialism to emerge (as in YouTube's worldwide setting that could signal North American cultural hegemony passing itself off as global). The present inquiry into the availability of non-Anglophone Shakespeare films highlights just some of the dilemmas posed by the global in YouTube Shakespeare, where search is located or regionalized. If YouTube is to be used as a teaching and learning resource, rather than automatically accepting the validity of predictive search, critical reflection about its status as archive will be necessary. Careful, deep and targeted searches are required in order to broaden what YouTube Shakespeare encompasses.

Non-English performances do appear in generic searches: under 'Hamlet', for example, though productions by the RSC, the Globe and American companies predominate, a user will also encounter a promotional trailer for Tomaz Pandur's visually inventive 2009 production at the Teatro Español.[193] However, for YouTube Shakespeare to become a discovery space requires an active user, one who is willing to defamiliarize their sense of Shakespeare. Among the numerous examples of the kind of discoveries possible is the case of the Thai film *Shakespeare Must Die*.[194] Set in a country resembling contemporary Thailand, the plot features an internalized

Shakespeare performance, a common device of movies that cite Shakespeare, in this case a theatre company embarking on a production of *Macbeth* that offends the country's autocratic regime. The meta-filmic plot device proved prescient: the Thai Film Censorship Board banned the film because in their assessment it contained 'content that causes divisiveness among the people of the nation'.[195] What was a promotional trailer on YouTube (uploaded 2 February 2012; 135,863 views) is now an indicator of state censorship, as well as a fascinating case of Shakespeare as a cipher through which national politics are negotiated and ideologies contested.[196]

*

YouTube crystallizes the contemporary moment as an attention economy characterized by an abundance of information that attains value depending on the attention it generates. Like the Internet more generally, it presents us with 'too much information and too few narratives that can tie it all together'.[197] In examining genres of YouTube Shakespeare, this chapter has undertaken an inquiry into the different kinds of patterns and themes that might be noticed amidst the flow of videos on the platform. As I have argued, YouTube presents us with a paradoxical combination of control (via its matrix of hyperlinks and the algorithmic determination of relevance) and capaciousness (in the sense of the depth and the accidental nature of its archive). Use is paradoxical too, entailing inattention, yet also serendipity. Rather than blindly accepting the opacity and internal validity of YouTube search, however, we need to bring to YouTube Shakespeare an awareness of the particular arrangements that run behind our searches – the algorithm, the default search location and IP address. Through critically reflective and deep searching, we might move from a sense of value based on view count – and thus a putative measure of attentiveness – towards one that takes in a range of criteria (such as genre, user-vernacular creativity and language). In short, value resides in exploiting

YouTube's copious content. Otherwise, YouTube Shakespeare risks being little more than an archive of Shakespeare film and performance clips. Through purposeful search, we might adapt the algorithm's mapping of our search preferences to our advantage and in the interests of a more plural set of results about Shakespeare. As much as the algorithm returns what we already know about Shakespeare based on our point of access to YouTube, we need to feed into its operations our own curiosities and interests, and reflect upon what it is *we* would like to know.

# 2

# Broadcast Your *Hamlet*: Convergence Culture, Shakespeare and Online Self-Expression

*Thine evermore, most dear lady, whilst this machine is to him. Hamlet.*

SHAKESPEARE, *HAMLET* (II.2.120)[1]

*To Tube or not to Tube, that is the question?*

XELANDERTHOMAS, *HAMLET PRINCE OF YOUTUBE*[2]

*I am a modern day Ophelia … living in the wrong era …*

POST ON JOSHJE777, *OPHELIA*[3]

*This is a rare find that only YouTube can provide.*

POST ON KENNETH DINKINS' *THE SHAKESPEARE TAPES*[4]

To search for, view and experience *Hamlet* on YouTube is to access the 'Hamletmachine'. The phrase alludes to Heiner Müller's 1977 play, where the remains of Shakespeare's tragedy

– or perhaps of Hamlet's description in the first epigraph above of his body as machine, an assembly of parts – provide the impetus for a series of terrifying fragments that express a nihilistic world.[5] It also derives from a student's assignment for a course I taught some years ago, where Müller's play was one of the prescribed texts.[6] As part of the assessment, students were invited to write a creative response to *Hamlet*. In one response, Shakespeare was a computer programmer charged with maintaining a giant cyborg called 'HAMLET', which churned out bite-size quotations as epigrams intended to create greater empathy in humans. With intertextual allusions to Asimov's 'The Immortal Bard' and Kubrick's *2001: A Space Odyssey*, the short story conveyed something of the status of both Shakespeare and also *Hamlet* (as synecdoche for the former) in contemporary culture as recycled and omnipresent, a pliable, but not always meaningful signifier.[7]

The ubiquity of *Hamlet* has resulted in parody, or the reduction of the character's philosophizing to bathos. For instance, the YouTube video *Cat Head Theatre* asks 'What would *Hamlet* look like if it were performed by cats?' Cue a short animation of three talking cat-heads, replete with cut-out Elizabethan attire, performing Hamlet's first meeting with Rosencrantz and Guildenstern, in a video that has had over 2.9 million views.[8] The allegorizing of Hamlet as a computer generated feline, or as automaton, is itself an unwitting repetition of a practice dating back to the nineteenth century, with the clockwork Hamlet and Ophelia of W. S. Gilbert's *The Mountebanks* (1892). This practice has been interpreted as emblematic of modernity itself, as expressive of the effects of mechanical repetition on cultural tradition and the dissipation of an aura.[9] However, Gilbert's mechanical Hamlet not only challenges the Romantic period conception of the 'uniquely rich if tortured subjectivity' Hamlet had come to stand in for,[10] but also reflects the necessity of envisaging a new way of imagining an already tradition-laden character and play to fit with the expressive technology of the time. Nonetheless, *Hamlet* goes on. 'The play lends itself to infinite

reprogramming', writes one critic, reminding us that theorizations of the modern subject, get 'fed into the machinery of the
play'.[11] YouTube's culture of vernacular production provides a
new space where the mythic capaciousness of the play can be
put to the test: anyone with a webcam or digital camera can
now share their Hamlet performance or production.

The search results for *Hamlet* indicate that many tubers
have done precisely that. A search under 'Shakespeare,
"Hamlet"' returns 66,800 results, an astonishing number,
its signifcance put all the more into perspective when set
beside figures for 'King Lear', which returns 12,700 results,
making *Hamlet*, numerically at least, a more popular play
than its traditional competitor for tragic excellence.[12] While
these numbers alone attest to the cultural reach of *Hamlet*,
my focus here is less about quantitative evaluations than
exploring iterations of the text by YouTubers through forms
of expression and participation native to YouTube itself. The
chapter identifies two dominant trends within YouTube's
self-generated *Hamlet*, namely videos concerned with 'To be,
or not to be' and with Ophelia's drowning. Of course, these
pivotal moments have developed an iconicity independent
of their host text. YouTube Shakespeare is no different:
it instances the association of *Hamlet* with repetition and
cultural entropy, as one video leads to another and another.
At the same time, however, YouTube's self-generated *Hamlets*
reflect a compulsion within our culture to make the text
anew. My concern here is to consider how and in what ways
YouTubers use *Hamlet* and to what extent the text facilitates
self-expression in an online setting. In becoming Hamlet or
Ophelia, or by associating their online alias or identity with
these characters, YouTubers make recourse to the rhetorical
figure of prosopopoeia, assuming the voice of an imagined
or absent person.[13] Hamlet and Ophelia emerge as figures of
repetition, perhaps reflecting a repetitive compulsion among
YouTubers to leave one's mark online – to be.

This chapter first considers the compulsion among tubers to
produce the play's signature speech as a fascinating negotiation

of derivation and the consequences of their own mediation. Second, questions of agency and origin are pursued through a detailed discussion of video responses to Ophelia. As with the soliloquy, Ophelia's iconicity is recycled within YouTube culture. Unlike the 'To be or not to be' videos, however, responses are predominantly by young women in ways that, I argue, suggest a frustration with over-determined constructions of gender and with those representations of women handed down by history. Nonetheless, YouTube Hamlet is a multivalent category, which evidences the extent to which Ophelia and Hamlet continue to generate responses and acquire new meanings. Moreover, YouTubers do not simply reproduce earlier iterations, but rather engage in forms of creative redaction. YouTube is becoming an increasingly important space where our exchange with *Hamlet* and Shakespeare can occur.

# 'To be or not to be remixed': Converging on the Hamletmachine

If *Hamlet* is indeed accessed on YouTube as if it were a machine, which provides ready-made templates (Hamlet and Ophelia) for online creative expression, then it is no different to any other text or data object that is grabbed, cited and shared by the user-consumer of media. However, this is not as stark a proposition as it first appears. Rather, it acknowledges that *Hamlet*, like Shakespeare more generally, is already embedded within YouTube's culture, which is to say our contemporary culture of media convergence. The model of convergence, which captures the interchange between old and new media content, as well as the asymmetrical relationship between the media producers and consumers, offers a useful way of formulating the practices and indeed politics of YouTube culture.[14] It also allows us to examine how YouTubers interact with and create *Hamlet* content.

Emphasizing the interconnections between an accessible digital media, user-generated content and media corporations, convergence culture is also a participatory culture (already explored in Chapter 1). It is less about a top-down or bottom-up understanding of media than an attempt to frame the complex interactions between multiple media agents. YouTube is, writes Alexandra Juhasz, a 'convergence superconductor', a phrase that captures its dual status as a databank of existing media content and also a host portal for spreading and sharing vernacular productions, productions that often draw from that existing content.[15] To freeze-frame the YouTube screen on a search 'Hamlet, "To be or not to be"', with the filter set to 'relevance', is to experience the dynamics of media convergence culture at first hand.[16] Contained in the list of videos is the mixture of media content that has become the hallmark of YouTube. We encounter content from existing media, such as excerpts from Shakespeare films shared on YouTube as favourite clips. These provide a ready-made archive of Hamlet performances (including Richard Burton, Lawrence Olivier, Kenneth Branagh, Ethan Hawke and David Tennant) and demonstrate how YouTube can function as a pedagogical resource for Shakespeareans. We also encounter amateur productions such as Dave McDevitt's high-speed performance, fandom with the Klingon 'To be, or not to be' (a homage to *Star Trek VI*) and Second Life *Hamlet*, all of which represent culture converging at high speed. Further convergences are provided by advertisements on the top left of the screen, which act as indices of the commercial interests that intersect with YouTube's participatory culture.

This is merely a snapshot of the web of connections enabled by YouTube's economy of tags, where a click from one video leads us to more and more content, and further and further away from the initial focus on the soliloquy. The unbounded nature of YouTube content can be daunting – even within the niche context of 'To be or not to be', more than 37,200 results are generated. The potential for saturation and the displacement of a grounding textual authority is self-evident. This is *Hamlet* in mixed company. However, YouTube also captures the complex hermeneutic field that is *Hamlet* and its cultural afterlife, allowing us to forge a productive dialogue between intertexts as they flow across new media.

We can further apprehend the implications of media convergence for *Hamlet* by way of a contrast with recent *Hamlet* films by Michael Almereyda (2000) and Alexander Fodor (2006). Shakespeare critics have noted how these films exhibit a consciousness of media forms and seem especially concerned to signal how their own relation to a putative original is heavily filtered through a set of intertexts.[17] In other words, these films negotiate the relation between *Hamlet* and the burden of its tradition. While the films provide one type of encounter with intertextuality – and complicate any singular notion of a stable original – YouTube affords a much more interactive and participatory encounter with the intertexts that constitute Shakespeare, including the movies mentioned above. Thus, if recent cinematic *Hamlet*s position us as spectators of Shakespeare's modern and postmodern manifestations, YouTube positions us as active users, free to navigate pathways through multiple *Hamlet*s, but also to create our own content. To experience *Hamlet* through YouTube is further differentiated from screen Shakespeare because navigation and creation occurs through the platform-specific features of the YouTube interface and its protocols (such as content rating, denoting favourites and commenting). Moreover, since content, however disparate, always appears 'YouTube branded', a supra-consciousness in the experience of the site is at work.[18] YouTube instances that interstitial space within convergence culture between the power of the media corporation (YouTube as brand) and the power of the media user (the invitation to broadcast, and thus to participate).

In responding to this invitation, users turn to practices of mashup and remix, which are well established among YouTube's community of users. The term 'mashup' refers to the use of audio-editing software to merge pop songs, but it can also entail the combination of one or more audio tracks with moving images. The term 'remix' refers to the digital manipulaiton of a musical text – for instance, the beat of a track might be altered to create a discernibly new sound. However, both practices come within remix culture and its attitude of media smash and grab that characterizes the digital age.[19] Through a bricolage of media objects, something new is produced. Such repurposing of media informs so much of online video creation. *Hamlet* is no exception. *To be or not to be remixed!* (uploaded 12 February 2009; 7,811 views) by Mrx2848 remixes performances from *Hamlet* films – in the order of Kenneth Branagh, Lawrence Olivier, Ethan Hawke and Mel Gibson.[20] Mrx2848's video nicely illustrates the convergence of amateur culture and commercial media content, activating the 'bardic function' through what has been described as the 'recontextualizing of found footage', in this instance Shakespeare films.[21] The video not only borrows from the films but also offers a critical commentary on them. This *Hamlet* remix offers a case study of four different treatments of the soliloquy, enabling viewers to make evaluative comparisons of performances and to perceive each one as remediations not only of Shakespeare's play but also of their filmic predecessors: Branagh's performance remediates Olivier's, and so on. The video captures Hamlet performances as a lineage, in which actors not only succeed each other, but Olivier in particular, since he marks the exemplary Hamlet, a kind of father figure that must be trumped. Within the video's succession of Hamlets, as the father (Oliver) gives way to his heir (Branagh), we might detect a replication of the play's own archetypal Oedipal story. There is also a sense of the cultural and historical specificities of character, of Hamlet in history, which unsettles any notion of character as stable or fixed.

The kind of history lesson that is available here is illustrative of a quality noted of mashups more generally. As Paul Booth argues, 'mashup textuality' or the the juxtapositioning of audio and image that are historically distinct from each other, importantly derives its effects from a sense of different cultural and historical time frames.[22] This 'multimix of temporalities' presupposes levels of user media literacy and viewer engagement with history, which give the lie to postmodernist understandings of individual media users as occupying an 'ever-changing now', or as impassive observers of the fragments of history.[23] *To be or not to be remixed!* keeps these two perspectives in play, capturing the difference of *Hamlet* in history, as well as its repetitiveness.

Repetition as a condition of remix is pursued in *Hamlet Soliloquy Remixed* (uploaded 29 September 2010; 111 views) by John Dishwater, which is posted in response to Mrx2848's video. Dishwater's film combines the audio of Simon Russell Beale's performance with a series of fragments on a loop, so that 'To be' becomes a refrain in search of an answer.[24] Unlike Mrx2848, however, this video does not take its cue from *Hamlet* movies, but instead uses animated typography to highlight phrases from the soliloquy, as well as black and white images from the late nineteenth-century expressionist artist Amedeo Modigliani. The primary effect is auditory rather than visual: broken up and on repeat, Beale's performance is overlaid with 'Elephant Song' (from Music of the Rain Forest Pygmies). This is 'To be' almost as a form of white noise.

In applying the logic of the remix and the mashup to *Hamlet*, YouTubers are not simply interested in mixing existing content; their productions also involve creative responses to the original, which are concerned with drawing it into the orbit of the user's present. For instance, in slittle's *hamlet: bad romance* (uploaded 17 January 2010; 6,769 views), Lady Gaga's track 'Bad Romance' becomes the score for the RSC/BBC *Hamlet* starring David Tennant, thus realizing a contemporary pop culture Shakespeare.[25] Gaga is of course a pop culture phenomenon – a measure of her reach is that she was one of the first pop stars to pass the 1 billion view count on YouTube for a single video – so it is neither surprising that she should become a mashable commodity nor that she figures in Shakespeare's contemporary formations.[26]

Hamlet mashed up, Hamlet remixed as a 'Bad Romance' video: we might well ask what there is of interest to

Shakespeareans, beyond noticing how such material shows how Shakespeare is the 'lingua franca of modern exchange', or a recurring, if potentially fatuous, cultural signifier.[27] As one critic observes, it is 'relatively easy to see Shakespeare in popular culture, much harder to know what exactly he is doing there'.[28] However, YouTube content is of value to the field of Shakespeare studies because it provides a point of connection between new media forms and Shakespeare, a connection that renders Shakespearean texts more accessible and relevant to the so called 'Generation M'. This connection is neither reductive nor superficial. To return to the example of *hamlet: bad romance*, the choice of Lady Gaga is interesting because she has been praised as a pop icon who pushes the boundaries of normative gender constructions within a mainstream setting.[29] As mashed with the BBC *Hamlet*, the track becomes a commentary on the diegesis. Hamlet and Ophelia are 'caught in a bad romance'. Gaga's lyrics work as a critique of *Hamlet*, told from the perspective of Ophelia: 'I want your love and I want your revenge.' However, the video could have amplified the value of its remix by mashing together images from Gaga's video with those from the BBC *Hamlet*.[30]

YouTubers consciously draw on other pop music genres, such as rap and hip hop, to perform the soliloquy. That these forms tend to be a feature in videos made for a school assignment is unsurprising, considering that the association of rap and hip hop with Shakespearean pedagogy is well established, and has found expression in such films as *Renaissance Man*.[31] It has even been satirized in *The Onion*, in the form of a teacher's use of street slang to introduce 'Big Willie Shakes'.[32] However, while a consciousness about remediating Shakespeare in seemingly 'hip' ways is useful, it is equally important to acknowledge that rap and hip hop are often key entry points for those coming to Shakespeare for the first time and allow a certain irreverence or freedom towards the texts. In *'To be or Not to be' Hamlet Rap* (uploaded 2 June 2009; 33,617 views), a video that stems from a school project but that, as viewer comments indicate, has subsequently become a classroom resource, the text of the soliloquy is mashed with a synthesized beat and rap lyrics.[33] While rap as a style is parodied, with the two performers mimicking the postures of male rap artists as they lip sync Hamlet's words, it is also used to present 'To be' as a refrain, thus parodying Hamlet's reflections. Surtitles provide a meta-commentary on the repetitious performance – 'Yeah, we get it already.' Of course, the iconic soliloquy is no stranger to parody, from Patrick Stewart's cameo in *Sesame Street* presenting the letter 'B' while dressed as Hamlet to Rowan Atkinson and Hugh Laurie's sketch *A Small Rewrite*, in which Shakespeare is told by his theatre manager to cut that 'stand-up stuff in the middle of the action', especially that 'dodgy' soliloquy.[34] In *Hamlet Rap*, parody self-consciously reverberates on the performers themselves, who use it to flag the averageness of their production, as compared to the technical accomplishments of commercial content.[35]

*Robbie Hamlet Rap* (uploaded 21 January 2010; 385 views) offers a less parodic approach to the soliloquy.[36] In this mashup by the self-styled 'dj Prince Hamlet', Shakespeare's text is dropped in favour of a hip-hop idiom: 'Is it better to be alive or dead?/"To be or not to be" is how it was said.' Although positioned in front of the camera, the performer opts to read rather than perform the piece, the text of which is displayed on screen. Even with the translation of Shakespearean language into the comparatively new medium of rap, mashed very effectively here with the instrumental of The Game's 'Hate it or Love it' (featuring 50 Cent), the performer retains the internal dynamic of Hamlet's soliloquy and the dilemmas it expresses. Responding to the video, one viewer posts, 'nice! why did you of all things choose to rap Hamlet?' It seems likely that this video is linked to a school assignment, although it need not be narrowly conceived as such. While school assignments provide a catalyst for online *Hamlet* productions, content is neither defined by institutional settings nor limited to school culture. Moreover, the video's circulation on YouTube brings it into contact with other types of non-professional Shakespeare performance. The decision to produce a Hamlet video could derive from an interest in Shakespeare that overlaps with a desire to display the performance as a means of media engagement, self-publication and presentation.

While videos reveal an engagement with Shakespeare, their logic of media smash-and-grab positions *Hamlet* as an amalgam of texts to be readily combined with other texts rather than as any anchoring or singular textual authority. As such, mashup culture has implications for the spectral quality of the Shakespearean 'original' and the dispersal of authority, questions that have been of significant interest within the field.[37] Derrida's discussion of the 'signature of the Thing "Shakespeare"' as that which renders adaptations, translations and interpretations 'possible and intelligible without ever being reducible to them' comes to mind.[38] More recently, Margaret Kidnie has addressed the spectre of the 'original' *Hamlet* that seems to ghost its cultural afterlife. She interestingly notes that in writing about productions or adaptations of the play, critics and reviewers often turn to a 'discourse of survival', as if the 'thing itself' survives the transforming capacities of a given performance or adaptation. 'The idea that *Hamlet* "survives" performance,' writes Kidnie, 'seems enabled by the unspoken belief that the play exists somewhere – or rather, somewhere *else* – apart from its (or perhaps just this) production.'[39]

With reference to mashups, however, questions about a Shakespearean original (and the implicit nostalgia for a lost aura that they evoke) could ultimately be redundant. For instance, in *To Be Or Not To Be* by Gr8bigtreehugger (uploaded 13 September 2006; 6,679 views), the 'signature of the Thing "Shakespeare"' is erased, as Hamlet is presented as a cyborg. The video combines CGI and artificial voice software – available through programs like iclone and CrazyTalk – to present Hamlet as an automaton, with the voice of Kenneth Branagh.[40] Hamlet's words merely provide data or text here to be inputted into a software program; the video is less about

'To be' than about showcasing the tuber's digital capabilities. By implication, the video also addresses the ubiquity of the speech and, as such, bears comparison to those nineteenth-century mechanical Hamlets that, as Richard Halpern notes, used mechanicity 'to mock and to evacuate Hamlet's famously anguished subjectivity'.[41] By casting Hamlet as a cyborg head perched on a pedestal, the video makes irony of the tradition of the tragic figure. In these terms, the video could interestingly function in a theatre production as a visual backdrop to the delivery by a live actor, a means of unsettling and defamiliarizing an audience's expectations of the soliloquy. Equally, the video teases its viewer with the possibility that, like its Hamlet, we are all cyborgs now. In this regard, it toys with those 'paranoid narratives ... that see technology as an external other that threatens the human'.[42]

Gr8bigtreehugger's *Shakespeare Superheroes* (uploaded 8 June 2006; 54,274 views) is similarly ironic and iconoclastic.[43] This upload features a CGI of the Incredible Hulk, the Marvel comic book and movie figure. The description explains how the Hulk 'gives up the tawdry world of superheroes and returns to his roots on the stage' and the ironic hyperbole continues through to the title sequence, documentary-style voice-over introducing 'Shakespeare superheroes' and the revelation of 'Hulk Hamlet'. The comparison is not unique – Edward Norton, who played the Hulk in the 2008 release, compared the role to Hamlet: 'it's a bit like Hamlet, lots of people can play ... and do their own interpretation'.[44] Mark Ruffalo, who played the Hulk in *The Avengers* (2012), remarks that 'the way I see it is that Ed has bequeathed this part to me. I look at it as my generation's Hamlet.'[45] While such claims are audacious, the vocabulary deployed here is a familiar one. Hamlet is called upon as touchstone of cultural value that is on a par with (while also elevating) the role of the Hulk. Hamlet also becomes a synecdoche for lineage and succession, in which the cultural primacy of the male transformation narrative is passed from one actor to another.

The sense of play to *Shakespeare Superheroes* reminds us that YouTube is predominantly an entertainment platform.

Content, as Alexandra Juhasz points out, is often concerned with the immediate (and immediate laughs), rather than the meaningful.[46] From the perspective of a Shakespearean looking at these uploads, however, I think there is something meaningful in the (knowing) reduction of such famous words in literature to the automated, robotic soundings of a computer-generated talking head. *Shakespeare Superheroes* and *To Be Or Not To Be* take what is merely implicit in other *Hamlet* videos – Hamlet as word machine – and amplify it through mashup and remix. While the videos lend themselves to interpretation as postmodern parody, their provocative renderings paradoxically constitute an attempt to reinvigorate the soliloquy. Unwittingly, then, the videos intervene in Hamlet's ongoing circulation, becoming parts in the Hamletmachine.

Other videos use mashup culture in ways that suggest that Hamlet's words can still elicit empathy. Jeff Maus's film short *Shakespeare's Hamlet – 'To be or not to be ...'* (uploaded 17 December 2007; 38,878 views) combines a series of images from film and TV with a voice-over, which is the audio of Kenneth Branagh's performance from his 1996 film.[47] The images variously suggest drug addiction, alcohol dependency and psychic disturbance.[48] Rather than compete with Hamlet's words, the montage of film images suggest an interpretation of the spoken dimension. The effect of the images, especially the opening shot of a man injecting himself and the close-up of a needle superimposed over other images of people drinking and in states of distress, is to imbue Branagh's somewhat dispassionate performance with pathos, as the viewer is prompted to reflect on suffering and psychological torment. *Hamlet* thus functions here as one of the intertexts – along with the remediated films and the Reed and Vonnegut quotes – that enable a reflection on the human death-drive. Viewer comments, a key feature of YouTube as an interactive platform and online community, afford us some insight into reactions to the upload:

A superb take on the famous soliloquy. It works perfectly; it has to be remembered just what was made when first written. Thanx for this ... another view of genius. Surreal, spine-tingling and very well made. A masterpiece [sic].

Thank you! I appreciate your sharing your vision with the world. I feel more enriched by having experienced your work. In the info you state this being somewhat out of context; I feel the context is taken to a whole, different level. Five Stars and Favorite!

As evidenced by these posts, YouTube material can be meaningful for some viewers or users. Equally, the comments reveal how we have moved from Hamlet's soliloquy and the ontology that it expresses into the realm of user posts, online identities and a sense of YouTube as an online community. The Hamletmachine can also be about mediating relations between humans.

# 'To vlog, to post, perchance to be featured': Remediating the soliloquy

Jeff Maus's upload could be interpreted as the video diary Hamlet might have made, if such technology had been available to him. As such, it recalls some recent *Hamlet* films already mentioned, among them Almereyda's starring Ethan Hawke, where 'the personal video' is, as Katherine Rowe notes, 'the technology of interiority among a variety of modern media, including telephones, television, photography, film, and so on'.[49] The technology available to Shakespeare was of course the soliloquy, that supreme device of the early modern stage, which gave audiences access to a character's motivations or thoughts, in the process insinuating a deeper self, or 'that within' (I.2.85). What Almereyda does is to update or overlay this earlier, Shakespearean medium with the newer medium of video, just as Shakespeare might be regarded as having reconfigured the direct address of medieval pageant and morality plays. This is the process of remediation, where a new form of representation authenticates itself in relation to 'earlier technologies of representation', or repurposes those technologies and their cultural functions.[50] The vlog should be regarded as a remediation of the soliloquy, silently harnessing the properties of the dramatic monologue for online performance. It is a well-established practice on YouTube, but with antecedents in the 1990s, such as the video diaries of Sadie Benning, as well as the more recent phenomenon of the webcam.[51] Enabling various forms of self-expression, self-referentiality and performance, the vlog captures much of what YouTube is about as 'a platform for nonprofessional, democratic media making'.[52] Typically, the video creator speaks directly into a webcam or hand-help camera, devices that within Web 2.0 have become empowering, since they enable media users to engage in media production.[53] Within these recordings, sometimes impromptu, sometimes carefully staged, users re-present the everyday. These presentations entail performances to a pop song, as in the now iconic examples of *Numa Numa* or Beyonce's 'All the Single Ladies', which go viral as they are emulated across the YouTube community.[54]

I would argue that *Hamlet*, and more specifically the soliloquy form, operates in the same way as these pop songs, providing a language or template for users to deploy for their own purposes. 'To Tube or not to Tube, that is the question?' asks Xelanderthomas in his video *Hamlet Prince of YouTube* (uploaded 2 January 2007; 120,762 views), modifying that most recognizable of lines to address online expression. 'Whether tis nobler in the mind to suffer the slings and arrows of asinine comments / Or to take arms against a sea of idiots / And, by posting, end them.'[55] The creator describes his video as 'a hopefully witty and humorous nod of support and encouragement to the courage it sometimes takes for some to upload a video' and as a defence of a 'barely surviving right we have … free speech'.[56] In the video itself, Xelanderthomas does not deliver his monologue direct to camera, opting instead for a sideways pose that suggests Rodin's The Thinker, an appropriate visual cue in the context of the performer's concerns.

Hamlet's metaphysical and ontological dilemmas are similarly recast in the service of vlogging by livingpassion in her *Hamlet the video blogger* (uploaded 18 March 2007; 608 views), the only Shakespeare-related piece by this YouTuber, whose channel includes over 100 vlogs. [57] The video opens by addressing the YouTube community: '*Hamlet – The Video Blogger. I'm sorry guys, I HAD to go nerdy for a minute*'; and the delivery of 'To be' is further prefaced with Hamlet's monologue, 'I have of late, but wherefore I know not, lost all my mirth' (II.2.260–75). Viewers respond in the language of vlogging: 'What a piece of work is vlogging, how uploaded and how true? To comment, or not to comment, that is the question. To vlog, to post, perchance to be featured; there's the rub! Tis a consummation devoutly to be wished … Great job!' For uploaders and viewers alike, being noticed or leaving a trace emerge as key motivating factors in online exchange and interaction.

YouTube also provides an effective platform for an individual to showcase his/her *Hamlet* performance. Accordingly, the site marks the latest phase of an established history of performances of Shakespeare's plays by people who are not theatrical professionals, but have nonetheless 'committed themselves to incorporating these plays into their own lives and those of their own immediate societies'.[58] 'This is something I was compelled to do', explains Rutherford Ashley in the byline to his video *Hamlet Act 3 Scene 1 – Navajo Poet Rutherford Ashley* (uploaded 7 January 2009; 1,323 views). 'It is a creepy monologue, but I find the drama of it a real challenge.'[59] The ensuing performance, delivered direct to camera, effects immediacy and intensity: for instance, before beginning, the performer says 'get this over with and I'm out the door'. As several viewers note, the performance includes errors, but it nonetheless reflects a desire to meet the challenge of iterating this most iconic of soliloquies. Rutherford seeks to present his own spin on the speech, interestingly extending out Hamlet's address to 'fair Ophelia' into a series of repetitions of 'remembered'.

Considering the availability of past performances, YouTubers like Rutherford have ample templates to choose from when producing their own *Hamlet* performance. However, the array of past Hamlets must be intimidating. How is a YouTuber to individualize his or her performance? This compares with stage actors playing Hamlet, who are conscious of 'a heritage of "points", that is details of stage business which had been introduced by their predecessors and had become in effect canonized as part of the acting tradition'.[60] Theatre is a memory machine, where every performance is potentially ghosted by what has gone before it.[61] On YouTube, however, where media objects are constantly grabbed and repurposed, originality may not be the most important motivation for would-be performers of Hamlet's soliloquy. Rather, a conscious acknowledgement of the process of remediation occurs, as if conceding from the outset that a performance of 'To be' is going to sound derivative. In *To Be or Not To Be, Shakespeare's Hamlet soliloquy, David Messulam* (uploaded 1 May 2012; 402 views), the performer combines the genre of the vlog with that of the movie trailer.[62] Title sequences introduce 'Messulam Films' and Hamlet as 'a man' who became, in the hyberbole of movie trailers, 'a legend'. There are also excerpts from the YouTuber's performance. In the performance itself, Messulam reads 'To be' from a computer screen. The effect of this framing device is to present the soliloquy as mediated and Shakespeare's tragic figure as filtered through the language of film and popular culture.

For the creators of these video performances, it is as if they are operating within a private space, yet it is an extraordinarily public one. As viewers looking at the vlog on a small screen within the YouTube interface, it is as if the person has opened a window onto his/her life or allowed us to eavesdrop on their performance. However, as the reference to the YouTube interface reminds us, the vlog is shared and experienced through a platform with its own specific features and disparate content. As such, although it appears to suggest immediacy and offer a kind of new media verisimilitude, the vlog is already a mediated event. At work here is a blurring of distinctions between the live and the mediatized, which Philip Auslander regards as a feature of contemporary cultural production.[63] YouTube vloggers have been especially adept at negotiating and blurring such boundaries, as well as those between public and private selves, the authentic and inauthentic. The case of *LonelyGirl15*, whose emotive vlogs turned out to be a project by two independent film-makers, is an extreme example of this.[64]

In watching *Hamlet* uploads, I would argue that we encounter a blurring of categories as traditional under-standings of the amateur and professional actor begin to shift. For some tubers, such as Shaktim, the self-styled 'Hamlet of YouTube', YouTube is a platform through which to display and archive their skills as an actor.[65] Shaktim (actor Tim Maloney) makes full use of YouTube, compiling his *Hamlet* performances, which run into the hundreds, into playlists. As he says of his playlist 'Hamlet 365', it affords 'YouTubers a unique insight into what it's actually like for an actor to "Work out a Character" using repetition as part of the rehearsal process'.[66] In *Hamlet 285 – The Only Living Boy* (uploaded 8 June 2009; 55 views), a reference to the Simon and Garfunkel track used in the upload, we see one way that Maloney prepares for the role.[67] However, the performance itself is preceded by a disclosure of the processes of filming as, webcam on, Maloney tries to find his frame. The sense of an immersive performance is thus unsettled, and perhaps deliberately so. For actors such as Maloney, for whom YouTube is a promotional platform, the imperative to do a stand-out rendition of 'To be' must remain strong. Thus, actor Kenneth Dinkins explains that he felt it necessary to add some Shakespeare to his demo reel as an actor. In his professionally produced performance *The Shakespeare Tapes: Hamlet Act*

*3, Scene 1* (uploaded 1 October 2012; 3,113 views), vlog culture meets the film short, with the conceit being that we are watching found footage of Hamlet's meditations, a device that recalls Almereyda's *Hamlet*. [68] The video is reminiscent of film technique more generally in its reliance on a score (in this instance Patsy Cline's 'Crazy' at the beginning and Jonny Cash's now more famous cover of the Nine-Inch Nails' song, 'Hurt', at the end). While these are thematically apposite to Hamlet's words, however, they also create narrow parameters that delimit Dinkins' treatment of Hamlet's thought processes. Actress Amy Walker adopts a different approach in her video *To Be Or Not To Be – Soliloquy from act III, scene I, of Shakespeare's Hamlet – 'Hamlet Flosses'* (uploaded 24 April 2008; 43,711 views).[69] She sets out to achieve immediacy by uttering the speech as a seemingly impromptu vlog from a bathroom. As one viewer notes, 'you put such a uniquely contemporary spin on a speech I've seen recited at least a million times'. The conceit of the performance is that the camera is the mirror, and Hamlet's reflections are presented as the verbalized thought processes of one individual as they go about such a mundane activity as flossing. In this domestication of *Hamlet*, the tendency within vernacular production to signal the everyday and the average is put to good effect.

The performer of *Hamlet on the Street* (uploaded 19 July 2007; 497,975 views) seeks to differentiate his Hamlet, in this instance the Hecuba speech, by performing it against the backdrop of some derelict buildings in his hometown of Camden, New Jersey. [70] For this young actor, YouTube is a platform to promote his talents.[71] Comments in response to the Hecuba performance are generally positive (and the video has 1,667 likes compared with 357 dislikes), with some viewers requesting a rendition of 'To be'. However, the video has also received negative posts that, in a lexicon typical of Internet trolls, deploy overtly racist ('hamlet is not black') and homophobic terms ('you my friend, are a flaming homosexual. but, I have one question for you, how did you perform hamlet on the streets on NJ and not get a few caps in your ass?'). As we will see in the next chapter, race becomes semiotically relevant in videos, especially when the performer is a person of colour. Posts concern location, referring to negative perceptions of Camden's crime rates. A viewer comment seeks to put the performance in context: 'My friend … is standing across the street from his high school. This is the amazingly stark reality of Camden NJ. This performance was not staged, it was impromptu and courageous.' Evident here is a discourse of authenticity, already gestured to in the title of the video, where the relocation of Hamlet to the street suggests a less institutionalized and revered Shakespeare than the one traditionally encountered onstage.[72] The suggestion of a Shakespeare from the 'streets' may not be especially unique, but the specificity of location (a neglected streetscape of Camden) is significant within the terms of its reception and also integral to the performer's self-presentation and sense of place. The young performer subsequently issued a video thanking YouTube viewers for their responses and, again speaking from the street, used the opportunity to express positive dimensions of his hometown.

YouTube represents a platform of mixed content, and performances within vlog culture can be playful and ironic. Where Hamlet's dilemma has him speak of a 'pause' (III.1.67), in videos such as *One Minute To Be Or Not To Be* by Dionfly (uploaded 17 October 2008; 1,013 views)[73] or DaveMcDevitt's *Fast Hamlet* (uploaded 15 September 2006; 9,724 views),[74] YouTube users speed up the thought process to the point of parody. While these latter examples reflect YouTube's association with entertainment and leisure, they have, as all culture does, however unconsciously or unintentionally, a political dimension. In relation to the home-dance video, for instance, Kathrin Peters and Andrea Seier argue that posting performances on YouTube is not only a strategy of self-expression but also one of 'self-distantiation beyond the exhaustive, hierarchical procedures of traditional media institutions'.[75] Perhaps something similar is at work when YouTube users turn to *Hamlet* and remediate the soliloquy.

Indeed, Hamlet offers an especially apposite figure to explore a scenario where self-expression occurs in a heavily mediated, secondary and even belated form: although he instances a striking individuality, paradoxically, he answers to and is interpellated by another's name, a name that marks him out as a derivation, as a copy. As Linda Charnes explains, 'To be a first-born son under primogeniture is one thing; to bear the father's name is a doubly derivative legacy that leaves little room for any kind of autonomy.'[76] Or, as Lee Edelman puts it, 'Hamlet is truly "too much i'th' sun" (1.2.67) too much, that is, his father's son.'[77] Hamlet's frustrations with a father that refuses to go away are deep and complex.[78] They find expression through to the end of the play, even after the demands of the Ghost for remembrance and revenge have finally been met, in his command to be remembered: 'in this harsh world draw thy breath in pain', he asks Horatio, 'To tell my story' (V.2.332–33). Here, 'as he lies dying, Hamlet discovers that he too wants to be remembered, wants to claim an identity that will stand at the centre of its own story rather than being merely ancillary to someone else's (his father's)'.[79] In a similar way, the inheriting actor gains identity and validation from the actor father. In this impulse towards self-narrative, we may discover a symbolic affinity between Hamlet's anxious desire to determine an identity for himself and YouTube's invitation to 'Broadcast Yourself'. The key point here is about the possibilities of the 'bardic function' or, more precisely, the kinds of agency afforded to individual media users by convergence culture. That call captures the extent to which YouTube is a participatory platform. Yet, as commentators have recognized, the YouTube strapline, together with its trademark icon, are bold reminders of the site's deep connections to corporate media. [80] With the purchase of YouTube by Google in October 2006, the coincidence of the 'two YouTubes', or the commercial imperatives of the site with those of the community, has become more pronounced, not least in the way that advertisement pop-ups and banners are now an inevitable feature of the browsing and viewing experience. Understood in these terms, YouTube becomes another example of the ways in which our (online) lives bear traces of mass media, the marks of the corporate in the form of adverts and sponsored features, the sense that our social identities and even modes of expression are conditioned by media images. 'The machine is us/ing us.'[81] An extreme instance of this is provided by the practice of some YouTubers who reproduce their own names with the font and icon of the YouTube logo, thus presenting their channel as a branded extension of themselves and of YouTube.[82]

There is a form of agency, one determined by the coordinates of the Internet and the digital that, as Lisa Nakamura argues, 'puts pressure on the formerly solid and anchoring notion of identity' to create 'images of identity and after-images'.[83] Such cyber-effects could be seen as an accentuation of what some critics have interpreted as the fate of creative production within the seemingly depthless culture of postmodernity.[84] In this culture, creativity is forced to reconcile itself to 'the world as an endless hall of mirrors, as a place where images constitute what we *are* ... and where images constitute all of what we *know*'.[85] Thus, while enabling creative expression and participation, YouTube also denotes at best a limited agency, at worst an imagined agency within mass-media consumer culture. We might say that this tension is crystallized in Hamlet's 'To be', which at once constitutes *the* words or speech to perform, yet also the words that can potentially signify anything and everything, such is their reduction to cliché or to postmodern parody.

That character and play can be said to express such a contemporary, postmodern understanding of the relation between individual identities and their cultural expressions, or that the play's ubiquity and endless repeatability has rendered it a 'fetishized cipher', will be a scenario familiar to Shakespeareans.[86] The character has always suggested a futurity, 'proleptically in tune with the latest present' and it is *we* who make him so.[87] The multiplicity of Hamlets on YouTube potentially points towards the realm of the simulacra and a dispersal of a Shakespearean aura. At the same time, the expropriation of the Shakespeare referent by YouTube users might also be interpreted as a form of nostalgia for a lost aura – 'when the real is no longer what it used to be, nostalgia assumes its full meaning' – and even, despite the parasitical logic of mashup, a nostalgia for a point of origin and a symbolic return to the authentic Shakespeare.[88] As a set of texts and intertexts, Shakespeare 'remains' in popular culture.[89] On YouTube, too, Hamlet never dies. In their productions, YouTubers partake in a Hamlet-like desire for story and for remembrance, a desire to leave a digital footprint in the contemporary mediascape, via the paternal Bard.

# Web 2.Ophelia: From remediation to remedy

We have seen how Hamlet is used in multiple and meaningful ways: as a small window on the YouTube interface and within the hypermedia spaces of contemporary culture, as a technology of narrative and as matter for online creative production and entertainment. The soliloquy, the medium that enables Hamlet's ontology, offers a template for creative expression via YouTube. Yet, within the reception of the play, Hamlet's ontology has been all to often gendered neutral, and thus taken as expressive of a transcendent human condition. The established tradition of female actors playing Hamlet – beginning in 1741 with Fanny Furnival at Dublin's Smock Alley Theatre – has helped to complicate, if not quite undo, such associations.[90] On YouTube, Hamlet cannot be said to be associated exclusively with a masculine identity, nor to script an essential human condition; videos frequently practise gender-blind casting, disrupting an alignment of character and actor. In surfing through videos, however, one also notices a certain gender trend: whereas performances of Hamlet are predominantly by men, those of Ophelia are predominantly by women. As such, one is left wondering to what extent the play's gender imbalance is replicated through YouTube. To put this another way, if Ophelia denotes gender-specific issues, to what extent are these progressive? In order to think further about these issues, I now turn to Ophelia productions on YouTube.

Ophelia has a cultural afterlife to rival that of Hamlet. With some 23,500 videos tagged with the name Ophelia, her image is a significant one on YouTube.[91] She features on Web 2.0 more generally, with pages devoted to her on the photo and media sharing sites Flickr and Tumblr.[92] In one sense, there is nothing especially new at work here: Ophelia's cultural afterlife, her propensity to signify outside of the play text, has been well documented.[93] Her multiple aftershocks have found elegiac expression in the lyrics of Natalie Merchant's song 'Ophelia', taken from her 1998 album of the same name, where Ophelia is explored through a number of feminine archetypes that require such regulation of women that female desire can only be constructed as haunting madness. The image of her death is an emotive one, cued in *Hamlet* itself with Laertes' poignant 'Too much of water hast thou, poor Ophelia, / And therefore I forbid my tears' (IV.7.183–84). It can also be fetishistic, eliciting a morbid fascination, what one critic calls 'NecrOphelia'.[94] Of course, her afterlife finds its most recognizable expression in Millais' painting, though Ophelia had inspired painters before the pre-Raphaelite image. After Millais, painters returned repeatedly to the iconic image of Ophelia lying on water, forever freeze-framed between static life (the viewer left wondering if her eyes were open) and death. The French poet Arthur Rimbaud captured the endurance of Ophelia's image when, to cite an English translation, he wrote 'For more than a thousand years sad Ophelia / Has passed, a white phantom, down the long black river.'[95]

However, it was the use of 'sad Ophelia' in Mary Pipher's social study of female adolescence, entitled *Reviving Ophelia*, which made Ophelia part of the modern vernacular.[96] Ophelia acts as a metaphor for cultural representations of women and has variously represented an ideal of femininity and beauty, the teenage girl-in-crisis, regulated female sexuality and the spectacularization of female death. Ophelia's image now floats among the currents of video-sharing sites, where users remediate Millais, or use film and other technologies to reproduce Ophelia's final moments, thus reanimating her. If these online productions mark a new phase in the history of Ophelia's reception, it may be because her delimited agency approximates to the paradoxical culture of online self-expression, where individual tubers broadcast a self in ways that can often seem derivative of, and indeed compliant with, mass media. As a figure whose self-expressions are defined by those around her, Ophelia provides YouTube users, especially female users, with an iconic text to negotiate their own self-expressions via mass media. She is also a space through which girls and their viewers can reflect critically on gender representations. In several videos, Ophelia functions as a metalanguage for a range of subjects, which may require a euphemistic or self-distancing treatment such as body image and (teen) suicide. There is certainly much evidence of strong identifications with Ophelia on YouTube.

Ophelia on Web 2.0 has already received some critical attention. Surveying Ophelia responses on Facebook and YouTube, for instance, Christy Desmet and Sujata Iyengar suggest that three subgenres 'stand out in contemporary YouTube culture': Ophelia elegies; Ophelia as tragic lover; and Drowning Ophelia. These indicate that Ophelia 'has not so much an afterlife as many parallel lives'.[97] In my own search through Ophelia videos, I have noticed similar thematic emphases and categories, though I am especially interested here in how YouTube culture itself shapes the form that responses to Ophelia take. Some of these responses are what one might call 'Ophelia-centric' in that their primary concern is with the character and her after-images. The mashup, already discussed in relation to 'To be or not to be' videos, is significant as a means of engaging with Ophelia as simulacrum. Other tubers use the slide-show, a simple but nonetheless effective way to produce a visual essay on Ophelia. Another genre is the film short, which reproduces or dramatizes Gertrude's description of Ophelia's death. Finally, there is the vlog, which is Ophelia-eccentric in its tendency to use Shakespeare's character as a starting point for creative expression. For anyone interested in recreating an Ophelia look, there is even a helpful 'how to' video available on YouTube: *Halloween Makeup tutorial: Ophelia – drowned body / nymph / waterspirit* (uploaded 1 November 2009; 4,363 views).[98]

Ophelia is a discourse, in the sense that she constitutes a language and space where constructions of femininity, girlhood and women's agency take place, and where they may also be challenged.[99] For Pipher, Ophelia provided a useful starting point for diagnosing 'the destructive forces that affect young women', including anxieties induced by peer pressure, as well as the damaging effects on self-esteem of media representations of the female body.[100] Ophelia becomes a synecdoche for girlhood in crisis, with the media taken to task for its 'girl hostile culture'.[101] It has been observed that while Pipher's book is about girls, ostensibly it is directed at adult women or their parents.[102] On YouTube, however, Ophelia is about girlhood and also a vehicle for *their* self-expressions. A video presentation by Pipher is available on YouTube (uploaded 4 October 2006; 118,470 views) and, through video tagging, it connects with such items as Natalie Merchant's song 'Ophelia', *Ophelia: the Evolution*, a compilation of clips from *Hamlet* films, as well as videos such as *Girls, Sexuality and the Media* and *Extreme (Photoshop) Makeover* which critique dominant representations of women in the media.[103] Thus, in looking at the YouTube interface, it is possible to apprehend the uses to which Ophelia has been put in vernacular culture as well as the set of issues regarding female adolescence and the machineries of representation that flow out from her name.

Considering the extent to which Ophelia has become a variegated text, all responses to her can appear to have an attenuated relationship to *Hamlet*. Of course, Ophelia comes to us in *Hamlet* as an already mediated representation, the circumstances of her death framed within Gertrude's careful, descriptive remembrance. Within the play's gendered scripting of the Ophelia–mother (in-law) dyad, there is no female lineage, no reproduction of female culture – Ophelia is not allowed 'to be'. Subsequent representations of Ophelia are quite often representations of Millais' Ophelia, a filmic *Hamlet*'s Ophelia or, in the case of references in pop music videos, reproductions of what has become a recognizable image within Western media and culture.[104] This is the 'phantom Ophelia', to borrow from the title of Rose Mahanor's painting and video, whose image is summoned again and again. In a short documentary video posted on YouTube (uploaded 4 November 2009; 568 views), Mahanor situates her painting within a wider cultural fascination with Ophelia, with some remarks on her representation in *Hamlet*. The video itself captures Ophelia's remediation, as we see images of sketches for Mahanor's painting as well as the finished piece itself. As a recurrent image, Ophelia displaces her Shakespearean beginnings: Shakespeare becomes one among a series of heavily mediated references or intertexts available to tubers. *Ophelia's Lullaby* (uploaded 16 March 2008; 5,750 views) captures Shakespeare's relative significance. The film reproduces Ophelia's death through a series of looping black and white images of hands in water, and selected quotation from *Hamlet*. A score is borrowed from the videogame *Silent Hill* and selected images from another videogame, *Kingdom Hearts*, which prove a draw for viewers: 'nice use of Kingdom Hearts ... surprisingly i [sic] have no idea who Ophelia is, but the Kingdom Heart i noticed right away'. This viewer encounters Ophelia not through an interest in Shakespeare, but through the video's sampling of a track from a videogame; no prior knowledge of Shakespeare's tragedy is required, let alone a sense of its neglected young girl and the significance of her drowning. Shakespeare is learnt through a videogame track remediated on a YouTube video.

Ophelia's mediated status is similarly conveyed in a series of videos by joshje777. In the first of the series (uploaded 5

January 2008; 20,801 views), the Ophelia of the title is less the character of Shakespeare's play, than the muse of Rimbaud's poem and of paintings by Millais and other artists.[105] The video takes the form of a slide-show, a noticeable genre of video-response to Ophelia.[106] Opening images of Ophelia are overlaid with excerpts from Rimbaud's poem, itself a text about Ophelia's after-images. This nicely establishes the repetition of Ophelia in painting and, by implication, conveys the distance from her representation in *Hamlet* itself. The images are scored to the track 'I asked for Love' by Lisa Gerrard and Patrick Cassidy, which lends a melancholic air to the successive images of Ophelia.[107] Joshje777's channel suggests a broad interest in art and especially painting, which may explain why the response to Ophelia is filtered through art history. However, the comments on the video, which are overwhelmingly enthusiastic, return the viewer to the play. Some viewers express a strong identification with Shakespeare's character: 'beautiful composition ... I have seen some of these works of art ... I have been quite taken with Ophelia since. I feel like her sometimes.' Joshje777 posts a comment, an excerpt from Elaine Showalter's essay 'Representing Ophelia', in which Showalter illustrates the gendered constructions of madness in the play and points to the suspicion with which it regards Ophelia's sexuality. Thus, questions about *Hamlet* are not as far from this iteration of Ophelia as they might initially appear to be.

More poignantly, the description accompanying the video includes a dedication to a friend. The video creator provides further context for this particular memorializing of Ophelia: 'the video is dedicated to a friend ... who's also drowned in the sea of sadness'. This is one of the more powerful deployments of Ophelia's story in online culture. It is also suggestive of the therapeutic potentiality latent within the concept of remediation itself. As Bolter and Grusin note, the word 'remediation' derives from the Latin *remederi*, 'to heal, to restore to health'. Outside of its specific meanings within media, remediation carries a suggestion of restoration, as in its use 'by environmental engineers to refer to "restoring" a damaged ecosystem'.[108] While Bolter and Grusin are suspicious of the improvement model suggested by such understandings of remediation – the relation between old and new media is, they argue, dialectical rather than linear – they do go on to note that remediation, as reform, can extend beyond the medium itself to 'imply reform in a social or political sense'.[109] Taking their cue from Bolter and Grusin, Christy Desmet and Sujata Iyengar suggest that we interpret Ophelia videos as remedying 'the perceived ills or omissions of earlier forms of art', so that Shakespeare's Ophelia is revivified through the process of remediation.[110]

I think we can take this a step further and see Ophelia revivals as explorations of a trauma. The trauma in question may be specific to the individual YouTuber, or Ophelia may represent the trauma of gender violence from organized religion, the state, other individuals or the violence of the diet industry. Ophelia may also speak to what some critics have regarded as the traumas generic to modern life. As Judith Halberstam writes (citing Mark Seltzer's work on America's 'wound culture'), 'we live in a society so preoccupied with scenes of violence and violation that trauma has become an "effect in search of a cause"'.[111] *Hamlet* itself details traumas of various sorts. We have already seen how Jeff Maus's film short addresses self-annihilation. However, representations of trauma can seem parasitical and minimize the psychic disturbance which a traumatic event or experience involves. Cathy Caruth refers to 'the difficulty of listening and responding to traumatic stories in a way that does not lose their impact, that does not reduce them to clichés or turn them all into versions of the same story'.[112] Nonetheless, it is important to confront the issues that emerge through Ophelia. The association of Ophelia and suicide is licensed by the play: she is seen onstage immediately after the audience (and perhaps Ophelia too?) has heard Hamlet contemplate how best to react against a 'sea of troubles' – it is in Ophelia that Hamlet's contemplation of death is literalized – and also because of the suggestive comments by the Gravedigger (V.1.1–2) and the Priest (V.1.216). Ophelia becomes a figure for trauma because her story hovers between the unfortunate accident of a traumatized young girl and the possibility that her distress led to her death. Gertrude's retrospective account may be a politically motivated suturing over of a hidden truth designed to appease an already incensed Laertes.

The issue of what happened to Ophelia – or rather what Ophelia may have done – is a feature of the reception of videos, where the subject of suicide and suicide ideation frames the acts of commemorating her. For instance, an exchange about suicide occurs in relation to the video *Ophelia's Crown – Autumn Tears* (uploaded 2 September 2007; 158,162 views). Posted as a response to the second in the series of joshje777's *Ophelia* slide-shows, this video exemplifies how Ophelia functions as community, and reminds us that YouTube is a network of YouTubers and viewers.[113] Like joshje777's video, *Ophelia's Crown* is also a slide-show, but here images of nature predominate over those of Ophelia, who features just four times. The title refers to the track 'Ophelia's Crown' by the band Autumn Tears, and viewer posts commend the tuber for complementing the atmosphere of the track. Posts mention the Shakespeare reference ('Grazie per la dolce, malinconica Ophelia ... lei è senza epoca ...' and 'Poetry in perfect Shakespearean theme'). Comments also turn more explicitly and bluntly to suicide: 'If you think it takes courage to kill yourself then you're a twat and shouldn't even be allowed near a computer or any people to spread your hateful crap', posts one viewer, initiating a lengthy exchange with two other viewers. There is an unfortunate lack of empathy here and the comments are most likely the work of Internet trolls. Nonetheless, the posts convey how Ophelia functions as a cipher through which the trauma of suicide is negotiated.

*Ophelia Drowning* (uploaded 24 September 2007; 43,443 views), a film short by Joey De Santino, also approaches the circumstances of Ophelia's death. Eschewing references to painted images of Ophelia, a feature of other dramatizations, the film opts for the contemporary setting of a private swimming pool. The opening shot is of a young woman's feet and her white dress gently blowing in the breeze, a movement echoed by the camera's circling motion as the Ophelia figure is brought fully into view, and we see her facing the pool. The absence of a score intensifies the sense of foreboding here, which is further suggested through a close-up of Ophelia tightening her fists and clutching at her dress. Through a point-of-view shot, we see Ophelia fixating on cascading water, before the camera cuts back to a close-up of a tear running down her face. In a later shot, we see Ophelia throw a single flower into the pool and a lingering shot of it floating on the water. Effective use is made of natural light in the film – the light blue sky of the opening shots gives way to dark clouds, as we see Ophelia slowly walk down the steps into the pool. As the woman immerses herself in the water, thus gesturing towards the iconic image of the floating Ophelia, the camera cuts to a close-up of a flower at the edge of the pool, followed by an image of the sky. This image dissolves to reveal Ophelia's face: eyes open, she looks up from what is presented here as her watery grave, as air bubbles and the lapping of water obscure her features. Viewer posts in response to the video are positive, with several commending the film-making itself. However, other viewers question the interpretation of Ophelia's drowning:

> Ophelia didn't pre-meditate her death. She fell into the water and decided not to struggle, allowing the weight of her wet dress to carry her downwards.
>     I like this interpretation. The idea of drowning to death immersed in water gives a feeling of a gradual loss of the will to live. I wouldn't imagine Ophelia vehemently thrashing about. In my mind she would be way too passive to commit suicide by shooting herself in the head for instance.

Evident here is a discourse of authenticity about Ophelia and an investment in the meaning that she carries, or is made to bear. For some viewers, it would seem, suicide is a spectre that should not be allowed to pass over her. While the film may be more equivocal than these posts indicate, it offers an interpretation of Ophelia, in which the subject of suicide is given visibility. Indeed, the issue of visibility may be the real concern in the above comments; as in the exchange on *Ophelia's Crown*, the concern is that Ophelia either marks a dangerous aestheticization of suicide, or becomes a point of identification and emulation for adolescents. If such anxieties are available as part of the reception of Ophelia, they overlap with discussions in society and media about approaches to teen suicide, especially in terms of avoiding sensationalist coverage, being mindful of the phenomenon of 'social contagion' or clustering (where a 'high-profile' suicide can augment suicide ideation), while also raising the issue as a means of addressing the complexities of the underlying causes.[114] *Ophelia's Drowning* opens up the possibility for Ophelia discourse to play a part in fostering awareness of teen suicide. In that sense, her remediation might in some small way be reforming, even remedying.

However, there are risks attached to dramatizing or recreating Ophelia's death, since such recreations can stand accused of exercising a morbid fascination with her, thus participating in scopophilia, or even necrophilia. By remediating the scene of her drowning, representations on Web 2.0 platforms 'repeat and perform her initial textual elision, consistently allowing representation to substitute for the absence of a real history/ story'.[115] The image of the near death, or dead, Ophelia has the potential to write over the other stories that might be told through her, thus posing the question, do recreations on YouTube replicate the reduction of Ophelia to an image of serene beauty that was a feature of nineteenth-century paintings? Magda Romanska elaborates on the implications of such images in late nineteenth-century art, suggesting a connection between the figuring of Ophelia's corpse as an erotic object and contemporary ideas of passive femininity in need of control: 'the representations of a self-destructive

Ophelia perpetuated power relations between the genders: stricken by an emotional malady seen as intrinsic to her very being, the female was incapable of independent existence'.[116] Furthermore, when contrasted with Hamlet, the epitome of human thought, representations of Ophelia tended to intensify power relations between the genders: 'Ophelia's intellectual agency became a matter of aesthetics, not an intellectual inquiry.'[117] Such gender dichotomies do find expression through YouTube *Hamlets*; contrasted with the remediation of 'To be or not to be', the text of Ophelia can seem superficial and less intellectual.

A similar concern that Ophelia discourse perpetuates superficial images of femininity has been raised in the context of popular psychology and the use of Ophelia as an idol or model for adolescent girls. While creating 'more spaces for young women to critically examine changing discourses of femininity', the use of Ophelia 'may, ironically, also be contributing to the proliferation of the girl-damaging media images through its own mass marketing'.[118] As the examples thus far have demonstrated, however, the vernacular culture of YouTube offers a much more dynamic Ophelia than either its nineteenth-century antecedents or the 'Reviving Ophelia' phenomenon. While taking their cue from Shakespeare's *Hamlet*, adaptations and reproductions on YouTube are critical and feminist reactions to that text. Through their emphasis on what is sidelined and silenced by the trajectory of Shakespeare's revenge plot, the videos provide a counterbalance to its gender politics. Videos can be Ophelian rather than Shakespearean.

Such reorientation of the play's dynamic is at work in *Ophelia's Suicide Soliloquy* (uploaded 2 July 2008; 10,358 views) by fidelis1400, which draws on the vlog, that technology of self-expression, to provide the soliloquy that Ophelia is denied by the play.[119] 'This [is] brilliant! if only it were in the real play', posts one viewer, identifying that motivating factor for Shakespearean adaptations – to redress perceived lacunae in the play. Ophelia speaks direct to camera, but despite the vlog-style performance and its promise of immediacy, the film does not offer full visibility: shot in black and white, Ophelia cuts a shadowy figure, with only the outline of her face and a white nightdress visible. As Ophelia delivers an apostrophe to the 'weeping brook' of Gertrude's description, the lapping of water can be heard and it becomes apparent that this Ophelia is speaking from a bath. The suggestion of a private space and the darkened frame conveys intimacy: this is Ophelia's final broadcast, as it were, of and by herself. It is delivered in a poetic style, most likely intended to sound authentic to Shakespeare's Ophelia. However, if some of the images appear strained and overwrought, perhaps it is appropriate: Ophelia's final soliloquy should sound a little tongue-tied. Resolving 'no longer to persist in poor company of myself', Ophelia urges the water nymphs to take her, though not before urging women 'Alas, do not allow shallow affection of men to enwrap you.' In her last words, imagined as a piece of Shakespeare apocrypha, Ophelia offers herself as a warning to women in history.

*Ophelia Drowns* by Bella1951 (uploaded 2 September 2007; 148,256 views) combines elements of the vlog with dramatization. Bella1951 introduces the film short with a direct address to camera, thus connecting her vernacular expression with the recreation of Ophelia.[120] The establishing shot reveals a creek, before cutting to a close-up of rushing water. Beethoven's Piano Sonata No. 14 in C Sharp is used as the score. We see Ophelia in a white dress with garlands in her hair, holding flowers in her hand. The naturalistic setting suggests not only a concern with visualizing Gertrude's description, provided here as a voice-over to the action, but also with presenting Ophelia as less of a mediated figure. Unlike *Ophelia's Drowning*, discussed earlier, this film follows Gertrude's account and presents her death as an accident. As Ophelia attempts to hang the garland on a tree, she falls into the 'weeping brook'. The camera lingers on her as she struggles against the current and tries to hold on to the rocks. This is Ophelia before she assumes the serene, angelic pose of Millais' painting. Remediating that image, the video asserts the efficacy of the filmic medium over its predecessor. *Ophelia Drowns* also critiques the Millais' image: whereas in the painting Ophelia's head and hands are raised above the water in a pose that resembles the Virgin Mary, Bella1951's adaptation has Ophelia fully submerged in the water, her arms stretched back, as her lifeless body is carried by the current. It has been argued that Ophelia's death has historically been rendered a sight of beauty because of a fundamental inability to comprehend it: 'the visual beauty of Ophelia's suicide and the glamorous, sensual, or erotic representation of her floating body fill in the gap in our cognition'.[121] Much like Gertrude's troubling reference to Ophelia as 'one incapable of her own distress' (IV.7.176), the image supplants a consideration of Ophelia's psychology. With Bella1951's video, however, we encounter an Ophelia who is not at one with the beautiful natural surroundings, but who quite literally clambers against it. The film tells a slightly different story to the traditional form beautiful Ophelia takes.

The significations of Ophelia images are further pursued through the slide-show, and though it lacks the simulated immediacy of the vlog, this form nonetheless deepens what Ophelia signifies. A key reference point for these videos is the music video for Natalie Merchant's track 'Ophelia', where Shakespeare's 'poor Ophelia' is discovered throughout history, from demi-goddess to suffragette to symbol of the nation, as an instance of the ideological work required of woman. *Marilyn Monroe – Ophelia* (uploaded 10 March 2009; 1,145 views) combines the slide-show with the fan-video, as we see looping images of the iconic actress set to Merchant's track.[122] Presented as a latter-day Ophelia, Monroe is elegized in the process. However, the video's lament carries a broader resonance. The description below the video includes Monroe's remark, 'I don't mind being in a man's world as long as I can be a woman in it', which, as applied to Ophelia, takes on an ironic note. Ophelia and Monroe are emblematic of women denied agency, and their stories must be told and told again in order to foreground the long history of gender inequality. At the same time, this troubling repetition suggests that both figures are trapped in a narrative loop that will not let them be.

Thus far, I have been suggesting that iterations of Ophelia on YouTube counter images of her as a serene, passive object inherited from the play via Millais and other artists. In presenting a different Ophelia, videos like *Ophelia Drowns* and *Ophelia Lullaby* interestingly parallel critical readings by feminist Shakespeare scholars, who have sought to revisit Ophelia and her representations. In her essay on the elision of Ophelia in three filmic *Hamlets*, for example, Carol Rutter outlines what a 'revisionist' representation of Ophelia's death and funeral might look like.[123] Her imagined film would offer a close-up of Gertrude's face as she recounts Ophelia's death, thus alerting spectators to 'the messy political business Gertrude's narrative has to do in the court' and, crucially, shots of Ophelia's body to trouble the play's emphasis on Hamlet.[124] Coppelia Kahn similarly pursues the question of how Ophelia might be read anew. Reflecting on the recurring images of a passive Ophelia in Western culture, Kahn returns to the play 'in search of another story, a different Ophelia – a subject more than an object'.[125] Kahn wonders what 'Ophelia's story without the drowning', that is to say, her full story, rather than the truncated version as represented by Millais and others, might look like.[126] What emerges from her inquiry is a play that 'emphasizes not so much Ophelia's subservience or weakness of character as the formidable powers of men who, instead of protecting here, manipulate and make use of her in their covert struggle to contain Hamlet'.[127] Both critics intervene in the play to eke out a less 'masculinist *Hamlet*', refusing to produce the sort of feminist criticism of Shakespeare that, as Katherine McLuskie once feared, could do little more than disclose its own exclusion from the man's world as envisaged in the works of the 'Patriarchal Bard'.[128] While Kahn's concern with mining the full texts of *Hamlet* for interpretative possibilities can appear dismissive

of creative Ophelia redactions, she does qualify matters with
her concluding remarks: 'As a feminist, I would prefer that
Ophelia, in whatever media she lives on, be self-consciously
performed, so that girls do not drown with her but rather,
wonder why, in the playworld of Hamlet, her girlhood ends
that way.'[129]

A number of YouTube videos answer this desire for a critically conscious performance of Ophelia. For instance, *Ophelia
– RM10* (uploaded 26 July 2010; 581 views) by artist Rebecca
Mellor subverts the iconicity of the death-like Ophelia.[130] A
single camera shot is used throughout to frame Ophelia, who
wears a floral dress and is laid out in a bathtub, with some
plants in the foreground. What is immediately noticeable
about this Ophelia, however, is 'her' heavy beard – when we
look again, it is apparent that the model is male. Mellor's use
of a male model serves to disrupt what might otherwise have
been a straightforward remediation of Millais' painting. Her
film is interested in the possibilities of video, described in the
accompanying text as possessing a 'painterly quality' that can
be lost through the use of 'digital effects'. While reflecting
on the stillness achieved in Millais' painting, the video also
points to the processes that enabled Millais' image and
parodies its heightened naturalism.[131] Mellor's video is more
than a remediation of the medium of painting; interesting
use is made of distorted sound effects, a kind of white noise,
which contrast with the stillness of the submerged body to
convey the distressed state of Ophelia. The comic incongruity
of represented role and the body beneath also nicely gestures
to the transvestism of the Shakespearean stage, to the body
of the boy actor who animated the fair Ophelia. As deployed
here by Mellor, drag has some of the disruptive, mocking and
subversive qualities, which Judith Butler has identified in her
work on gender performativity.[132] Following Butler, I would
argue that Ophelia in drag disrupts the heterosexual coherence
of Millais's image to subvert its implicit scopophilia. Mellor's
film defamiliarizes Ophelia, her image and even gender itself.
Ophelia becomes the site of a critical examination of the

'mediatized (female) body, onto which beauty ideals have been violently inscribed throughout history'.[133]

As with Mellor's video, harolore's *Ophelia Drowns* (uploaded 11 January 2009; 7,346 views) eschews a naturalistic presentation.[134] Here, the stillness associated with Ophelia is subverted through the use of interpretative dance. Movement is the key effect of this video, from its opening shot of floating fabric to the flowing white dress of the dancer as she moves to music, a haunting track, 'Honey, Honey' by Feist. There is subtlety to this performance, with its figurative representation of Ophelia's watery associations – for instance, through the use of close-ups, bubbles appear to dance off the performer's hands, and water is further suggested through floating blue balloons. While Ophelia remains an object of beauty, and the drowning is imagined as a beauteous act, she is also depicted as vibrant and energetic. The film is acutely aware that its 'live' Ophelia is as mediatized as any of her predecessors: in the third frame of the video, we get a split-second view of the clapperboard, a visual cue to the remediated liveness under construction here.

If these videos deploy Ophelia to critique mediatized images of femininity, in the process revealing a cynical attitude to the 'original', the work of other YouTubers seems more thoroughly postmodern as it foregrounds parody and embraces the surface of representation. In an early YouTube video, *Hamlet – The Death of Ophelia – Director's Cut* (uploaded 15 December 2006; 1,701 views) by Edits538, Ophelia dramatizations are parodied: in this video, the iconic death scene involves a wooden doll on a perilous journey across a bathtub.[135] The opening title sequences, which parody the MGM icon and score it to the title music for 20th Century Fox, set the tone for this comic treatment of Ophelia. Indeterminate on the question of whether this doll-Ophelia jumps or falls, the video lends bathos to the scene by scoring it to canned laughter and 'The End' by The Doors. Yet, despite the reduction of Ophelia's death to an absurdity, or perhaps because of it, the video comments on Ophelia's objectification and malleability.

There may, then, be some meaning or depth beyond the gag of Ophelia as a wooden doll. By contrast, Barbie doll recreations appear to offer little in the way of critical reflectiveness on the significance of the dead Ophelia. In *Hamlet: Ophelia's Death*, toy dolls are used to act out the sequence of events leading to her drowning: *Ophelia's Death#13* (uploaded 29 September 2008; 208 views) depicts it as an unfortunate 'accident' in a basin of water, as a human hand holds down the doll.[136] *Barbie Hamlet: the Musical* (uploaded 20 May 2009; 77 views) presents the entire play using dolls. In the final instalment, Ophelia meets her watery end in a food blender, Hamlet proving too late to the rescue.[137] Originating as high-school assignments, these videos reflect one type of response to Shakespeare that such projects can take. Given this context, and perhaps unsurprisingly, the play is filtered through a series of film and popular culture references, with the sensationalist treatment of Ophelia's death straight out of movies like *Final Destination*.[138] These responses should not be dismissed too readily, however, and it is important to be mindful that they represent early engagements with Shakespeare. The videos also reflect the images and narratives available to students to negotiate their gender and sexuality and to work through the cultural value of being in one body or another. As responses from a certain demographic, the Barbie Ophelias may express a sense of distance from the play, and to the limited agency that it affords women. In other words, laughter provides an entirely appropriate reaction to the patriarchal matrix of *Hamlet*. Yet the use of Barbie is of further significance: the doll is emblematic of a feminine ideal and its commodification in popular culture, an 'unobtainable representation of an imaginary femaleness'.[139] At once preposterously slender and immaculately presented, Barbie has been critiqued for epitomizing and reinforcing women's positioning in capitalist culture as objects to be consumed, styled and manipulated. From this viewpoint, Barbie is an apt surrogate for that version of Ophelia that interprets her as another ideal of femininity. It is small wonder that killing Barbie might prove desirable, an updated version of killing the 'angel in the house'.[140]

However, Barbie has been read as a more complex text than her all-important look might first imply. Kim Toffoletti argues that Barbie instantiates a hyperfemininity that discloses gender itself as a simulation. Further, she represents a 'precursor to the post-human; a type of plastic transformer who embodies the potential for identity to be mutable and unfixed'.[141] Indeed, Barbie's very plasticity signals a potentiality that 'invalidates a notion of the material body as the limit point of subjectivity'.[142] Such large claims cannot be substantiated solely based on selected YouTube videos that engage with a Shakespearean character through a form of (child's) play. Nonetheless, Toffoletti's formulation reminds us that Barbie is not the predictable signifier that her starring role in these parodic relocations of Ophelia might at first suggest. By using Barbie, these videos entail a potentially radical unpacking of those images of a passive, static Ophelia, disrupting the kind of over-identification with Ophelia that naturalistic reproductions can elicit.

Barbie's image also features in another Ophelian context with *Ophelia's Vlogs* (uploaded 8 January 2012; 192 views) by dancingqueenajm.[143] In these one-woman performances, Ophelia is played as a type of Barbie girl (with a hint of Marilyn Monroe) who delivers her diary digests directly to her webcam. The description below the video provides some context: 'we explored Ophelia's character in relation to teenage girls, using the book *Reviving Ophelia* by Mary Pipher. It's also a satire about white teenage girls.' As with the Barbie parodies, the video borrows from popular culture, especially films like *Clueless* and *Mean Girls*. There are five vlogs, which are separated by titles and also by physical adjustments – Ophelia's blond, Barbie-style hair changes from vlog to vlog. These are further individuated through song choice, each one appropriate to Ophelia's evolving revelations. So, in the first piece to camera, as Ophelia speaks of her romance for Hamlet, Rick Astley's 1980s pop-factory hit

'Never Gonna Give You Up' is playing in the background. In the third vlog, as Hamlet seems a far less stable prospect – 'Hamlet is, like totally rich, but like totally nuts' – Avril Lavinge's 'Happy Ending' takes on an ironic twist. The tone throughout is parodic of the play's representation of Ophelia: 'I was sitting next to Hamlet because, like, sometimes I need a guy, like, to tell me what's going on in the play, you know.' This is a clueless Ophelia – she signs off by revealing plans to go 'down to the river and take a swim for awhile'.

Other vlog-style performances work from the text itself to redress the limited degree of agency afforded to Ophelia, as in *Holli Dillon Modern Adaptation of Ophelia Monologue: 'I've been so affrighted'* (uploaded 20 February 2012; 70 views).[144] In the play, Ophelia's account to her father of Hamlet's behaviour (II.1.84–97) is a moment of dramatic irony, since the audience has previously witnessed Hamlet being visited by the Ghost. Ophelia's thoughts and emotions do find expression, but are ultimately overshadowed by the subject of her description (Hamlet) and its receiver (Polonius). In Holli Dillon's video, Ophelia's account is isolated from the scene; and while some context is provided in the description – 'A modern adaptation of Ophelia, set in the punk era in East London. Ophelia has come to find her father at the night club in Hackney. She's quite shaken and doesn't know what to do' – there is no Polonius to audit her thoughts. The camera focuses on Ophelia, and effective use is made of close-ups and also direct looks into the camera by Dillon to create a sense of immediacy and a private, troubled revelation. As the final shot lingers on an upset Ophelia, the viewer knows this is only the beginning of her story.

# Who owns Ophelia?

Questions of gender representation and agency are central to Web 2.0 iterations of Ophelia that are involved, sometimes explicitly so, in recuperating the character of Shakespeare's play. Ophelia emerges as a catalyst for various forms of online production, participation and expression. She is a text of fandom, the locus of an actor's self-promotion, or a free space on to which a performative self can be grafted. For other tubers, YouTubers Ophelia is quite simply an alias for online expression, the connection to Shakespeare going no further than the use of his character's name as shorthand for a series of vlogs or for YouTube channels, as in *Opheliasays*[145] and *OpheliasaysWhaaaa*.[146]

In speaking through Ophelia, these vloggers participate in that discourse of Ophelia referred to at the outset, the Ophelia of Mary Pipher's *Reviving Ophelia*. Marnina Gonick argues that the Reviving Ophelia discourse overlaps with a discourse of Girl Power, with its message of a self-determining woman, to produce the 'neoliberal girl subject'. At work in these discourses are 'processes of individualization that ... direct attention from structural explanations for inequality toward explanations of personal circumstances and personality traits'.[147] In other words, Ophelia is a 'technology for the production of certain kinds of persons'.[148] On YouTube, the Reviving Ophelia discourse cannot be separated from the Shakespearean Ophelia: they are contiguous and interlinked. Ophelia constitutes a crucial reference point for tubers, primarily adolescent girls, and is the site through which they can explore representations of women and thus the machineries of gender inequality at work in culture. Their interventions bear comparison to the critical possibilities that Theresa Senft has noted of some webcams, which some women use as a 'means to speak back to the new media industry'.[149] The slide-show videos discussed earlier, with Ophelia featured as a point of connection to other women in history, suggest another way in which Ophelia iconography has critical purchase.

That Ophelia productions draw on a range of references is not in itself remarkable, especially when one considers how image sampling is such a feature of online expression.

Such borrowings reflect the workings of the culture industry, where content is consumed and replicated. They also instance the logic of mashup, where YouTubers repurpose existing media content, sometimes in a critical fashion, sometimes in a celebratory one. However, that logic places the kinds of vernacular expression this chapter has been discussing at risk; after all, in their smash and grab attitude to media, YouTubers infringe copyright on several fronts. YouTube is already responding to this.[150] The YouTube algorithm operates content identification systems to detect copyright infringement. To take one example, *Ophelia Immortal* – a mashup of Branagh's *Hamlet* and the track 'My Immortal' by Evanescence – has fallen foul of such content detection. A message pops up, with an unhappy emoticon, 'This video contains content from MC for Warner Bros. and EMI, one or more of whom have blocked it in your country on copyright grounds.'[151]

Virginia Kuhn has interestingly explored the implications of copyright enforcement for vernacular expression, media literacy and digital pedagogy.[152] While condemning pirating outright, Kuhn calls for a more nuanced attitude to online creation that features copyrighted material. She develops Henry Jenkins' earlier call, in relation to fandom, for media corporations and content holders to make distinctions between 'commercial competition and amateur appropriation, between for-profit use and the barter economy of the Web, between creative repurposing and piracy'.[153] The problem, as Kuhn sees it, is that the enforcement of copyright violations, which is currently ad hoc, will ultimately lead to a culture of fear and self-censorship, discouraging YouTubers from engaging in mashup and remix. Kuhn defends these activities as crucial for developing critical media literacy: 'we ought to be more concerned about a critical impulse and large-scale literacy rather than passive consumption of content created by a few media conglomerates'.[154] YouTubers frequently endeavour to pre-empt accusations of copyright violation by including a disclaimer such as 'no infringement intended' in the description below their videos. YouTube itself provides a detailed guide on copyright for its users, explaining infringement, how users might detect it and suggesting ways of avoiding it. [155] Most of these, if followed to the letter, would make for a very different YouTube to the one we currently know. Kuhn advocates a less censorious reaction to copyright infringement, one that takes account of 'fair use' (for example, the use of prefabricated content for academic or scholarly purposes). Some copyright owners overlook infringements, implicitly recognizing the indirect promotional benefits that can accrue from citation within grassroots and fan culture. [156] However, a culture of uncertainty pervades the interactions between corporate media and those users who actively seek to repurpose media content.

I would argue that Ophelia and YouTube Shakespeare productions more generally should be considered as fair use of copyright. There needs to be a broader recognition of the value of such media sampling, which involves creative redaction and digital knowledge rather than personal aggrandizement. Another mashup, *Possession* (uploaded 19 June 2008; 60,429 views), created by the same YouTuber as the video mentioned above, using Sarah McLachlan's track as a score to Branagh's film to give 'Hamlet's perspective on Ophelia's death', goes undetected, at least for now. [157] The video is a good illustration of Kuhn's argument that as forms of media literacy and critique, YouTube mashups should be defended. *Possession* works as a critical reading of *Hamlet* (Shakespeare's and Branagh's), making effective use of the incorporated media, especially McLachlan's song, to convey Hamlet's love for Ophelia as poised between a genuine passion and a suffocating control. In foregrounding Hamlet's perspective, *Possession* not only reiterates Branagh's interest in motifs of looking and spying in the play itself, but also makes its viewer think about that controlling optic as gendered male.

YouTubers also sample each other's work, and as with performances of 'To be or not to be', similarities are evident across Ophelia videos. Yet, some YouTubers violate the culture of community by copying rather than sampling another's content. *Kula Shaker - Ophelia* (uploaded 29 July 2010; 63,786 views) presents itself as a fan video to the track 'Ophelia' from Kula Shaker's album *Pilgrim's Progress* (2010).[158] The film, in which a girl dives into a pool, makes good use of rewind effects, transitions between monochrome and colour backgrounds and looping images to convey movement. However, in viewer comments this YouTuber has been accused of appropriating footage that was originally filmed and uploaded as *Ophelia Dance Video backup* (uploaded 11 November 2008; 1,873 views).[159] Considering how common sampling is within YouTube culture, there is an irony in tubers berating their peers. There are no viewer comments on the copyright infringement involved in using Kula Shaker's track. It may be the case that different criteria apply when borrowing from amateur content as opposed to commercial or professional productions. For viewers, the distinction may be that *Kula Shaker - Ophelia* is a straightforward appropriation of *Ophelia Dance Video backup*. Had the logic of mashup been applied, with the film edited or remixed or creatively altered, and acknowledgement made to its provenance, in all likelihood there would not have been the same objection, or dispute over provenance. On YouTube, Ophelia is a free space, available to everyone to recreate and recuperate. In this sense, no one owns her. Where such productions and engagements draw on copyrighted content, Ophelia enters into spaces that are potentially contested, and which may lead to her erasure. The range and citational depth of Ophelia performances would be severely compromised were copyright holders to track infringements and require offending content to be removed. If Ophelia has denoted an ideal of femininity that is challenged through YouTube creations, and as such has been a significant technology in the production of more diverse subject positions for women, the next phase of her afterlife may involve a defence of her media convergences.

\*

In tracing *Hamlet*'s remediation on YouTube, part of my objective has been to consider what type of Shakespeare emerges and the uses to which it is put. In one sense, Shakespeare is diluted by virtue of being one among a number of texts available across a dense mediascape. In another, it is clear that YouTubers do indeed have something to say about and do with this text, perhaps by building on that 'fundamental commitment to expression' prized as the hallmark of the Shakespearean canon.[160] For emerging actors, 'To be or not to be' is an essential text to master, often in terms that suggest a symbolic desire to inherit and sustain masculine cultural primacy (one Hamlet begets and succeeds another). At the same time as they position *Hamlet* as a culturally valorized vocabulary for self-expression, however, YouTubers also suggest that its form and politics require updating.

A second objective was to explore to what extent an old gendered dichotomy of the intellectual Hamlet versus the emotional, beautiful Ophelia is replayed through the vernacular culture of YouTube. That Shakespearean 'commitment to expression' is, as engagements with Ophelia indicate, contingent on a number of factors, including dramatic form and gender hierarchies. Ophelia videos are about redressing lacunae in the play, imbuing her with private thoughts – an intellectual life. Through processes of relocation or surrogation, videos contest those inherited images of Ophelia as the embodiment of an idealized femininity. As the examples essayed in this chapter indicate, the soliloquy becomes the medium for self-expression, though iterations of Ophelia reveal similar concerns. Yet, while the gender of the performer(s) does not always neatly coalesce with the Shakespearean figure being cited, it is important to note the specificities of gender that the discourse of Ophelia entails. She is a signifying agent in terms of girlhood, forms of femininity and body image. We have also seen how she is a catalyst for empowered gender self-consciousness. Creative responses to Ophelia thus go beyond gendered representations in Shakespeare to encompass broader representations as they circulate in media and popular culture. That these issues pertain to Ophelia, in ways that they do not in relation to Hamlet, is a function of the pervasiveness of gender inequalities in dominant culture. Vernacular expression on YouTube still has some way to go on this front. There are other challenges ahead for tubing itself, in light of issues about copyright infringement, which threaten creative uses of found media. However, the Hamlets and Ophelias analysed here reveal some of the fascinating ways YouTubers are combining the affordances of YouTube with the signifying capacities of Shakespeare to pursue modes of self-expression and creative engagement that are entertaining, meaningful and critically astute.

# 3

# Race in YouTube Shakespeare: Ways of Seeing

*There is no raw, untrained perception dwellng in the body. The human sensorium has had to be educated to the appreciation of racial difference.*

PAUL GILROY[1]

*don't be afraid to do other characters. It's not necessary to be white to do Hamlet o[r] Macbeth.*

POST ON MARCUS SYKES, *SHAKESPEARE IN THE GHETTO*[2]

*… how things are represented and the 'machineries' and regimes of representation in a culture do play a consitutive, and not merely a reflexive, after-the-event, role.*

STUART HALL[3]

*When I teach Shakespeare … when I see a contemporary Shakespearean production on film, stage*

*... or the Internet ... I see race: whiteness, blackness, Hispanic-ness, Asian-ness, the normatively raced, and the deviantly raced. It is always there; it is always present; it always impacts the way Shakespeare is being employed.*

AYANNA THOMPSON[4]

The example of YouTube *Hamlet* discussed in the previous chapter offers insight into the various forms of creative self-expression and identity-performance that are fostered through YouTube's culture of vernacular participation. What emerges when, as in the second epigraph above, our attention turns to the issue of race in that context? Can online participatory culture foster any degree of cultural and racial diversity? Indeed, considering the disembodied nature of online encounter, can race be said to happen or occur in that setting? Of course, any discussion of race is always problematic, challenging and contentious, not least because the term itself is a slippery one that encompasses several registers of difference. First, race is 'at one and the same time visible and invisible, a component of biological identity and a trope of cultural and religious difference'.[5] Second, writing about race causes certain anxieties. Even as we follow Paul Gilroy, cited above, and make the important recognition that race is an insidious form of discrimination which has no essence, we must also note the ways in which 'a racial epidermal schema' marks the body discursively.[6] Thus in focusing on the indexes of race we, somewhat paradoxically, run the risk of activating its scopic power and essentializing it further. Toni Morrison captures this dilemma when she considers how we might 'enunciate race while depriving it of its lethal cling?'[7] Her adroit observation foregrounds the difficulties which plague claims that we are 'beyond' race, made with regard to the utopian possibilties associated with the Internet in its infancy, or talk of a post-racial world, for some exemplified in an American context by the election of Barack Obama as president.[8] To suggest that race no longer has the powers of categorical demaraction it previously held is to betray 'those groups whose oppositional, legal, and even democratic claims have come to rest on identities and solidarities forged at great cost from the categories given to them by their oppressors'.[9]

The Internet and online culture further complicates these questions by bringing with them a peculiar, but connected, set of dilemmas and issues. As noted in Chapter 1, the Internet and YouTube instance enhanced levels of vernacular participation as users work with network digital objects. One of the most incisive treatments of online and interactive mediums produced to date is the work of Lisa Nakamura, who has convincingly demonstrated that race happens online, despite the disembodied nature of online exchange.[10] Attending to the 'visual cultures of race', Nakamura explores how individuals make use of the participative and interactive tools of the digital and the Internet to 'actively visualize themselves', producing what she calls 'a visual culture expressive of racial and ethnic identity' (and does so despite neo-liberal claims that 'race doesn't matter').[11] By locating the 'racio-visual logic of new media identity', as she calls it, Nakamura argues 'that anyone who can take a picture can upload a file and can create visual images of race or commentaries on its visualization'; significantly, this can be read as a form of resistance which actively defies 'a neo-liberal stance that tries to disappear race'.[12] There are profound implications here for YouTube Shakespeare. In this context, users quite often actively approach the subject of race in Shakespeare in ways that are both dynamic and challenging. By extension, individuals within the online community use the Shakespeare text as a ready-made template through which to express their own racial identity.

Yet, as Nakamura also notices, interaction and expression online entails the use of aliases that frequently operate along overtly racist and sexist lines: 'performances online', she writes, use 'race and gender as amusing prostheses to be donned and shed without "real life" consequences'.[13]

Uploading and sharing content on YouTube involves exposure to the judgement of viewers, including those who may exploit the anonymity afforded by online posting. In his important analysis of YouTube, Michael Wesch presents this in diagram form: 'anonymity + physical distance + rare & ephemeral dialogue = hatred as public performance'.[14] The nexus of conditions marking online expresssion and interaction becomes especially acute in relation to race or raced representations. Moreover, while users can flag a video or a comment as offensive, the openness of YouTube militates against a sustained or systematic control of hate speech. If race is about recognizing and challenging dominant ways of seeing, online culture presents peculiar difficulties. The combination of the unseen viewer with the immediacy of response give rise to a kind of casual or detached phobia; online, the 'lethal cling' of racial discourse is hard to evade.

YouTube is, then, a paradoxical space where racism occurs (through hateful or phobic comments) and also where, recalling Stuart Hall's formulation, the 'machineries or regimes of representation' that enable and sustain racialized thinking are interrogated and unpacked. Racialized aesthetics are addressed in the now iconic YouTube video *Chocolate Rain* (uploaded 27 April 2007; 85,083,237 views).[15] The work of the 1491s, a comedy sketch group, is equally important for its interrogation of racialized aesthetics, especially with reference to representations of Native Americans.[16] A search under 'race and racism' will bring over 83,000 results, so it is certainly a category on YouTube. These facts alone would appear to suggest that, when dealing with online media, we should regard race and racism as categories in their own right. I would argue, then, that it is important to locate YouTube Shakespeare and race as a discursive category within that context. Despite this, it is also the case that 'questions of race are hard to pin down on YouTube', as Anandan Kavoori observes, perhaps because of the ephemerality of some content in this setting or a certain propensity towards superficiality. As such, 'identity politics almost always plays suitor to the goals of entertainment', a reality that results in race becoming 'a subtext rather than a dominant leitmotif' in YouTube videos.[17] Indeed, race has not been a predominant concern in any of the critical studies of YouTube published to date. The result is that various energies – both constructive and deleterious – are displaced in this setting. As Alexandra Juhasz notes, popular videos tend to express the attitudes and tastes of mainstream media and culture. Juhasz cites a research project conducted by her students and highlighted in their knowingly yet provocatively titled video, *Where are all the Blacks on YouTube* (subsequently removed from YouTube). The project revealed that 'the most popular videos about black people reflect and reinforce the standard views of our society (about hypersexuality, low intelligence, and gonzo violence)'.[18] Searching for critical alternatives to this racial stereotyping involves entering the 'niche Tube', the term employed by Juhasz to describe the cache of less popular videos that 'immediately falls off the radar, underserved and unobserved by YouTube's systems of ranking'.[19] While Juhasz posits too stark a binary here between mainstream and niche content on YouTube, her argument is nonetheless instructive, since it alerts us to ways of seeing on YouTube that may implicitly privilege whiteness, or serve to further marginalize racial minorties.

Shakespeare – as writer and as signifier – has long been recognized as a dynamic and contested space, where race is constructed, negotiated and challenged. As Ayanna Thompson's refreshingly reflective and important remark (cited in the fourth epigraph above) reminds us, 'race always impacts the way Shakespeare is being employed'. The plays contain distinct early modern vocabularies of difference, including lineage, family, colour prejudice, religion and xenophobia, to which audiences and readers bring their own ideas and attitudes regarding race.[20] Maya Angelou's playful claim that 'Nobody else understands it, but I know Shakespeare was a black woman' is just one of the ways that racial formations in the texts have been reimagined by those who may have felt at a distance from a Bard that, historically, seemed all too white.[21]

An 'extraordinarily powerful medium between generations and culture', as noted by Ania Loomba, the plays have even acted as 'a conduit for transmitting and shaping ideas about colonialism and race'.[22] YouTube may signal a new phase in these interrelated processes. One particularly interesting form of transmission that has occurred on the platform is the 'classroom inspired performance video', a genre of broadcast that, according to Thompson, 'offers a unique space to analyse the ways in which this generation negotiates performances of Shakespeare and performances of race'.[23] As an archive, YouTube consequently has the capacity to contribute to the meanings of race in Shakespeare. Indeed, by compiling videos into a playlist, one could easily produce a visual micro-history of the racial markings of Shakespeare performance: Olivier in blackface (uploaded 29 March 2007; 56,736 views);[24] Paul Robeson reflecting on the signifcance of playing Othello (uploaded 11 April 2008; 37,367 views);[25] James Earl Jones reciting Shakespeare in the presence of President Barack Obama (uploaded 25 September 2012; 204 views).[26] These videos constitute important indices of race in Shakespeare. They are also demonstrate the extent to which the plays have functioned as transmitters of and commentators *on* race. As Thompson's recent work insists, however, we should not assume that Shakespeare is necessarily a conducive medium, or metaphor, for '*contemporary* race relations'.[27]

These issues and questions are pursued through this chapter as it analyses expressions of race in a variety of YouTube Shakespeare videos, including the music video, the monologue and the film short. Close consideration is given to viewer comments, since these form a significant part of the reception context. If YouTube is susceptible to trolls, who deliberately set out to disrupt the sense of community made possible by the platform-as-social-network, it is necessary to confront such comments, however disquieting, since they bear witness to the conditions and realities of online expression. Comments feature in the first section of the chapter where I analyse reactions to Marcus Sykes' *Shakespeare in the Ghetto* series, locating his videos in the context of recent work on the semiotics of racial performance.[28] Remaining with questions regarding blackface and colour-blind casting, the chapter turns to a series of videos that reference, or engage directly, with *Othello* and its cultural meanings, from vernacular productions to commercially oriented videos such as *The Story of Othello* and Sassy Gay Friend's *Othello*. *Romeo and Juliet* also features as a reference point for an exploration of an interracial relationship in a film short and also a music video. In moving across different geographic and cultural locations (of the videos, 8 are from North America, 2 from Britain, and 1 from Ireland), the chapter places emphasis on the semiotics of a set of videos and aims to probe the racial politics of their iterations. I am especially interested in exploring to what extent Shakespeare emerges as an indeterminate metalanguage for race within YouTube culture, at once enabling and inadequate.

# Interpreting race in (YouTube) Shakespeare: Colour blindness and online posting

Race can emerge overtly in YouTube Shakespeare, especially where students are encouraged to use online culture to pursue racial thematics in the plays. *Shakespeare and race – 4* (uploaded 19 February 2008; 59 views) is one in a series of YouTube videos made by two American high-school students in the style of impromtu interviews or vox pops about the relation between Shakespeare and racial stereotypes.[29] In this video, two female interviewers question a male friend. After an opening question about stereotypes of African Americans, they ask the male teen 'So, does Shakespeare have any lessons to teach us about race?' After some laughter, he replies, 'Shakespeare's racist.' When questioned further about why he has made this particular statement, he laughs and says 'Cos he is.' When his friends berate him for 'being boring', he elaborates: 'Shakespeare is racist because he was talking about Othello as thick lipped.' The comment in the video need not be taken literally since an element of self-conscious performance and playfulness is evident with the interviewee. Nonetheless, it is interesting to note the presumptive correlation here between authorial intention and dramatic representation, which seems to hinge on a loose idea of Shakespeare's cultural authority, or the phenomenon of 'Shakespeare says'.[30] In interrogating race as a category within the plays, Shakespeareans have pointed to the anachronistic application of racist appelations to texts conceived before the 'terminology of race was invented'; this has exonerated Shakespeare from precisely the kind of casual claim made in the video above.[31] Of the 16 uses of the word 'race' in Shakespeare, none imply skin colour, nor is 'race' ever used with reference to black characters like Othello or Aaron. Yet, several plays (including, most notably, *Othello*) reveal 'a strong colour-consciousness – or, more specifically, a black-and-white colour consciousness'.[32]

Furthermore, reading race in Shakespeare requires critical reflection, so as to avoid easy assumptions about which texts are deemed to be about race and which ones are not. 'Shakespeare penned only three racially marked adult male roles,' writes Celia Daileader, 'Aaron in *Titus Andronicus*, the Prince of Morrocco in *The Merchant of Venice* and Othello.'[33] While these texts have traditionally been understood as containing what Margo Hendricks refers to as 'the obvious markers of race', they should not be the definitive bookends for a consideration of race in Shakespeare.[34] At stake here are important questions about the thematic and conceptual categories applied to certain texts.[35] *Romeo and Juliet* is the archetypal story of tragic love, but the fact that its protagonists are white does *not* mean that the play is race neutral. As I demonstrate later, it can be deployed as a vocabulary to examine interracial relationships. Thus, the (racial) marking of some texts, in terms of those that contain non-white people and the unmarking of those that do not, is an issue within the wider field of representation of which Shakespeare's works are a part, namely the positioning of whiteness as if it is the 'normalized centre',[36] or a generic identity that is 'non-raced'.[37] As Richard Dyer argues, 'Race is not only attributable to people who are not white, nor is the imagery of non-white people the only racial imagery'. Addressing the representational ubiquity of whiteness and 'seeing the racing of whites' is, Dyer insists, a necessary step towards dislodging 'them/us from the postion of power, with all the inequities, oppression, privileges, and suffering in its stream'.[38] It has been argued that 'racism and racial insecurities persist even when everyone is racialized (white, brown, and black)'.[39] Similarly, it has been suggested that the increased visibility of non-whites within cultural representation and a critical alertness to it does not necessarily correlate with greater empowerment.[40] As Stuart Hall noted some years ago, 'I know that what replaces invisibility is a kind of carefully regulated, segregated visibility.'[41] For all of these reasons, we must continue to foster critical thinking about racial visibility and access to representation. The bid to do so not only remains vital work for cultural studies scholars; it also needs to be extended to the culture of vernacular participation and anonymous comment signalled by YouTube and other new media platforms.[42]

Debates surrounding colour-blind or non-traditional casting within Shakespeare studies have done much to challenge assumptions about representations of race and difference in the texts. They have also contributed to the kind of complication or critical interrogation of whiteness that Dyer calls for. More particularly, theorizations about non-traditional casting in Shakespeare performance on stage and screen provide a useful starting point for thinking about the semiotics of race in YouTube Shakespeare. These theories have great significance for what critics such as Ayanna Thompson and Lisa Anderson have described as the 'semiotic (ir)relevance' of race in a given production or performance. They might also help us to consider the extent to which 'an actor's race is endowed with any meaning within a performance'.[43] Before pursuing these questions with specific reference to *Shakespeare in the Ghetto*, the video performances by Marcus Sykes, an African-American actor, a brief consideration of some of the issues raised by colour-blind casting will be helpful.

On a fundamental level, colour-blind casting banished the historical practice of blackface or racial impersonation (an issue that I will return to later) from Shakespearean theatre, hence the designation 'non-traditional' casting.[44] As Joseph Papp, who pioneered the practice in 1960s New York, explains, 'I was thinking of ways to eliminate colour as a factor in casting, but ... be very aware of colour on the stage.'[45] Beyond such foundational objectives, however, the politics of colour-blind practices have been questioned. While welcomed by some as an effective means of unsettling constructions and perceptions of race – and as a necessary recognition of the achievements of actors of colour – colour-blind practices have been regarded as a form of tokenistic representation. Here, a limited form of visibility runs the risk of reifying the actor of colour's body, often construing it as a spectacular or fetishized object.[46] For that reason we might suggest that non-traditional casting poses deeper questions about the possibilities, as well as the potential risks, of colour blindness in society. As Christy Burns argues, colour blindness is 'a legitimate hope for the future', but its advocates may unwittingly trade in a 'kind of utopianism.' '[W]ere we to elide all awareness of race,' she writes, 'we would not only lose cultures that do matter, but we might also return to even deeper forms of racism.'[47] This is the double-bind of colour blindess: in attempting to promote a disregard for race, the practice unwittingly erases difference and our capacity to disclose racism, thereby limiting the capacity to challenge it.

That colour-blind casting can potentially elide race, or delimit attention to it, is a point that has been pursued by other critics. With reference to productions at the RSC, Ayanna Thompson found that reviewers tended to overlook the question of race altogether, even when it was a demonstrative aspect of the production, prompting her to ask, 'Is it better to notice or not to notice race?'[48] Thompson offers an expansion of this question where she draws upon Susan Bennett's idea of a 'production–reception contract' between the play in performance and its audience. In this formulation, the immediate conditions of reception – the set of conditions in which the play is made available to, and experienced by, the audience – are accompanied by 'a larger, multilayered history of viewing', in which an audience thinks about 'which bodies have historically been made objects, [and] which bodies have historically been allowed to be spectators'.[49] In other words, audience members may receive a performance through a lens that encourages them to view their cultural and/or racial Others in fixed, stereotypical or uncritical ways. However, the presence or inclusion of bodies that have been traditionally viewed racially can also produce a supra-consciousness about race, as Anderson observes:

> The actor's blackness precedes him or her, evokes the history of race in our culture; without any effort, the meanings of blackness filter through our consciousness. We work to ascertain the meaning of this particular blackness, while other meanings remain present.[50]

For Anderson, then, an audience will habitually notice race, even where it is not envisaged as semiotically relevant to the production. Hence, '[t]o assume that we can watch a theatrical production and ignore the racial identities of the actors onstage is to assume the impossible'.[51]

While both Thompson's and Anderson's reflections pertain to theatre, a medium with its own particular set of conditions that situate and shape audience response, their observations also have a wider application in terms of the relation between a viewer and the racialized body. As Anderson emphasizes, 'We are not blind to race (colour); it is one of the ways in which we categorize our lives.'[52] And, as K. Anthony Appiah puts it, the 'label works despite the absence of the essence'.[53]

There is, therefore, an inevitability to seeing race, even in the the context of disembodied online exchange. It is one of those 'modes of othering' that, along with gender and sexuality, is simplified and 'reduced to the perception of visible differences, whose social meaning is taken to be obvious, immediate, and intelligible to the naked eye'.[54] With this in mind, I turn now to a consideration of the visibility of race and its semiotic significance in Sykes's YouTube videos.

There are 9 videos in total, with the earliest posted in April 2006 and the most recent dating from February 2011. With the exception of performances of sonnets 8 and 119, the performances are of iconic speeches from the plays: Jaques's 'All the world's a stage' (II.7.140–67) from *As You Like It*; Angelo's 'What's this? What's this? Is this her fault, or mine?' (II.2.163–87) from *Measure for Measure*; extracts from Aaron's monologues in *Titus Andronicus*; Shylock's 'Hath not a Jew eyes' (III.1.48–66); Othello's 'Her father loved me' (I.3.129–70) and also his response to Iago's mention of jealousy, 'Why, why is this? (III.3.179–93). The first *Othello* performance has the highest view count of the entire series. Sykes's material is akin to those performances of 'To be or not to be' discussed in the previous chapter; as with *Hamlet* uploads, Sykes uses a vlog-style direct address to camera and remediates the Shakespearean speech in the interests of a self-reflexive performance, which combines a display of acting talents with participation in an online broadcast community. A sense of community is evident in Sykes's use of YouTube to disseminate his Shakespeare performances. He encourages viewers to make requests, and posts left in response to his videos often include suggestions for future performances.[55] To the extent that viewer comments offer a barometer of response to Sykes's videos, it is interesting to note that while his performances of Aaron and Othello elicit comments about race, his Angelo and Jacques monologues do not.[56] This contrasting degree of reaction may reflect culturally ingrained perceptions about certain Shakespearean characters as racially marked, with viewers less likely to notice race in

Shakespeare where a performance involves white characters, than they are in relation to one that involves characters written as black.[57]

Additionally, race may come to the fore in Sykes's Othello and Aaron performances because of a perceived alignment of dramatic character and performer; in other words, race becomes especially noticeable, or is deemed semiotically relevant in conditions where a performer is a person of colour. 'There is something in Othello with which you identify, isn't there?' posts a viewer in response to *Shakespeare in the Ghetto – Othello* (uploaded 23 November 2007; 319,637 views).[58] Another viewer comments 'This really strikes me as truly Othello. Yes, Othello is "a Moor," meaning he was from Africa so your ancestry is a natural part of the realism, but there's more. I love this.' Sykes's own response indicates an empathy with the character: 'yea were [sic] both black i love Shakespeare but there are few black heros [sic] in his work so i feel most comfortable in this role.' The stated identification with Othello has a degree of familiarity to it, especially considering the established history of black actors, such as Paul Robeson, claiming an affinity with the role which came to be seen as a prerequisite for 'the black performer's admission to the professional ranks of the Western dramatic stage'.[59] Furthermore, the title of the series signals a certain attitude to Shakespeare, a sort of Shakespeare from and for the street, or even a 'black' Shakespeare. Yet, at the same time, it is also important to remember, as Richard Burt has argued in relation to citations of the plays in American television and films, that there is no longer anything approaching an authentic black appropriation of the Bard which can be measured against a putatively classical or traditional version. Within our contemporary mediatized landscape, the texts have become quotable commodities or 'Shakesbites'.[60] Nonetheless, a language of authenticity is evident in viewers' comments about Sykes's videos, with several criticizing his performances for not being sufficientlly 'ghetto'. One viewer helpfully broadens out the meanings of the title:

> For all who don't understand the title Shakespeare in the Ghetto: there might be all sorts of reasons why the artist calls his work by this name ... He might be saying that HE was born and raised in the ghetto, or that he performs his art in the ghetto, or he might be calling it 'ghetto' to get a reaction of some sort from the audience. If this is the case, he is successful! An artist provokes thought from his audience.

Sykes himself offers the following account: 'some of my monologues were actually meant to be funny, and are inaccurate on purpose to be honest'.[61] A degree of self-deprecation, or a strategic distancing of the material from the negative, offensive and controversial comments it has garnered, might be at work here. While focusing on Sykes's videos risks ghettoizing his material, I think it is important to note how race emerges as an over-determined category within the reception of his performance. Furthermore, by attending to his performance, we can contribute to what Manthia Diawara argues is the necessary and important recognition of black performance 'as a way out of the circuit of white appropriation, spectacularization, and enactment of dominance that has seemed to mark so much of the representational history of black subjects in the West'.[62]

Sykes's video *Shakespeare in the Ghetto – Othello* captures this critical potential of black performance, as well as the difficulties of unpacking racialized thinking. The film is shot in black and white, with Sykes looking upwards and directly into a fixed camera, as he delivers a redacted performance of Othello's account to the Senate of his first encounter with Desdemona (I.3.129–70). The effect here is to provide a close-up of facial expressions, though as Sykes moves backwards his naked torso is partially visible. Several of the comments are evaluative, with observations about Sykes's enunciation of Shakespearean language, or his shortening of the speech. Others praise his empathetic performance, implicitly suggesting some affinity between actor and character in terms that presume an essentialized black subject or that narrowly categorize the range of roles in Shakespeare along colour lines, so that black actors become fetishistically associated with the figures of Aaron or Othello, in a phenomenon Celia Daileader dubs 'Othellophilia'.[63] Some posts challenge such ways of seeing: 'don't be afraid to do other characters. It's not necessary to be white to do Hamlet o[r] Macbeth.' Elsewhere, however, viewer comments bring race to the surface in more explicit, problematic ways:

There's nothing hotter than Shakespeare.

I know, even if its from a Afro African American black guy.

this guy sux [sic] bad instead sykesmarcus you should go pop a '40 cal' or go 'chill' with your 'homies' and cheat on your 'babymama' or go 'pop a gat' or a 'ratchet'.

Fucking stupid niggers ruining white literature.

Commenting on videos is native to the culture of YouTube and a key dimension of the reception context for any video. The platform encourages immediate evaluation, as viewers can rate content at the click of the thumbs up/thumbs down icon. YouTube has also updated its comment feature, prioritizing posts that viewers have 'liked' within an otherwise chronological arrangement. It is possible to follow the exchange between viewers by clicking on the link 'Show the comment' (those comments flagged as inappropriate by viewers are hidden and replaced with the line 'This comment has received too many negative votes'). A YouTuber can elect to disable the comment feature for his/her video; and a commentator can delete posts retrospectively. However, where posting does occur, it is marked by a paradox: while the race of the individual featured in the video is viewable, or available as part of the semiotics of the piece, even in cases where an alias has been used, the race of the person leaving the comment is not. As such, online posting has not created racism anew, but rather exacerbated it.[64] By uploading his Othello performance, Sykes enters into the free-for-all culture of online posting, where anonymity confers licence on individuals to comment overtly and phobically. The deployment of online aliases is a function of online identity more generally where, as Nakamura argues, interaction and expression occurs through 'cybertypes' or 'images of identity and afterimages' that are frequently phobic. Images of 'race and gender [are treated] as amusing prostheses to be donned and shed without "real life" consequences'.[65] Wesch's point about the deliberately provocative and offensive nature of online commenting, or 'hatred as public performance', has already been noted.[66] This is the downside of the YouTube invitation to 'Broadcast Yourself', where uploading a video involves exposure to trolls.

There is a wider issue here about YouTube culture – its production of a community of one, that individual anonymous user, who sees videos as content rather than as the work of another person. In such a scenario, where there are after-images of identity, the possibilties for empathy are short-circuited. As Juhasz writes,

> YouTube serves the decentering mandate of post-identity politics by creating a logic of dispersal and network. Yet it fails to relink these decentered fragments in any rational or sustaining way. There is no possibility to make collectives through its architecture. Information cannot become knowledge without a map, a structure, and an ethics.'[67]

With reference to classroom-inspired Shakespeare performance videos, it is as if some 'respondents are channeling Iago's racism and sexism'.[68] Understood in relation to Internet culture, we can begin to see how established cultural sterotypes about black people form part of the reception of Sykes's video and how they are read onto his performance, or how racist language, including the 'n-word', is used freely in comments, a reminder (if one were needed) that the racist rhetoric and attitudes that *Othello* unleashes through Iago are disturbingly present.[69]

In *Shakespeare in the Ghetto – Aaron* (uploaded 6 May 2010; 677 views), race once again emerges in posts as a noticeable aspect of Sykes's performance.[70] As with his other videos, Sykes uses a title sequence in which Shakespeare's name is variously spelt as 'Shakespheer' or 'Shakesphere', branding his adaptation of the Bard while also punning on Shakespeare's international dimension (as in 'sphere') and enacting a playful levelling and differentiation (peer/fear). In the video, Sykes offers a redacted version of Aaron's speech in which, now captured, the Moor details his mischievous plotting (V.1.98–120, 124–44). Surtitles – somewhat in the style of silent film – are used to convey two interrogatives by Lucius ('Art thou not sorry / for these hanis [sic] deeds?'), and by one of his men ('What! / Canst thou say all this and never blush?'), which punctuate Aaron's boast. As with the *Othello* video, Sykes's performance of another Shakespearean stage Moor gives rise to posts in which the colour of Sykes's skin is read as available for comment and judgement:

> That was AWFUL! The only thing 'ghetto' about your monologue was it's [sic] mediocrity. Are you one of those black guys who thinks he should get a pat on the head just for reading lines from the Bard? Cause that is all you did, READ! Dude there is nothing 'affirmative action like' in Aaron the Moor's personality. He's an ass beater, not a stoner/slacker. You played Aaron as if you'd just finished smoking a joint, so I think I'll just ... puff, puff, ... pass on you.

Most critics would probably agree that in its representation of Aaron, Shakespeare's early tragedy offers little in the way of ambivalence.[71] Not only does Aaron boast of his motiveless villainy, but he also firmly links it to his skin colour so that the latter is read as an indelible mark of the former.[72] However, for the viewer quoted above, Sykes's video is about a futile attempt to redeem the role – as if such a project is the primary or inevitable motivating factor for an actor of colour – or an appropriation of Shakespeare's cultural power in order to ameliorate inequality based on race. Disquietingly, the evaluation of Sykes's acting abilities turns to matters of skin colour: race is not only noticed here, but is invoked in comments as a pre-loaded signifier, an ocular placeholder, through which the meaning of a performance is determined.

Online posts may well reflect attitudes to race that find more muted expression offline, but significantly they can also be formative in challenging racism. To return to Juhasz's argument about the potentially alienating effects of the YouTube network, I would argue that it is possible to forge collectives through directed use of the site as facilitated by category-specific searches (as in YouTube Shakespeare) and also via channels and channel subscriptions. Furthermore, as Juhasz herself acknowledges, there are those 'niche' tubes at work within the matrix of YouTube more generally that denote a more interactive and critically engaged relationship to content and to other users. As Gary Younge argues, racism need not be an inevitable part of the Internet, even if 'people have made it so'. In fact, because viewer responses have a particular form of agency and power, suggests Younge, 'people can make it otherwise'.[73] Fortunately, we can see signs of collective self-censorship in action. Comments like those cited above are widely criticized, with viewers directly addressing ignorance, prejudice and phobic sentiment. For instance, in response to the phobic post on Sykes's Othello video, a viewer comments: 'why so angry, do you hate yourself? how sad you must not like your life poor little white boy I feel sorry for someone like you because you must hate your life.' Such correctives to hate-posts, and the chain of assumptions underpinning them, suggest that critical awareness does occur, a reality that possibly controverts claims that YouTube produces an impassive viewer and is 'more about the immediate' than 'the meaningful'.[74] In this regard, YouTube Shakespeare becomes an open, public space, where nakedly visible (re)articulations of static racial stereotypes are challenged and resisted in all kinds of crucial and reflective ways. The value of the YouTube comment feature is thus evident – it discloses, democratizes and deals with the manifold effects of a Shakespearean text.

However, there may be a more specific value for Shakespearean pedagogy. As Thompson has argued, viewer posts 'highlight some uncomfortable aspects of the texts that are often glossed over in the classroom, specifically the dynamics of race and gender in Shakespearean performance'.[75] This strategy is not without risks, since one cannot predict how race will signify in a classroom setting, any more than Sykes can control the extent to which blackness will function as a criterion in evaluations of his performance in an online setting. By participating in YouTube's culture of vernacular production, Sykes opens his work and indeed himself to the opinions of his online peers who set the terms of reception. Race emerges in the videos as semiotically relevant, an incontrovertible dimension of interpretation. Indeed, as the posts suggest, it seems to function as an *a priori* dimension of evaluation. To upload a video is to enter into a volatile interpretative terrain, especially where a performance is by an actor of colour.

# Playing blackface: Racial (dis)closures and the risks of parody

Reactions to *Shakespeare in the Ghetto* reveal how race emerges as an over-determined category, and suggest the limits of YouTube and the Internet to fully disrupt racialized ways of viewing. However, the series also represents the possibilities of online production and it is important to acknowledge the contribution it makes to the showcasing of racial matters both in and through Shakespearean performance. The next set of videos turns more explicitly to structures of seeing by focusing on *Othello* and that play's historical associations with blackface. *Othello blacking up* (uploaded 19 January 2011; 93 views) is a film short, shot in black and white.[76] The participants feature in other videos about *Othello*, which take the form of pre-rehearsal workshops and discussions about the play's central dynamics. YouTube functions here as a convenient way to share the video among the group members and to intervene in modes of representation more generally. As there are no viewer comments, it is not possible to pursue the reception context as in the case of Sykes' videos. Nevertheless, it is extremely interesting to note how the reference to blackface in the title connects this video with prominent examples of blackfaced performance, such as Olivier's (in Stuart Burge's 1965 film), and clips from notorious minstrel show films like *Yes Sir, Mr Bones*, featuring Cotton Watts in blackface.[77] At one point, *Othello blacking up* seems to reference Olivier's performance, namely the scene where his black make-up rubs off on Maggie Smith's Desdemona. *Othello blacking up* is significant as a response both to the foundational place of blackface in the performance history of *Othello* and to some of its legacies, in particular minstrelesy.[78] Indeed, the video would be an interesting classroom resource for exploring blackface in Shakespeare and addressing racialized representations in culture.

The establishing shot firmly introduces the Shakespearean context, with a close-up of a copy of the Arden edition of *Othello*, make-up and applicator, and a partially visible white hand, while the use of Verdi's *Otello* as a score throughout serves to complement the diegesis (primarily because blackface continued in opera long after it had become unacceptable in theatre).[79] In the next frame, we see a white male actor sitting before a mirror, as a make-up artist begins the process of applying black pancake, a process that is repeated on a white female actor. To my mind, this structure and development opens up some rich interpretative possibilities, since these two actors can be read as Othello and Desdemona figures, and the actor applying the make-up as the Iago figure. The entire film literalizes the play's discourse of blackness, namely, the racist rhetoric emanating from Iago, which obscures Othello's perception of Desdemona and metaphorically darkens her honour.

*Othello blacking up* situates itself in relation to debates about the politics of impersonating the Moor. On the Shakespearean stage, as Dympna Callaghan reminds us, the representation of racial difference was enabled by stage properties such as costume, but primarily cosmetics. The use of blackface, which 'concealed under the sign of negritude a host of ethnicities', contrasted with the use of whiteface to produce a stark demarcation of difference based on skin colour.[80] As Callaghan elaborates, blackface was not only predicated on the exclusion of non-whites from the representational spectrum – 'Othello was a white man' – but was also one of the ways through which whiteness was essentialized and privileged. In modern performances, 'the question of how to cast *Othello* without entertaining its racist stereotypes remains' unresolved.[81] As noted earlier, colour-blind casting, and the concomitant departure from the original practices of the Shakespearean stage, offer the clearest way of circumventing the spectre of blackface associated with *Othello*. Accordingly, the established tradition of casting a black actor in the role is defended by the writer Ben Okri, who sees it as crucial to the avoidance of minstrelesy, or the activation of what he calls the 'white man's myth of the Black man'.[82]

Casting an actor of colour can also lead to the audience overidentifying the actor with the role – the Othellophilia that haunts the play in performance. Thus, Hugh Macrae Richmond questions the claim that casting non-Caucasian actors realizes a less condescending portrayal of Othello: 'the irony is that such casting invites a non-aesthetic identification with the actors as truly representatives of the historical victims of just such condescension'.[83] The actor Hugh Quarshie echoes such views when he asks 'if a black actor plays Othello does he not risk making racial stereotypes seem legitimate and even true? When a black actor plays a role written for a white actor in black make-up and for a predominatly white audience, does he not encourage the white way, or rather the wrong way, of looking at black men?'[84] Yet, others have argued that blackface is effective in alerting audiences to the 'indirect production of whiteness', since it fosters a double-consciousness in the audience about the white body that lies beneath a cosmeticized blackness.[85] Advocating selected blackface performances, Virginia Mason Vaughan suggests that where students are reminded that the eponymous hero was written with a white actor in mind, a less essentialized idea of the Moor and of blackness is likely to emerge. 'Only when we see that Othello is not real – that he is not a valid portrayal of any black man who ever lived but a creation of actors like Burbage, Olivier, Fishburne – can we begin to understand the "fear and desires" that have been superimposed on his persona.'[86]

Claims concerning the deconstructive potentiality of racial impersonation are also pursued by Thompson, who analyses the effects of several modern performances of blackface in American film and television, including those by black actors and directors who attempt to revisit the historical legacies of blackface.[87] What emerges from the analysis is that regardless of the intentions behind such productions, the semiotic significance of an actor donning black pancake cannot be controlled and, more often than not, easily slips into racial stereotype.[88] For Thompson, the unpredictability involved in playing with blackface is a function of 'Shakespeare's cultural capital rather than any inherent problems with the performance of blackface itself', since the authority that comes with the Bard foreshortens the potential 'reception ranges' for blackface: 'we will have to dispense with the cultural force of Bardolatry before we can advance creating and enabling an oppositional gaze for blackface performance'.[89] Yet, Shakespeare's cultural prestige possibly *does* provide a space to explore racial difference, so long as it is supplemented by what Karin deGravelles has described as 'an ethical relationship' to text like *Othello*. DeGravelles envisages a mode of reading and teaching that attends to the text's association with the historical traumas of racism and colonization. She argues that 'it is important that our responsibility in engaging the play be to those who have been harmed rather than to the text itself, its characters, or its author', especially when one considers the play's histories and its 'unclear political stance'.[90] Shakespeare's tragedy of the Moor, deGravelles concludes, 'is, and should be, a profoundly difficult play to read, watch, and teach'.[91]

The fact that the difficult business of watching *Othello* calls for sensitive and sophisticated responses is directly confronted in *Othello blacking up*. The video explores the legacy of blackface responsibly and self-consciously, and does so through an emphasis on perspective, on the act of seeing racial difference. The film's central device of the mirror is significant here. The use of the dressing room mirror is not merely contextually appropriate (gesturing as it does to the theatrical conditions of Shakespeare's play), but also draws our attention to the processes that precede and enable the impersonation of racial difference. It is richly suggestive in a number of ways. In Lacanian terms, the mirror marks a key phase of identity formation, whereby the infant, perceiving its own reflection, comes to identify with the illusory completeness of the mirrored image.[92] This image acts as a supplement to the fragmented sense of the body with which it contrasts so strikingly. As such, the video makes available a psychoanalytical reading of Shakespeare's characters and may, more pointedly, be alluding to the aggression that Lacan holds is fundamental to the ego. This aggression originates from a false or misrecognition on the part of the infant with the mirrored image of his body, which is glimpsed in the reflection as a putatively whole, or complete, self that he frustratingly desires to assimilate. By placing the actors in front of a mirror, and by depicting the Othello figure rejecting the woman's embrace, and then pushing away her head with his hand (as if horrified by her newly darkened face), the video offers an account of Othello's aggression towards Desdemona as a form of sublimated anger about a lost wholeness that never was. Additionally, the rejection of a blackened Desdemona figure, with the emphasis on the lingering touch of the white hand on her cosmetically altered skin, intertwines with those interpretations of the play that suggest that what Othello secretly desires all along is not Desdemona herself, but whiteness and its culturally valorized associations of privilege, respectability and acceptance.[93]

On a broader level, the video's use of the mirror and of blackface captures the extent to which race is primarily a matter of the visual. '"Look, a Negro!"', Fanon's evocative and powerful recollection of how his body becomes legible through the racialized gaze, while historically particular to his narrative of colonial Algeria, still resonates.[94] Moreover, Fanon's experience – 'the corporeal schema crumbled, its place taken by a racial epidermal schema' – requires that we qualify Lacan's account of identity and identification, which as Shannon Winnubust argues, is problematically universalizing and white. As Winnubust writes, Fanon's 'image of his own body, a foundational site for his ego-and-subject formation, is interpellated by the cultural symbolic in which it is located. The black infant attempts to gather himself into a "whole body", but can see himself only as he is seen by the white racist world.'[95] Ever conscious of the white gaze, the black subject is 'denied entry into the alterity which Lacan sees as grounding the necessary fiction of the unified self'.[96] The video gestures towards the debilitating effects of internalizing the white gaze, as the Othello figure stares at his image, and later rejects Desdemona. *Othello blacking up* thus promotes a consideration of racialized viewing through its focus on the cosmeticization of racial difference in Shakespearean theatre as well as on acts of looking (and the near scopophilic gaze or simple act of looking is, of course, a leitmotif in the film). In the penultimate frame, as the make-up artist turns out the lights, an action evocative of Othello's 'Put out the light, and then put out thy light!' (V.2.7), we see the Othello and Desdemona figures sitting in semi-darkness. In the final frame, in which the make-up applicator is brought towards and then covers the camera lens, the viewer is fully implicated in the act of looking. The effect is to disrupt the distance between the blackfaced performers and ourselves as viewers. Ultimately, however, the film's attempt to unsettle a racialized perspective is only partially succesful, since there is no attempt to problematize whiteness to the same extent. Indeed, the film could stand accused of replicating the racial politics of Renaissance blackface by presuming an original and essential whiteness beneath.[97] By using whiteface as part of the exploration of racial cosmetics in *Othello*, the performers might have complicated race more thoroughly.

Blackface is also thematically central in another YouTube video, *Shakespeare Abridged Promo – Othello Rap* (uploaded 6 June 2010; 942 views), a promotional video for a performance by a group of four actors that took place at the Dublin Shakespeare Festival in June 2010.[98] Whereas *Othello blacking up* adopts a historical approach in alluding to the original practice of Shakespearean theatre, this video demonstrates a more contemporizing impulse in its use of rap. We can detect the influence of the Reduced Shakespeare Company here, since their performances turned rap into *the* medium through which a more accessible, putatively relevant and immediate Shakespeare could be achieved.[99] As used to remediate Shakespeare, rap and hip hop become surrogates for the text and suggest that the process of remediation entails a departure from an older medium, as if to say that it lacks the requisite contemporary resonance. *Shakespeare Abridged* includes a performance of Reduced's *Othello Rap* and, as in that production, the rap itself is prefaced by a short explanatory scene. In the case of Reduced, the pre-rap dialogue confronts that difficult business of *Othello* referred to earlier: 'the part was written for a black actor', they explain to their audience, so as an all-white crew, they are 'racially challenged' to impersonate Shakespeare's Moor.[100] For Reduced, blackface is not an option; instead, the performers dismiss the practice of Shakespeare's theatre and adopt the safer mode of irony to address race, and at the same time to circumvent it, though the rap itself goes on to trade in stereotypes about black male sexual prowess.[101] In the *Shakespeare Abridged* video, the performers do not engage in full blackface, but they do address the cosmeticization of race in Shakespeare's theatre quite explicitly.

The video opens in the style of the vlog or video diary and also of reality televison, especially in terms of the fabricated spontaneity and authenticity associated with the latter genre. One of the male performers speaks directly to a hand-held camera as he moves about a house, calling out the name of the female performer. She is discovered eating from a tin of chocolate powder. This is the primary gag of the video and it is signposted, both with the question 'So we have to be black to do Othello and you bought me hot chocolate?', and also visually as the male performer precedes to dab chocolate powder on his torso.[102] Viewer posts praise the performance for its humour, which in one sense does highlight the act of blacking up as an absurdity.

In contrast to *Othello blacking up*, however, *Shakespeare Abridged* does not forge the kind of ethical relationship to *Othello* that deGravelles calls for. That race and racial difference are subjects of laughter in the video suggests a level of 'post-raciality', and the performers belong to that demographic that is sometimes believed to operate outside of, or beyond, narrow identity politics based on race, gender or class.[103] Yet, the comic treatment of Othello's skin colour serves less to destabilize racial impersonation on the Shakespearean stage than to minimize the association of blackface with histories of minstrelesy, where blackness is offered as a commodity for the entertainment of white audiences. Thus, the video downplays the extent to which blackface involved the elision or exclusion of black actors from the field of representation.[104] A number of factors account for the political unconscious of this video, from a lack of consideration of the politics of *Othello* itself, to a more generic white blindness that, in turn, references matters of racial difference in culture.[105] Whereas *Othello blacking up* suggests that the Shakespearean text is partially successful as a medium for regarding racial difference as a function of the visual and of perspective, *Shakespeare Abridged* unwittingly instantiates the risks of performing Shakespearean blackface. As deployed comically in this video, the effect is to reinforce, rather than unsettle, a racialized gaze.

*The Story of Othello* (uploaded 1 May 2010; 26,654 views) is also a promotion for a stage performance, this time for an American theatre company, and it too borrows from Reduced's *Othello* to contemporize Shakespeare. While avoiding blackface, the video contains a number of racial markers and also plays with the semiotics of race.[106] The text of Reduced's rap is updated through contemporary urban music, especially R&B. Thus, while implicitly recognizing that the Shakespearean text offers a metalanguage for exploring race, at the same time *The Story of Othello* suggests that the text requires a contemporary slant that supplements the original with a newer medium and its lexicon. Billed as a trailer for the Red Door Theater's production of 'The Complete Works of William Shakespeare [abridged]', *The Story of Othello* was commissioned by the theatre company as a backdrop to the live performance, suggesting the blurring of the 'live' and the mediatized, which Philip Auslander regards as a characteristic of contemporary cultural production.[107] As posted on YouTube, the video is an example of how the platform is used as a promotional space for theatre productions. The comic reduction of Shakespeare's tragic plot is likely to provoke laughter: a nice touch is the use of Shakespeare's image (from the Folio) as a bleep icon for expletives in the rap. However, it is necessary to look behind the humour in order to consider what the video says about *Othello* and what it reveals about the cultural work that the remediated text performs on YouTube.

The video exemplifies a form of response to *Othello* in which the play's complex interweaving of race and sex is treated comically through parody and exaggerated performance. Directed by Derrick Acosta of Mega64, *The Story of Othello* riffs off Reduced's *Othello Rap*, reworking its opening lines and including visual cues to their Shakespearean-style costumes, themselves parodies of 'proper' Elizabethan attire (for instance, two of the rappers wear breeches).[108] There are further gestures to period detail, with Desdemona played by a man in drag. The video's dominant aesthetic comes from the music video, or rather a parody of that particular cultural form. Two specific genres are targeted, namely the hip-hop and the boy-band music video. Various signifiers indicate these genres, from the exaggerated dance moves and bodily gestures of the performers (suggesting a parody of artists such as Snoop Dogg or Pharrell, as well as boy bands) to the street wear (hoodie, track-suit top, basketball vest and sunglasses) and the lined up cars, headlights blazing, which backlight the performance.[109] Combined with the appearance of the rapper Dallas and the professional quality of the production, these references most likely account for the appeal of the video among a particular cohort.[110] Another draw for viewers of *The Story of Othello* is its urban, MTV-style Shakespeare, certainly familiar to those conversant with such films as Blake Nelson's *O* and Luhrmann's *Romeo + Juliet*.[111] With aspects of their style and pace borrowed from the music video, these films have sometimes been too readily dismissed as Shakespeare for the MTV viewer. As Julie Sanders points out, however, the targeted audience is adept at 'reading visuals mediated through a musical or auditory frame'.[112] The *Story of Othello* similarly presumes audience recognition of a number of cultural forms and as such is a semiotically dense text.

In *The Story of Othello*, the characterization of Othello is semiotically loaded with a specific cue, since the white actor (Shaun Conde) wears an Afro wig. His direct performance to camera, another device from the music video that is patently parodied here, is interspersed with close-ups introducing the characters and title sequences which emphasize the narrative aspects of the rap. For instance, in the line 'Othello met a girl she was totally white / He liked her so much, he made her his wife', the words 'totally white' appear as capitalized surtitles beside Desdemona. The borrowings from Reduced's *Othello Rap* signal a parodic take on the primary sexual and interracial dynamic of Shakespeare's play that develops throughout the video. The video belongs to a category of Shakespearean parody characterized by incongruity. As Stephen Purcell notes, plots or characters are transposed into unlikely settings or performed in an inappropriate style.[113] Purcell elaborates on the effects of parody, suggesting that the 'comic incongruities between Shakespeare and popular forms' can reinforce a sense of the former's inaccessibility to popular audiences, while at the same time affording a creative and critical detachment that serves to disrupt distinctions between 'high' and 'popular' culture.[114] Of relevance here is Linda Hutcheon's argument that 'parody works to distance and, at the same time, to involve the reader in a participatory hermeneutic activity'.[115] Parody also offers a licensed, or culturally safe, mode for addressing issues such as race and sexuality that still prove sensitive in society. For example, in a reading of YouTube videos directly tackle racial identity, such as *Top 60 Ghetto Names* (uploaded 9 January 2009; 28,269,719 views), Kavoori notes that comedy serves to negotiate a line between 'the affirmation of stereotypes and the pleasure that parody offers' and, moreover does so in a way that is both permissible and part of a 'wider conversation about political correctness and race'.[116]

That said, it is also important to consider the limitations of this particular mode of address, which tends to nullify the efficacy of the content. Much generic content on YouTube produces a 'new structure of viewing that is neither sharp nor critical' – especially where videos rely on irony, as in the case of the mockumentary genre.[117] Simply put, this restructuring returns us to the point about representation and racism: both the tropes and the biases that irony aims to identify and dissasemble once again become dominant or, worse still, indiscernible and/or undistinguishable from those videos that are, in fact, chauvinistic and phobic. In the case of *The Story of Othello,* then, irony has the potential to put into circulation in an uncritical way a series of racial stereotypes and an inflexible attitude to sexuality.

The comic treatment of Othello's sexual desire for white women is illustrative here, with the refrain of the song playfully establishing Othello's obsessive tendencies: 'He said girl, you know I think you're fine / Girl I'm gonna make you mine / Desdemona you're making me groana / You're the hottest white woman on this side of Verona.' The specificities of Othello's sexual preferences are further suggested, as we see a close-up of a lustful Othello, before the video cuts back to the rappers making pelvic thrusts to camera at the thought of Desdemona, followed by the rapper Dallas's direct address to camera: 'White women, where you at?' In this treatment of what in Shakespeare's play is initially presented as the mutual love of Othello and Desdemona, Othello is presented as obsessively desiring Desdemona and the whiteness that she symbolizes for him. In these scenes, the video offers a parody of the gender politics of *Othello*, and also of hip-hop videos, especially the privileging of the male gaze and the positioning of woman as the object of desire, which Paul Gilroy and others have explored as a problematic dimension of black vernacular expression.[118]

If there is any disruption of the play's patriarchal economy here, the video also trades in a set of stereotypes of voracious black male sexuality and the threat of rape that it has carried in the (white) cultural imagination. While the narrative establishes Iago as the root of marital destruction – 'There was a bad dude / Iago, such a menace / He didn't like Othello, the Moor of Venice' – it simultaneously dwells on Othello's destructive obsessiveness, both in an action sequence in which Othello leans over and smothers a sleeping Desdemona, and through a revised chorus: 'Girl, you know I think you're fine / Girl, I'm gonna make you mine / You're the hottest dead woman on this side of Verona.' The place name may be a reference to Verona Beach, Florida, rather than to the setting of *Romeo and Juliet*, though it works as an intertextual allusion to that tragedy about another, if less obsessive, lover. The gestures and dance moves accompanying the final chorus signal a performative attitude to, and parody of, the hyper-masculinity of R&B and its address to women. However, as the video cuts to an image of Othello hanging from a doorframe – 'Yo, then he killed himself too, peace' – it is not clear how such playfulness and irony applies to his story and its racialized baggage.

While the video critiques male obsession and desire as exemplified by Othello, it also trades in Othellophilia. In such exaggerations of the Othello story, there is no Shakespeare tragedy and perhaps not even much concern with the figure of the black male, but rather an ideology and its system of representation that is 'about women – white women explictly, as the subjects of representation; black women, implicitly, as the abjected'.[119] *Othello* becomes a narrative about the surveillance of female sexuality. A viewer tellingly comments 'I like how you couldn't get an actual woman to go along with this.' Ultimately, *The Story of Othello* is a confusing text, its ironic aesthetic at once facilitating the disclosure of cultural stereotypes about race and sexuality as found in Shakespeare, or contemporary urban music, yet also producing problematic associations between blackness and violence against women.

# Gender and interracial couplings in YouTube Shakespeare

One consequence of the comic rendering of *Othello* is to highlight the ideological work of Shakespeare's play. As paired down to the rudiments of its plot, denuded of pathos, *Othello* reads as a story about the interdependency of patriarchal power, the regulation of female desire and male abusiveness.[120] Several videos draw out such base effects: *Othello Modern play* (uploaded 16 May 2010; 354 views) fixates on the violence of the final scene. Based on the accompanying description ('acted out by teens in a modern day Hispanic society'), this video appears to be part of a high-school assignment.[121] The Othello figure (played by a young Latino man) lies over his Desdemona (played by a white girl) on a bed and starts to smother her with a cushion. While the participants can barely control their laughter, one is left wondering about the impact of such participation in the play's violence. Does it foster a direct address of the play's subtexts, encouraging students to think about *Othello* as a story of domestic abuse (which the hero's status as tragic hero can potentially obscure)? Or, might it provide a catalyst for a discussion about domestic violence in contemporary society? With such possibilities comes the risk of treating violence as representation, without any consideration of its lived realities.

Shakespeare's tragedy is reimagined as a distinctly domestic scenario in a film short, *Othello* (uploaded 20 March 2008; 6,579 views). In this instance, the cast involves a white couple: Otto is a psychopath who confronts his partner Des about her alleged affair with Cassio.[122] Forcing her against a door, Otto clasps Des's neck before drowning her in a toilet bowl. The video serves less as a critique of the violence that marks the climax of the inherited Shakespeare plot, than as a spectacularization of domestic abuse. Perhaps the film is merely amplifying the play's own pornographic perspective, a perspective the audience is invited to adopt, in ways that generate a voyeuristic excitement about the coupling of Othello and Desdemona.[123] However, in presenting an all-white couple, the video removes what in Shakespeare's play is a fascination with the bed as the primary 'site of racial transgression', the fulcrum of its fantasies and fears that find their most perverse expression in Iago's racially inflected image of 'an old black ram ... tupping your white ewe' (I.1.87–88).[124]

That Desdemona emerges in video adaptations of *Othello* as passive and silent alerts one to the intersection of race and gender in Shakespeare's text. This, in turn, could be said to shore up white patriarchal ideology, rather than challenge it. By implication, the racialized cross-dressing of the play's original theatrical conditions (boy actors in whiteface playing the female parts, a white actor in blackface playing Othello) further valorizes 'white masculinity' as the ineluctable essence

beneath.[125] In its modern iterations, the play does not necessarily enact such privilege, but it can still bring to the surface
attitudes latent within its audiences, because 'it uncannily
seems to play out what they think they already know, what
they have been taught, about race and sex: about black men's
fundamental irreconcilability to the values of civilized society
and about what happens to nice young (white) girls who defy
their father's wishes'.[126] As a text that can all too easily become
an archetype of dominant gender and racial ideologies, it
should come as no surprise that *Othello* is among the texts to
feature in *Sassy Gay Friend*, a series by Second City Network
that has become something of a YouTube phenomenon. In the
videos, iconic women from history and literature – including
Eve, Ophelia and Desdemona – are visited from the future by
a gay best friend, who alerts them to the absurdity of the plot
conventions, cultural myths and patriarchal ideologies that
they are at once contained by and also shore up. Of the videos
discussed in this chapter, *Sassy Gay Friend: Othello* (uploaded
28 March 2010; 3,212,893 views) has the most views on
YouTube.[127] Focusing as it does on the climactic scene of the
play, the action appropriately takes place in a bedroom.

In the establishing shot, we see Desdemona on her bed,
as a voice-over, in a mock-serious tone, explains: 'Meet
Desdemona from Shakespeare's Othello. She is waiting in
her bed to be murdered by her husband. This fate could
have been avoided if she had had a Sassy Gay Friend.' Cue
the emergence from a closet – the humour is not especially
subtle – of the eponymous gay friend, played by Brian
Gallivan, and the series title sequence and music. This fast-
paced video presumes a broad familiarity with the play's plot,
comically distilled into its core elements as Sassy Gay Friend
explains matters to Desdemona – her perceived unfaithfulness,
Othello's jealousy – and repeatedly urges her to leave: 'Tina
Turner, we gotta private dance it out of here.' On one level,
the pun on Turner's song is indicative of the sketch's easy
humour. On another, the reference to the singer (who endured
an abusive relationship at the hands of her partner Ike Turner)

and to this particular song (about a woman who makes her living by dancing for the pleasure of men) has the effect of reading *Othello* as a text of male domestic violence and of the objectification of women.[128] Puns also emphasize the implausibility of aspects of Shakespeare's plot, with the business of the misplaced handkerchief at Cassio's ('now Othello thinks your fingers have been all over Cassio's keyboard, so we gotta go') not only being played for laughs, but also highlighting the absurdities of Othello's gender politics: 'Some guy ends up with your handkerchief and he gets to murder you?' Other puns knowingly exploit established racial stereotypes about black men: 'Does Moor mean more?' he asks Desdemona and, as she laughs, adds, 'Now I'm being racist.' The video ends with the series' catchphrase, 'Now I'm being a stupid bitch … I'm such a stupid bitch.'

As its idiom and catchphrases suggest, *Sassy Gay Friend* is largely about the gags and, as such, seems less interested in offering its audience a queering of gender in key literary texts than in using recognizable cultural references and types to poke fun at archetypal representations of women and, by implication, men in culture. Arguably, it offers a fairly safe form of queerness and of homosexuality, one that presents the gay man as possessing a valuable commodity (his savvy attitude), to be extended back in time to literature's clueless heroines. However, the laughter is dependent on the queer advice that Desdemona receives, and the video ultimately *does* involve a queer reading of *Othello* – one that parodies traditional masculinity, while simultaneously questioning the role assigned to women by the forms of heterosexual desire that are signified in Shakespeare's tragedy. As deployed in *Sassy Gay Friend*, parody becomes an instinctively queer form, encouraging us to look again or anew. High camp, fast-paced, *Sassy Gay Friend: Othello* is a self-conscious text that deploys a postmodern knowingness to debunk the canonical Shakespeare and its complicity with such grand narratives as patriarchy. Nonetheless, the video, like the series more generally, recognizes the enduring cultural draw of the Bard.

A similar sense of Shakespeare as a cipher is evident in two YouTube uploads which draw on *Romeo and Juliet* to examine interracial relationships: a film short, *ColourBlind (a romeo and juliet story)*, and *Poetry n Motion – Romeo and Juliet (1998)*. In these videos, the essentials of Shakespeare's tragic plot are turned directly towards race and the iconic story of young love mined with a view to the possibilities it offers for rescripting static, phobic and repressive cultural formations of race. *Romeo and Juliet*, already discussed in Chapter 1, as an example of the fan-made video, has a rich afterlife on YouTube, which counts among the media spaces through which that story is repeated, used or challenged. Of 'the play's cultural ubiquity', Marjorie Garber suggests that the story not only appeals to youth, but at certain points in modern history may even have contributed to the production of the idea of youth.[129] There is also the 'readiness for appropriation' of the play's 'ancient grudge' (Prologue, 3) between two families.[130] *West Side Story* is among the earliest of a host of adaptations that root the play's feud between the Montagues and the Capulets in inter-cultural or racial tensions. Luhrmann's *Romeo + Juliet* also suggests a racialized dimension to the feud. However, while its *mise en scène* variously implies the multicultural and multi-ethnic make-up of contemporary world cities, the emphasis on the star vehicles of Daines and DiCaprio means that this story of the 'star-crossed lovers' is ultimately a traditional, racially conservative one.[131] Non-Anglophone adaptations have proved more willing to probe the possibilities of the play's central dynamic. [132]

In *ColourBlind* (uploaded 10 October 2009; 2,892 views), Shakespeare's play provides the narrative impetus for a film short that explores an interracial relationship, in this case between a Mexican girl and John, a young black man.[133] The opening shot establishes the objection to the relationship as rooted in parental vigilance and control, which is what a viewer familiar with the story of Romeo and Juliet (as it is remembered in popular culture) might expect. A young Mexican woman – the sister of the film's Juliet figure Desiree

– sits in a parked car talking on a mobile phone: 'Yeh Mom, she's here ... Si, Señora ... I'll take care of it.' The extra diegetic element of the title *ColourBlind* establishes race as another layer to such parental disapproval and familial protectiveness; it also crosses generational lines, from mother to daughter. The film immediately cuts to a close-up of the Romeo figure as he waits for Desiree.[134] As the lovers recline on a hill, John tells Desiree he has written something for her, which turns out to be a recasting of Romeo's 'But soft, what light through yonder window breaks? / It is the east, and Juliet is the sun' (II.2.2–3). The intertextual allusion to the play's first encounter scene is deftly handled and, as repurposed here, Romeo's lines acquire an immediacy that seems entirely specific to the situation of these two teens. Romeo's figuring of Juliet as the sun – 'Arise, fair sun, and kill the envious moon' (II.2.4) – is interpolated with the line 'Forget about your Mamma and all her endless drama' so that the lines 'sick and pale with grief / That thou her maid art far more fair than she' (II.2.4–6) apply to Desiree's mother. The central motif (the transgression of parental authority and the bonds of family) is further established as the lovers are interrupted by Desiree's sister, the woman of the opening scene. A heated exchange between the siblings ensues, with Desiree asserting her choice and independence. Here, as in other representations in film and music, the Juliet figure is imbued with an agency that reflects 'shifting notions and self-images of girlhood and young womanhood'.[135] Desiree's self-determinism is contrasted with the sister's conformity to parental authority and attitudes, a conformity that is shown to be damaging as, in Spanish, she refers to John in racist terms: 'Hold up, hold up, who are you calling a dirty black Negro?' he asks.

Such racially inflammatory language is, however, rebuked in the film, as it deploys that dominant association of its Shakespearean intertext, love triumphant: 'Love ain't got no colour, remember that shit', John says. As he does so, Desiree steps into the frame and stands beside him; this suggests their alignment and common stance against the attitudes of

Desiree's sister, who is quite literally minimized in the shot. He begins to recite Martin Luther King's 'I have a dream', moving between English and Spanish. The use of King as an intertext offers an alternative narrative authority to that of the Shakespearean intertext, suggesting the possibility of love across a racial divide rather than its tragic ending. Equally important is the use of Mexican music throughout as a score. This is not simply a backdrop to the diegesis but rather a 'meta-diegetic' element in that it 'contributes to the interpretation or understanding of what is being witnessed on screen'.[136] The film closes with Desiree's sister seemingly won over by John's echoing of King's plea for tolerance, mutual respect and inclusion. However, a degree of uncertainty remains as to whether the objections of the absent mother, established at the outset, can be similarly appeased.

*Poetry n Motion – Romeo and Juliet* (uploaded 10 January 2009; 205,662 views) is the music video for the song by the 1990s group whose members included Michael Ameer Williams and Garland Hatten.[137] From its Shakespearean intertext, the song takes the theme of patriarchal control (as expressed in Old Capulet's insistence that Juliet marry Paris) to tell a story of racial prejudice. 'So goes our story about Romeo and Juliet.' In Poetry'n'Motion's telling, prejudice can be vanquished, 'Today I challenge thee / Have faith in things that you can't see,' goes the chorus, 'Respect the power and you'll see / How strong love can be.' The *mise en scène* of the video furthers the Shakespearean association of the lyrics: the opening shot is of a curtain rising on a production rehearsal. After a close-up of an actress, the Juliet figure, and then of the principal singer, we have a montage of the rehearsals for a play, which involves an interracial relationship between the Juliet figure and her Romeo, here a stage hand, that the girl's father disapproves of. As a viewer posts, 'Romeo was black??? Wtf?' This may reflect an ironic stance on colour-blind casting – as if to say 'Why wouldn't Romeo be played by a non-white actor?' – or the interrogative gestures towards a chain of assumptions about the representational boundaries for Shakespearean characters – as if to say 'How could Romeo be anything other than white?' Film adaptations of the play have used the device of the internal performance before. In this instance, the framing device positions the three singers in the roles of directors, and thus as interpreters of the onstage action; the song becomes a meta-commentary on the Romeo and Juliet story. The action cuts between images of the onstage Romeo and Juliet, whose pairing ends tragically, and the same couple embracing offstage. Through these looping images, the video keeps in play the two associations of its Shakespearean intertext, the obstacles faced by love, and its fatal endurance: 'Together in eternal rest / no more stress / Do you have it yet / Romeo and Juliet.' Drawing from the iconicity of this Shakespearean pairing, the video grants visibility to interracial couplings, while also suggesting that such couplings may continue to face familial and cultural obstacles. As in the case of *ColorBlind*, *Poetry n Motion* creates a new narrative out of the Shakespearean text that seeks to extend its capacity to unsettle racial prejudice.

*

In surveying race in selected YouTube Shakespeare, I have sought to trace and then foreground the various ways that Shakespeare's texts provide a metalanguage through which race is examined. While Shakespeare is implicitly, and in some instances explicitly, called upon as a significant cultural authority or useful cipher, the videos discussed here variously instance Shakespeare's (in)adequacy as platform, placeholder or medium for addressing race in a contemporary setting. At once authoritative presence and shifting cultural space, Shakespeare does not quite manange to unpack race as a cultural construct or to ameliorate racial tensions, but rather requires contemporizing. Race emerges again and again as an unpredictable signifier, at once fully in view, yet also intangible and enigmatic, a sceptre that fuels ideas of race as an essence. 'Like Shakespeare, race remains, as a leftover which both does and does not signify.'[138] Race in YouTube Shakespeare can mean many different things and can produce varying effects. As *Shakespeare in the Ghetto* indicates, race can become semiotically integral to meaning in ways that a performer like Sykes can neither pre-empt nor police. In other uploads that explore the association of Shakespearean theatre with racial exclusion, we encountered the shaping force of what Stuart Hall describes as the 'machineries' and 'regimes' of representation. 'How things are represented,' he argues, 'play a constitutive, and not merely a reflexive, after-the-event role.'[139] Videos like *Shakespeare Abridged Promotional* and *The Story of Othello* warrant close reading and critique for this very reason. We need to think about the effect of representational modes with regard to race; as these videos reveal, parody and irony can prove counterproductive, with the stereotype reactivated rather than critiqued. Other instances, as in those user comments that refute hate posts, reveal the efficacy and vital importance of intervening in the field of representation.

Within these contrasting examples lie the limits and possibilites of YouTube culture. It can promote greater diversity and meaningful multiculturalism. Yet, the openness of online culture does not necessarily equate with an openness of attitude. As a catalyst for vernacular participation, as a social network and as an influential space where things are represented, and thus where discourses of race occur and circulate, YouTube matters. It is a space where we must critically reflect on representations. For Shakespeare studies, we can readily explore the racial histories of the texts and of their various cultural afterlives (online vernacular video production and performance, citation in music videos, theatre promotions). There are valuable opportunities to produce visual archives of race in Shakespearean texts through collection, curatorship and the annotation of videos. Moreover, this is important work for sustaining a crucial critical alertness about how and when race enters discursive spaces. However, the responsibility remains with us, as viewers and users, to reflect on race in (YouTube) Shakespeare in order that we might continue to challenge its unpredictable and insidious reverberations.

# 4

# Medium Play, Queer Erasures: Shakespeare's *Sonnets* on YouTube

*It is impossible to read this fulsome panegyrick,
addressed to a male object, without an equal mixture
of disgust and indignation.*

GEORGE STEEVENS, NOTE ON SONNET 20[1]

*sonnet 18 is about a man. you probably should have
checked that out.*

POST ON *WILLIAM SHAKESPEARE'S SONNET 18 ANIMATED*[2]

*Who will believe my verse in time to come
If it were filled with your most high deserts?*

SHAKESPEARE, SONNET 17[3]

Analytical sorties into YouTube Shakespeare have largely been concerned with responses to Shakespearean drama, a situation that reflects the volume of videos responding to the plays in contrast to those responding to the *Sonnets*.[4] It might also reflect a broader cultural association of Shakespeare as playwright rather than poet.[5] Furthermore, for those YouTubers who create a Shakespeare video, an important catalyst is the Shakespeare movie, which provides ready-made content to be adapted. There is no immediately recognizable filmic equivalent of the *Sonnets*, unless we include Samuel Parker's film short, *Shakespeare's Sonnets* (2005), based on the novella of the same title, or citations in such films as *Sense and Sensibility* (1995), where both Marianne and Willoughby possess a copy of the poems, or *Dead Poet's Society* (1989) and *Venus* (2006), both of which feature a recital of Sonnet 18.[6] Yet, the sonnet is argubaly well suited to the medium of YouTube. As Don Patterson suggests, the shape of the sonnet can be described as a square.[7] It is a 'tight little block of print on a page', which the reader can behold at once and 'read in less than a minute'.[8] Of course, accessing a sonnet through the potentially distracting screens of YouTube might militate against reading in the deeper, interpretative sense of the word. As one writer puts it, 'it takes a lifetime to read a Shakespeare sonnet'.[9] However, the pleasures and challenges of the *Sonnets* are not jettisoned within YouTube Shakespeare. Rather, the culture of vernacular production marks a further phase of their reception.[10] YouTubers are using the platform to showcase the application of digital technologies, for example, with text displayed through kinetic typography. YouTube is also a pedagogical resource, and students are being encouraged to record a reading, to visualize a sonnet, or to use video creation to work closely with poetic form.

This chapter shows how the medium of the sonnet is being adapted on YouTube and suggests that videos offer some dynamic ways of thinking about textuality and medium. It is also concerned with examining the reconfiguration of those sonnets addressed to the young man. Three sets of samples have been examined and these case studies are discussed in order to disclose what appears to be quite a widespread phenomenon on YouTube, the erasure of the male object of address. On the one hand, adapting a flexible attitude to the subject of address and/or the addressee's gender has its pay-offs. It takes account of the indeterminacy of gender dynamics in the sequence, while also allowing for the indeterminacy of reader responses to the text. There are certainly numerous examples of sonnet remixes, which are neither beholden to the gender dynamics of the sequence nor seek to reassign them. For instance, *The Three Project – William Shakespeare, Sonnet 18* (uploaded 14 August 2008; 1,472 views) mashes images from *No Country for Old Men* with the audio of Peter O'Toole's recital from *Venus* to produce an emotive film short that pursues the poem's concerns, without determining the 'thee' of the final line.[11] On the other hand, however, given the 'scandal' or embarrassment that has marked the historical reception of the *Sonnets*, from the shocked outrage of eighteenth-century editors like George Steevens to more recent obfuscations about the potentially queer business to the love expressed by the lover-poet in the sequence, the practice of displacing the gender of the addressee is a cause for concern.[12] It involves the kind of transcendentalizing long associated with Shakespeare, a problematic phenomenon that is predicated on at best an unwitting presumptive heterosexuality, at worst a silent erasure of non-heterosexual love and desires. Indeed those responses that play with form might also stand accused of similarly circumventing the male object of address.

While it is important to be attentive to the freeplay of vernacular remix culture and to the ways a YouTube videographer makes meaning of the *Sonnets*, it is equally important that we remain critically alert to the political (un)conscious of such interventions. Moreover, because YouTube is being presented by teachers as a learning space, where students not only access Shakespeare but actively partake in the texts by making and uploading their own content, it is crucial, as with the category of race discussed in the previous chapter, to address the kind of meanings surrounding the *Sonnets* that are being put into circulation on the platform. At stake here is a potential disconnect between Shakespeare criticism and vernacular or personalized responses on YouTube. Viewed from the perspective of the former, especially in terms of recent work on sexuality and gender, some sonnet videos appear to be surpisingly conservative. A further issue regards the categories of gender and sexuality as they are constructed within the *Sonnets*, in particular the question of what one regards as being under erasure. For instance, can we speak of homosexual desire in a late sixteenth-century sequence, when the demarcation and institutionalization of the categories 'heterosexual' and 'homosexual' is generally placed in the eighteenth? However, as Madhavi Menon has argued, we need to begin disrupting such historical and conceptual boundaries, to '"queer" a time that, like Shakespeare's own, is traditionally taken as "before" the homosexual'.[13] 'What we understand by Shakespeare', she writes, 'needs to be shaken up rather than being taken for granted.'[14] The process envisaged here is not at the level of the author – after all, such a focus would be contrary to queer theory's critique of 'the bounded individual and of unitary subjectivity' – but in relation to the texts and to critical reception.[15] YouTube can become an important space in broadening and challenging what Shakespeare and the *Sonnets* signify. YouTube Shakespeare might also be harnessed in the interests of what has been called a 'gender-aware pedagogy', where more flexible attitudes with regard to sexual identities are promoted through the text.[16] Shakespeare criticism has a role to play in advancing more progressive forms of video creation on YouTube and in connecting such activities to the hermeneutics of the *Sonnets*. Realizing these possibilities, however, will require a queering of the *Sonnets* on YouTube, so as to avoid old interpretations resurfacing on new platforms.

# Playing the medium

At each point of their reception, the *Sonnets* are reinter-preted and a new set of priorities attached to their meanings. Richard Halpern captures the changing state of interpretation when he remarks 'On the one hand, openly addressing homoerotic themes when discussing Shakespeare's *Sonnets* is now perfectly acceptable, indeed unavoidable ... On the other, I would be rendered squirmingly uncomfortable were I told to teach a class on the beauty of Shakespeare's *Sonnets*.'[17] The relationship between the form of the *Sonnets* and their content has long been a source of critical tension, especially where content denotes those poems address to the young man. Indeed, it is a tension that the sequence itself might be said to confront, as in sonnet 17 cited above, where the lover-poet contemplates the reception of his poetics of praise for the young man, or in sonnet 20, where succesive puns blur the boundaries between the homosocial and the homoerotic.[18] Reflecting on the hermeneutics of the *Sonnets*, Adena Rosmarin suggests that part of the problem is the established critical tendency of interpreting the texts through a Romantic period conception of poetry as the expression of emotion, as opposed to 'the Renaissance definition of the poet as maker'.[19] During the Renaissance, she reminds us, writers were 'enamoured of the word as thing' and Shakespeare's sequence itself explores the interplay between verba and res, of language and thought, of how form shapes or might wholly determine content. In other words, any sharp distinction between form and theme will be a false one. For some critics, however, attention to form can equate too readily with aesthetic evaluations that, as in the case of Halpern above, produce an understandable nervousness, precisely because the suggestion of a concentration on the less (sexy) subject of form has so often been a way of circumventing discussion about desire and its different expressions in the sequence. Part of my objective here is to consider to what extent mining the web of connected videos tagged under 'Sonnets' on YouTube can enable a greater sense of the kind of interplay between form and theme that runs through the sequence. Initially, however, I want to consider how YouTubers approach the medium of the *Sonnets*.

In exploring sonnet videos on YouTube, an intriguing correlation between the platform and the sequence suggests itself. Both involve processes of (re)mediation, YouTube in the sense of remediating other media (such as television or film), in the process appropriating some of their cultural functions, the *Sonnets* in the sense that they remediate earlier sequences, and established rhetorical devices (such as the inexpress-ibility topos).[20] The poems are also acts of remediation in the sense that they frame and narrativize the dynamic of lover, young man and dark lady, engrafting them new (to borrow from sonnet 15) with each sonnet. Both YouTube and the sequence also contain elements that encourage us to read them as hypermedia environments. In other words, in contrast to media that seek to disguise their form and create an illusion of 'immediacy', they alert the user to their medium. With websites such as YouTube, 'the user as a subject is constantly present, clicking on buttons, choosing menu items'.[21] A level of medium-consciousness is also embedded in the *Sonnets*. Even as the sequence fosters the illusion of immediate expression – as Sidney's *Astrophil and Stella* did beforehand – Shakespeare also unfolds several intermedial cues to the lover-poet's *medium* of expression. Whether it is those claims as to the incommensurability of verse and emotion ('Who will believe my verse in time to come' (sonnet 17)), or the use of similes from other forms ('Music to hear, why hear'st thou music sadly?' (sonnet 8)), 'As an unperfect actor on the stage' (sonnet 23)),[22] or the interrogation of poetic method ('How can my Muse want subject to invent / While thou dost breathe' (sonnet 38)), 'Why is my verse so barren of new pride' (sonnet 76)), or claims for the immortality of verse over time ('Not marble, nor the gilded monuments / Of princes, shall outlive this powerful rhyme' (sonnet 55)), 'Like as the waves make toward the pebbled shore, / So do our minutes hasten to their end' (sonnet 60)), 'in black ink my love may still shine bright' (sonnet 65)), Shakespeare's *Sonnets* repeatedly seem to suggest that the 'medium is the message'.[23]

These intermedial turns are integral to the fictive scenario of the lover-poet as he seeks to find appropriate modes to express himself. They are not especially Shakespearean – Sidney uses similar tropes – but are rather indicative of that Renaissance understanding of the poet as maker, one who invites the reader to take pleasure in the 'word as thing'. As if taking their cue from this Renaissance concept, responses to the *Sonnets* on YouTube focus on medium and on text as artful object. An interesting genre of sonnet upload in this regard is the text visualization or kinetic typography video. These videos make use of digital technologies, such as Flash as well as programmes like Wordle and TextArc, to visualize the poem word by word or line by line. For example, Chrisdavey's *BBC Shakespeare Sonnet* (uploaded 19 June 2007; 3,459 views) visualizes the full text of sonnet 30 ('When to the sessions of sweet silent thought'). The title and additional information indicate that the video was made as part of an assignment – an ident for BBC television – for a graphic design module[24]. With the upload just 36 seconds long, the type moves very quickly – perhaps too quickly to be read – but the pace is arguably appropriate, conveying the movement of a sonnet that is itself about the swift passage of time.

The effect of the moving type (scored to a piece of unidentified synthesized music) is similar to that achieved by software such as TextArc, where words and word frequency can be conveyed visually and emphasized through larger or different fonts. As Anne Cranny-Francis reminds us, type and fonts are not simply decorative; indeed, their apparent superficiality is something of a fallacy as they carry in them associations and connotations. By playing with type and fonts, 'the visuality of the written text once again becomes visible'.[25] In Chrisdavey's video, the 'thought' of line 1 is highlighted through the use of a shadow or 3-D effect. In line 4 ('And with old woes new wail my dear time's waste'), the final word is capitalized and enlarged. These font effects foreground the lover-poet's 'remembrance of things past' (line 2). Kinetic typography is used to visualize a thought that the poem's lines verbalize: so the words in line 5 – 'Then can I drown an eye (unused to flow)' – do indeed seem to flow, like water drops or more appropriately tear-drops. As one viewer comments: 'Exactly what to do with a sonnet!' A potential impact of these and other text effects, such as type in vertical and horizontal motion, is to disrupt a traditional reading of the text from left to right. The eye is drawn to the appearance of words and also their interaction.

In one sense, this video exemplifies YouTube's reduced attention economy and that of Web 2.0 technologies more generally, with the brevity of videos, as well as the exhaustive menu of choice, propelling the viewer towards distraction. Anandan Kavoori characterizes the potential for inattention as 'digital play': rather than simply watching YouTube, we play the medium. 'Patience is not an option in this game – if the video is poor, the sound bad, and the context problematic, it is time to play something else.'[26] User selection and choice are some of the elements accounting for the appeal of YouTube, but the downside is a 'partial – and somewhat unfocused – consumption'.[27] However, as Kavoori's term 'digital play' perhaps already implies, the experiential predations of YouTube need to be offset against the potential pleasures afforded by the platform and the specificities of user or viewer interests (individual viewers will most likely have their own sense of 'play' vis-à-vis other viewers). Furthermore, videos like Chrisdavey's *BBC Shakespeare Sonnet* are themselves forms of digital play that, to borrow from a description of the impact of filmic adaptations on literary texts, become 'a means of prolonging the pleasure of the original representation, and repeating the production of a memory'.[28] The video affords the viewer the pleasure of remembering sonnet 30, but doing so differently. It thus stands as an adaptation of sonnet 30 and as its own piece of visual art.[29]

Digital play is also on offer in *Shakespeare's Sonnet 12* (uploaded 11 November 2006; 12,575 views) by user siblmp, where kinetic tyopgraphy is deployed to create the effect of words floating on water.[30] The video opens with a close-up shot of water; we then see words appear to form the lines of the poem. There is an accompanying score, which in the description of the video is acknowledged as being by

Alessandro Gwis; appropriately for a sonnet about time, the piece includes the faint ticking of a clock. As with the upload by chrisdavey, this video's broad effect is to focus the viewer's attention on the words of the poem. However, the editing that has been undertaken, with 14 lines cut to just five, compromises the Shakespearean form of three quatrains and a closing rhyming couplet:

> When I do count the clock that tells the time
> And see the brave day sunk in hideous night
> When I behold the violet past prime
> Then of thy beauty do I question make
> That thou among the wastes of time must go.

Clearly, despite the attribution in its title, this video does not present Shakespeare's poem. As such, it may not be the best recommendation for students wishing to learn about the organization and rhyming scheme of the Shakespearean sonnet. Yet, the video offers an interesting interpretation of the poem, conveying how, as in other sonnets, the dilemmas and frustrations posed in the three quatrains are insufficiently resolved by the concluding couplet. 'The effect [of this sonnet] is almost self-cancelling,' notes Katherine Duncan Jones, 'for the poetic evocation of time's all inclusive operation is so persuasive as to leave the remedy in doubt.'[31] Similarly, Stephen Booth points out that the couplet's 'optimistic conclusion' does not seem to grow logically out of the poem.[32] The video makes extensive use of blank spaces, of what comes after Shakespeare's lines, or in place of them; the lingering shots of the water, with the shadow of clouds visibile, perhaps intimate that beauty cannot necessarily be encompassed in the written word. An incomplete version of sonnet 12, this video thrives on visual effects, but it also works as a rejection of the poem's internal argument, a rejection that is boldly asserted through creative redaction.

In their use of technologies to create word-effects, flows and loops, these uploads bear some similarity to what has

been termed kinetic digital poetry or videopoetry.[33] These
effects are largely contingent on the computer – it is, after
all, the technology of the computer and its language of
code that makes kinetic poetry possible in the first instance.
However, while it is code that enables us to make a poetry 'in
which letters and words can dance across the screen before
the reader's eyes', there is a human agent at work in the
sense of making choices and imputting commands.[34] As N.
Katherine Hayles remarks, 'complex feedback loops connect
humans and machines, old technolgies and new language and
code'.[35] Furthermore, although e-poetry has been dismissed
as indicative of a postmodern aesthetic of the spectacle, it
is more usefully regarded as a form of creative expression
through new media. It has some antecedents in concrete, or
pattern poetry, but, in its fullest manifestations, digital poetry
presumes greater levels of viewer interaction.[36] As Roberto
Simanowski argues, by playing with text and the materiality of
words, digital poetry 'implies reflection on the use of language
and increases our sensitivity towards, and ability to discover
and reject, all attempts at instrumentalizing language'.[37]
Digital poetry achieves its effect, Simanowski explains, not
by bringing about a 'change of perception, a change from the
semiotic system of reading typical of literature to the semiotic
system of viewing typical of visual art'.[38] Its visuality thus
resides in the addition of 'the optical gesture of the word to its
semantic meaning: as completion, expansion, or negation'.[39]
Similarly, Janez Strehovec argues that in e-poetry, words
are not always rendered beautifully, but can be shown as
unstable and fragmented.[40] Such insights into the potentiality
of seemingly surface effects suggest that we read – or rather
*view* – YouTube sonnet videopoetry not simply as instances of
online creative expression via Shakespeare, but also as forms
of textual work.

The interplay between the hidden technologies of the
computer and human imput emerges in *Shakespeare Sonnet
81 – Animated Typography* (uploaded 1 June 2008; 6,197
views) by froj2002. The video disrupts Shakespeare's poem to

elaborate on the 'optical gesture' inherit in its words. Kinetic type is combined with what the user describes as a 'motion gra[p]hics "reel" using photographs of hand made type'.[41] As in the earlier upload, we have moving type but, at one minute longer, froj2002's upload is at a slower pace. Especially interesting is the inclusion of the images of hand-made type. For instance, in the visualization of line 3 ('From hence your memory death cannot take'), the word 'memory' is emphasized and rendered in a shadowy font; with line 6 ('Though I, once gone, to all the world must die'), 'die' is spelt out in charred matchsticks; with line 10 ('Which eyes not yet created shall o'er-read'), the word 'eyes' has been inked onto a closed eyelid; in line 12 ('When all the breathers of this world are dead'), 'this' is displayed in a font reminiscent of Elizabethan longhand; and, in the final line ('Where breath most breathes, ev'n in the mouths of men'), we see 'breathes' as breath on a mirror. Some of these visuals may be of an overly literal kind, but the video establishes a suggestive contrast between the two visual effects, recognizable type and hand-made or created text-images. Through this contrast between word as print and as handwritten, one senses something of the original form of the Renaissance sonnet, that is as texts that circulated in manuscript, or were inscribed onto miniature portraits, but were not necessarily intended to appear in printed form.[42] The manuscript form of the sonnet becomes a spectral presence in the video. 'You shall live, such virtue hath my pen' (line 13), states the lover-poet. 'Pen' is here used as a metonym for verse, and for the efficacy of the written word, but it also points to the sonnet's *pre*-print status. Within this process of remediation – a process that applies to both YouTube and the *Sonnets* – the old medium may dissappear, creating a sense of 'immediacy'. However, layering the new medium onto an existing one, in this case print, produces 'hypermediacy', or an awareness of media and forms. '[T]he artist ... strives to make the viewer acknowledge the medium as a medium and to delight in that acknowledgement.'[43] Comments suggest that these textual-visual effects are appreciated:

this is absolutely beautiful
cannot stop watching this
Great job! Lovely piano and very interesting typography
great helping me to memorize this junk.

Sonnet videopoetry on YouTube can act as a catalyst towards thinking formally. As with the uploads of the plays, where the 'aggregation of past performances available on YouTube fosters historical consciousness', and thus function as a pedagogical resource, sonnet visualizations present interesting opportunities for student-centred learning.[44] The final comment, despite the pejorative, concedes as much. YouTube Shakespeare emerges here less as a subsitute for close reading of the text, than as a supplementary learning resource. The next chapter elaborates on the implications of YouTube for Shakespeare pedagogy, but for now I want to suggest that sonnet videos could be interestingly deployed by students to consider word play and sound patterns. Such an exercise could be illuminating and instructive, focusing attention on the significance of the typographical arrangement and layout to a sonnet's meaning.

Furthermore, YouTube content presents opportunities to address questions about the order of the sequence and its narrative coherence, issues that have been a feature of critical reception.[45] If we follow Kathryn Schwarz's formulation, and think of the *Sonnets* less as a cohesive narrative, than about 'a desire for narrative', or as 'oblique provocateurs of our own impulse toward story', then YouTube provides a platform to create personalized versions of Shakespeare's sequence.[46] Several tubers have already undertaken this, with channels such as TheSonnetProject by Australian actor David Meadows offering all 154 poems.[47] These projects indicate opportunities for experiential learning. For instance, students could make use of the playlist function of a YouTube channel to catalogue and annotate videos and to pursue various arrangements and patterns by organizing the poems themati-cally, or by addressee, or by the order of the 1609 sequence.

As playlists can be set to loop automatically, it is possible to have a continuous flow of sonnets and to review the results of such experiments.

More generally, YouTube Shakespeareans might explore and enact what has been described as the *Sonnets*' own machine-like properties, or their presentation of 'rhetorical software that renders their readers and the historical worlds those readers posit "lively"'.[48] The recurrent motif in the sequence about the endurance of poetry over time is interesting here. It imbues the text with a futurity and a capacity to anticipate its subsequent readers, as in sonnet 81, 'Your momument shall be my gentle verse, / Which eyes not yet created shall o'er-read' (lines 9–10). In such terms, each reading or upload of a sonnet is simultaneously an activation and an appropriation of the propelling mechanism within the sequence itself, the mechanism that not only 'begets' the young man, but also maintains his liveness, the 'living record of your memory' (sonnet 55, line 8), again and again, sonnet after sonnet. On YouTube, too, the sonnets go on, and propel new stories.

## Queer erasures?

If uploading a sonnet or cataloguing a video within a playlist is a means towards story, and self-presentation on YouTube, sonnet videos can seem curiously traditional, or unwilling to mine the possibilties of the texts, especially in terms of their queer potential. This is at odds with recent criticism. In a provocative essay, for example, Aranye Fradenburg suggests that the overarching effect of the sequence 'can strike readers as queer, and not just because they are about a man and a woman, or maybe the other kind of ass kissing'.[49] The queer effect also derives from the 'linking of elaborate language about feeling to wordless infantile experience' in the poems.[50] Fradenburg goes on to prompt the reader to give in to the

*Sonnets'* coupling of the beautiful and the taboo, and their tendency towards what she playfully describes as 'the love you feel for inappropriate objects … The kind of love that makes a fool, a pervert, a stalker of you.'[51] This is not to suggest that Shakespeare was some sort of sexual radical, but is rather a function of early modern concepts of sexuality and gender, the 'ordinary currency' of which, to borrow Alan Sinfield's formulation, might be 'sexy to us'.[52] Whereas YouTube Shakespeare suggests possibilities for experimentation with the form and sequencing of the *Sonnets*, it offers a comparatively disappointing degree of experimentation or sense of play with regard to the poems' liasions, especially those that fall outside of a heterosexual schema.

Evident across both vernacular and commercially produced videos is a tendency either to circumvent the male object of address, or to erase him altogether. Admittedly, the division of the *Sonnets* along two objects of address – the young man and the dark lady – is arbitrary; there is, one critic suggests, a 'gender undecidability' at work.[53] Perhaps taking advantage of these dual objects of address, as well as uncertainities regarding the order of the sequence, adaptations recontextualize the *Sonnets*. This practice predates vernacular production on YouTube – one can think of Marianne in the film *Sense and Sensibility* reciting Sonnet 116 as she looks out over the estate of the man who has betrayed her. The incorporation of this intertext may be director Ang Lee's nod to Austen's own reworking of the plots of Shakespearean comedy, but can also be understood in the context of responses to Shakespeare by women writers, who often sought to foster a sense of women's relationship to, rather than a distance from, the Bard.[54] Several videos feature young women assuming the position of subject directing a male object of desire, for instance. In this regard, iterations of the *Sonnets* are no different to other forms of Shakespeare adaptation on the site, in that they are about discovering a perspective on the text, or departing from it altogether. That said, we need to notice that recontextualizations of the *Sonnets* on YouTube can involve forms of inattention and erasure, which delimit the range of subtexts available within the poem and imply conservative attitudes to the texts.

An illustrative example of the politics of recontextualizing the *Sonnets* is the commercially produced video vignette of sonnet 29, 'When in disgrace with fortune and men's eyes' (uploaded 10 June 2008; 181,227 views), originally made for a DVD called *Essential Poems*, featuring actor Matthew Macfadyen.[55] Comments praise Macfadyen's enunciation of the poem. The film puts the sonnet in a modern, urban setting: Macfadyen sits 'alone' in a café, beweeping his 'outcast state'. As the speaker wishes himself 'like to one more rich in hope' (line 5), we see a flashback of Macfadyen on the street, passing by posters of American rappers. However, the most significant aspect of the film's interpretation of the poem occurs at the end – a text message is received, coinciding with the line 'Haply I think on thee' (line 10) and shortly afterwards a young woman enters the frame. In the final shot, the couple hug. As this iteration of sonnet 29 would have it, the object of address, the 'thee' (line 10) and 'thy sweet love' (13), the thought of which lifts the speaker, such that he would 'scorn to change [his] state with kings' (line 14), is most certainly a woman. The video evidences a discomfort, which places it within a long line of readerly embrasssment as to the potentially queer directions desire takes in the *Sonnets*.[56] An interpretative bed-swap is enacted, the young man replaced with a young woman. This manoeuvre could be seen as an echo of the movement in the sequence itself from male to female addressee and, by implication, from homosocial bonds to heterosexual relations. Despite this apparently straight trajectory, however, the sequence, as Valerie Traub reminds us, 'treats heteroeroticism as a vehicle for the erotic bonds between men'.[57] Sonnet 29 exhibits what Traub describes as a 'homerotics of similitude', where the lover-poet's focus on the differences of age, status and beauty between himself and the young man paradoxically produces a homogeneity that proves the catalyst for poetic expression. Within this homogeneity of male bodies, the figure of woman, though addressed in later sonnets to the so-called 'dark lady', is necessarily found wanting or irrelevant. Viewed in such terms, the video offers a corrective to the patriarchal economy of the sequence.

Yet, precisely because of the alterations it performs, the sonnet 29 video offers an interesting discursive starting point about how some forms of desire find cultural expression and valorization, while others do not. It evidences an appropriation of the *Sonnets* in the interests of what Judith Butler has termed 'compulsory heterosexuality', thus directing us towards the hermeneutics of the gender and sexual dynamic of the sequence itself.[58] On the one hand, the text is hardly reducible to this dynamic: 'sexual difference is only one differential category in these poems', writes Margreta de Grazia; class, age, reputation and marital status are there too.[59] To this list, one should add whiteness as a racial signifier.[60] On the other hand, indifference to sexual difference can look a lot like the old classroom tactic of diverting attention away from gender trouble towards the safer subjects of patronage, generational rivalry and poetic reputation. Of course when their early modern specificities are taken into account, these subjects loop back to the homosociality of the sequence itself, a homosociality that, as noted above, already implies a homoerotic charge. With the video of sonnet 29, however, such available meanings are occluded: diversionary tactics are being replayed in new formats. As a poem deemed 'essential', it must be remembered as a text of heterosexual love, with any suggestion of homosocial bonds and non-reproductive sexuality erased.

The Macfadyen video has the second highest view count of sonnet videos on YouTube after *Shakespeare Sonnet 29* by lyra000 (uploaded 27 July 2007; 222,078 views).[61] This is a fan-made tribute to Macfadyen, mashing images of his starring role in the film *Pride and Prejudice* with a vocal performance of sonnet 29 by Rufus Rainwright. Through its selections of close-ups of prospective heterosexual pairings from the film, however, this fan text also enacts an intepretation of the poem. Admittedly, the heterosexual focus here might be a function of the inherited Austen narrative, but the implication for the Shakespearean intertext is less than progressive. At issue is less the shortcomings of an isolated vernacular production, or in the case of the Macfadyen vignette, the loss of subtextual layers that the recontextualization involves, than the presumptive heteronormativity at work in several adaptations and interpretations.

Responses to the *Sonnets* from within vernacular culture reveal a similar disregard towards the male object of address, and a displacement or erasure of the homoerotic subtext of the sequence. In order to arrive at a case study of such a response, three sets of videos were selected. The first sample selected slide-show, or image-based, responses to sonnet 18, with the earliest upload from September 2006 and the latest from January 2013. Of the 20 videos within the group, only 1 openly alludes to the male object of address. In a second sample, again from a broad time span, but in this instance relating to responses to sonnets 55, 66, 94, 95 and 114, only 2 out of the 10 videos acknowledge the young man. Within this sample is a subset of school-based assignments by a group of Dutch students, available on a single channel.[62] Of these videos – which respond to sonnets 43, 60, 66 and 94 – only 1 treats the male-to-male subtext of the poems.[63] A third sample returns similar results; of 12 videos uploaded on a single channel, and responding to a variety of sonnets, only 1 alludes to the male addressee.[64]

These student video assignments take the form of a slide-show presentation, a genre of video already noted in relation to Ophelia. Frequently, the images used to visualize the text are literal, with Google Images and Photobucket providing easily accessible databanks. Such literalizing of a sonnet's metaphors may suggest that the videos have a mnemonic function for their creators, enabling students to remember the text through direct engagement and recontextualization. For example, the paratactic structure of sonnet 66, with its repetitious complaints about worldly and material corrosiveness, lends itself to montage. In *Shakespeare, Sonnet 66* (uploaded 15 December 2011; 750 views), the video-makers repurpose Shakespeare's lines towards contemporary issues. The line 'And folly, doctor-like, controlling skill' is set to an image of Arnold Schwarzenegger as Governor of California.[65] *Sonnet 66 Illumination* (uploaded 15 December 2011; 131 views) also turns to American political life, selecting an image of George W. Bush, sitting beside a child in a classroom, with the President holding a book, which is upside down.[66] While the frustrations articulated in sonnet 66 allow students to engage in critical commentary on aspects of contemporary society, this critique nonetheless has its blind spots. When it comes to the figure of the male addressee, the visual literalism of the videos gives way to a form of visual displacement and substitution. In *Shakespeare, Sonnet 66,* and the related class-assignment video *Film_0002.mv* (uploaded 15 December 2011; 28 views), the poem's closing couplet – 'Tired with all these, from these would I be gone, / Save that to die I leave my love alone' – is synced with an image of a man and a woman embracing.[67] The exception here is *Sonnet 66 Illumination*, which ends with an image of two men holding hands. In the third sample of videos, there is also one exception, *Sonnet 29* (uploaded 9 January 2011; 507 views), a mashup of Rufus Wainright's vocal performance with a slide-show of images, which closely attend to the lover-poet's jealousy of the young-man's youthful beauty and, unlike the Macfadyen video, figure the 'thee' (line 10) and 'thy' (line 13) of the sonnet as masculine.[68] The video concludes with an image of two men holding hands.

As the numbers outlined above suggest, however, there is a tendency to erase the male addressee or to include images of a straight couple and thus (un)consciously superimpose a heteronormativity on the text; it is as if the embarrassment of those eighteenth-century editors continues in new forms. *Shakespeare Sonnet 43* (uploaded 16 December 2011; 43 views), for example, synchronizes a reading of the poem ('When most I wink, then do mine eyes best see') with images from two films featuring Audrey Tatou – *Les Amants* and

*Le Fableux Destin.*[69] The video is effective in conveying the sonnet's unfolding conceit about eyes and perspective, but it neglects to consider that the lover-poet is addressing the young man. Sonnet 18 videos also seek to straighten out matters. LMV666's *Shakespeare – Shall I compare thee to a summers day* (uploaded 22 March 2009; 3,926 views) offers the following explanatory note: 'William falls in love with a lady in higher status, and writes his love for her.'[70] Such neglect may be attributed to a number of factors. First, the influence of professionally produced videos, especially student-learning resources like Socratica, which are freely available on YouTube, might account for the oversights within amateur or student productions. Socratica's channel includes a set of text-based presentations of the *Sonnets*, with fonts suggestive of early modern type. An image of a woman is included above the text for sonnet 18.[71] A similar move is evident in the video for Sonnet 1, which features an image of two women. This may be a literalization of the 'fairest creatures' of the poem's opening line, but the visual nonetheless functions as a denial of the male object of address, and of the poem's concern with male reproduction.

Second, the tenor of amateur creative responses can be framed in terms of conservative teaching approaches, in particular a reluctance among teachers to interpret the texts outside of a circuit of Bardolatry – a concern, perhaps, not to trouble the canonical figure of Shakespeare with the queer business of poems addressed to a young man – as well as a potential reticence among students themselves to openly address what might appear to be gay subject matter in a school context. Within that context, at least in its Westernized and Anglophone forms, 'gay' is not limited to its primary cultural associations with homosexuality, but can also signify perjorative peer judgement; as such, a student might be quite understandably reluctant to risk, or invite, such labelling. The *Sonnets* offer a potential space where such attitudes can be addressed. Teachers have a role to play here, not only in developing a responsible approach to issues of gender and sexuality as they emerge in literary texts, but in encouraging students to make their own interventions into the poems. Through the playful, or even iconoclastic, stance towards Shakespeare, students might come to think critically about the politics of representation, and to consider how the cultural valorization of the Bard serves certain interests and desires, while occluding others.

There are some encouraging signs that YouTube Shakespeare can provide this kind of open, interpretative space. The comment feature entails a meta-commentary on videos, and viewers do occasionally remark on the disappearance of the young man, as in reactions to *William Shakespeare's Sonnet 18 animated* (uploaded 11 November 2007; 63,169 views) by ladyzahl. The video, which uses CGI to accompany David Tennant's reading of the poem, opens with a portrait of Shakespeare, before unfolding a virtual landscape and close-up of a virtual beloved, a female avatar resembling Lara Croft. The opening image of Shakespeare himself makes sense in terms of the video's concluding shots of a computer-generated lover-poet at his writing desk, gazing on the image of the woman: the Bard's poetic expressiveness is, the video suggests, decidedly heterosexual. Comments provide further insight into the alteration that has been undertaken:

very beautiful video ... my fave sonnet from Shakespeare

this is great. however, sonnet 18 is about a man. you probably should have checked that out. or maybe read the line 'and often HIS ... dimmed'. please dont think im trying to destroy your work though. its really well done. and definately [sic] a favourite.

I knew it was about a man, but I wanted it to be about a woman. I just took a bit of creative license with it. But I am glad that you know Shakespeare and I am very happy that you enjoyed it! Thank you.

yeah. i love shakspeares [sic] work. im sorry btw, my original comment seems abit cocky on second reading. great video! keep up the good work!

The 'his' in that line refers to the sun, not the poet's lover. 'Sometime too hot the eye of heaven (the sun) shines, and often is his (the sun's) gold complexion dimmed'.

You're right, however, Shakespeare did wrote [sic] the sonnet for a 'his' ... his nephew.[72]

Various fallacies about the *Sonnets* emerge here, as well as speculations regarding Shakespeare's sexual orientation, an issue that has long ghosted approaches to the sequence, as if the liasions and desires explored therein can be ascribed to the singular author. The videographer claims 'creative license' in amending the poem, a claim in tandem with YouTube's 'Broadcast Yourself' mantra and the culture of 'vernacular creativity' that underpins it. [73] Furthermore, the use of aliases to post comments suggests a virtual identity, perhaps even a type of *post*-identity, with online spaces facilitating the broadcasting of a self unfettered by gender, or class, or race, or any other set of demarcations that pertain in the 'real' world. From this perspective, the alterations to the *Sonnets* may no longer seem to matter that much; indeed, they may reflect a move beyond identity politics, where designations such as 'straight', 'gay' or 'bi' not only seem overly restrictive, but belated. As Judith Halberstam reminds us, 'Many young gays and lesbians think of themselves as part of a "post-gender" world and for them the idea of "labelling" becomes a sign of oppression that they have happily cast off in order to move into the pluralistic world of infinite diversity.'[74]

As Halberstam demonstrates more generally, however, the cultural production and representation of queerness is more complex than the post-gender formulation allows. For one thing, this 'new homonormativity' runs the risk of depoliti-cizing gay culture, thus leaving 'dominant heteronormative assumptions and institutions' uncontested.[75] Moreover, while the digital appears to signal a labile space where gender is left behind, established stereotypes are never far from view in that setting, where the combination of viewer anonymity with instantaneous response generates phobic or deliberately provocative observations.[76] For a variety of reasons, then, including access to, and equity within, the field of representation and the development of a gender-conscious pedagogy, it matters considerably whether or not the gender of the addressee gets erased in the reception of the poems. Otherwise a sense of the historical and cultural conditions of Shakespeare's *Sonnets* is blurred. It is necessary that we remain alert to the various particularities of their subtexts – misogyny, whiteness/darkness, homosociality, homoeroticism – however challenging these may be.[77]

Without the young man, we also lose sight of how the *Sonnets* have, as Eve Sedgwick explains, 'figured importantly in the formation of a specifically homosexual (not just homosocial) male intertextuality'.[78] Shakespeare's *Sonnets* have for so long been appropriated in the interests of a generalized, universal love, implicitly conceived of as heterosexual, that it would be naïve to think that any silencing of their address, however casual or seemingly without consequence, is insignificant. For texts whose putative transcendence is hard to shake off, the anxious desire to write out anything queer about the poems reminds us that heteronormativity has a history, a textual trace. To acknowledge that things are otherwise, is to spotlight those lives and identities that do not operate within the institutions or conventions of heterosexuality and its timeline, and thus offer what Halberstam calls 'the potential to open up new life narratives and alternative relations to time and space'.[79] YouTube iterations of the *Sonnets* essayed thus far suggest that Halberstam's call for a critique of heterotemporalities is as urgent as ever.

However, my suggestion that the sublimating tendencies associated with the reception of the *Sonnets* are being replayed on YouTube needs to be balanced against the unbounded nature of YouTube content, as well as the features of the site, which have the effect of locating any one upload alongside a series of 'Suggestions' generated by the initial search. For instance, on the watch page for *Shakespeare Sonnet 29* discussed above, suggested videos include others featuring Rufus Wainwright's vocal performance of this sonnet.[80] Within YouTube's system of linked videos, a viewer could find themselves moving through video clips from Wainwright's collaboration with Bob Wilson for the Berliner Ensemble's dramatization of the *Sonnets*, a production that explores both the homo- and hetero-erotics of the sequence.[81] This is illustrative of the ways in which any one sonnet video intersects with a range of discourses, genres or cultures encountered on YouTube, discourses that may require us to qualify any conclusive sense of what the *Sonnets* mean in that setting.

We have already seen how the sonnet 29 video circulates within the discourse of fandom surrounding the actor Matthew Macfadyen. In another fan production, frescadp's *Kirk/Spock: The Marriage of True Minds* (uploaded 23 April 2009; 3,169 views), sonnet 116 ('Let me not to the marriage of true minds / Admit impediments') intersects with *Star Trek*.[82] In this union of intertexts, however, the male object of address remains. The video sets each line to a series of stills from the original *Star Trek* TV series and from the 2009 film (and the entire piece is scored to Bach's Suite for Cello No. 1 in G Major: Prelude). Extra-diegetic material is provided in the form of introductory subtitles: 'A slow afternoon on the Enterprise', followed by Spock's question, 'I found a poem that you might like, Captain?' After the poem itself, Captain Kirk's reply is provided in subtitles: 'Why, Spock, I'm touched, it's just like me and ... My ship.' Shakespeare and the world of *Star Trek* have some prior intertextual associations (for example the Klingon claim to the 'original' *Hamlet* in *Star Trek VI*).[83] The video's combination of diverse elements – a text, film and music – operates within the logic of media convergence, where users regard every object on the mediascape as available for appropriation.

The Shakespeare intertext of *Kirk/Spock: The Marriage of True Minds* needs to be understood more specifically as part of the culture of Slash. As Henry Jenkins explains, this term 'specifies a genre of fan stories positing homoerotic affairs between two series protagonists'; it owes its origins to the practice of placing a 'slash' between two names, as in Kirk/Spock, who may well be the first Slash pairing.[84] Imagining deep bonds of friendship aboard the *Enterprise*, Slash seeks out, and then amplifies, that which is only available on a subtextual level in the series proper. Importantly, Slash emphasizes an emotional connectedness between the characters that may lead to a sexually consumated relationship; in this emphasis, Slash 'is not so much a genre about sex as it is a genre about the limitations of traditional masculinity and about reconfiguring male identity'.[85] In presenting sexual identity as indeterminate, Slash has much to offer online creators of the *Sonnets*. *Kirk/Spock: The Marriage of True Minds* elaborates on a relationship well established in fan culture by overlaying it with Shakespeare's sonnet, which I would suggest functions here less as an authorizing presence than as a complementary text of homosociality and male-to-male desire. The video is to be welcomed for making available on YouTube an approach to the *Sonnets*, where forms of desire outside of a heterosexual schema are playfully envisioned, rather than silently erased. As such, it could be interestingly used as a teaching resource, providing the catalyst for a discussion about homosociality in Shakespeare's *Sonnets* and indeed its relationship to a patriarchal system in which women are scripted as little more than ciphers for intra-male relations.

Within school-based assignments, too, there are some encouraging signs of a willingness to at least allude to the young man of the *Sonnets*. For instance, in *Shakespeare's sonnets gay?* (uploaded 6 May 2010; 180 views), sonnet 15 ('When I consider everything that grows') is adapted as a high-school boy's crush on a fellow student. The poem itself is presented as a voice-over and with a degree of pathos that is at odds with the performers, who struggle to hold back their laughter.[86] Of the sample of sonnet 18 videos, only one suggests the homosocial and homoerotic subtexts of the poems – *Sonnet 18 Illustrated* (uploaded 12 February 2011; 92 views).[87] As in the other slide-show videos, the poem is treated quite literally, and we encounter the familiar image of a man and woman embracing. However, a playful interpretation of the line 'And often is his gold complexion dimmed; / And every fair from fair sometime declines', is offered, with a diptych of two toned male torsos, one bearing a cut-out of Shakespeare's head, complete with love-heart eyes. The semiotic significance of casting the Bard as gym bunny would remain little more than a nice visual gimmick were it not for the fact that so many other videos of sonnet 18 casually erase any suggestion of a homosocial or homoerotic dimension. The humour presumes some prior sense of those dimensions to Shakespeare's *Sonnets* and while it may invoke certain stereotyoes of gay men, it goes some way to countering the prevailing heteronormativity of sonnet videopoetry on YouTube.

While playful in their approach, ultimately these videos may not go far enough, since there is a risk that as they move towards humour and parody, they imply that the subject matter of male-to-male attraction does not have to be taken seriously. By way of contrast, however, the Czech film short *Nahrazuje* (uploaded 11 June 2010; 650 views), which adapts sonnet 20 ('A woman's face with nature's own hand painted'), offers a more profound critique.[88] This poem has been interpreted as crucial in determining the representation of same-sex relations in the sequence, not least because its opening comparison with 'A woman's face' establishes the gender of the addressee as male, but also because the wordplay – such as 'one thing' and 'nothing' (line 12) – implies the lover-poet's tacit recognition of an erotic frisson in relation to the young man, a frisson that the reader is implicitly drawn into. In its contemporary adaptation, *Nahrazuje* (or 'Replaced') pursues the desires of the lover-poet through a story of the unrequited love of Will for his flatmate Henri. Through close-ups of Henri and his girlfriend Miree kissing, the film establishes Will's desire; indeed, the close-ups constitute the filmic equivalent to the lover-poet's fixation on the young man in the poem. The ambivalence of the sonnet's closing couplet – in which the possibility of physical desire between men is kept in play, even as platonic love is asserted – is also captured in the film through its open ending, with Will seemingly caught between loss and a more promising future.

*

The videos discussed in this chapter reveal various levels of creativity, each feasible through the digital, Web 2.0 applications and YouTube's culture of vernacular share and display. As this chapter has emphasized, videos are also iterations of the poems and raise their own set of interpretative issues that, as readers of Shakespeare's *Sonnets*, we need to critically address. In tracing forms of erasure across videos, my objective has not been to claim an exclusivity for a narrowly gay reading of the *Sonnets* – to do so would be to engage in the appropriative tendencies noted of earlier formalist criticism – any more than it has been about faithfulness, or lack thereof, to the anchoring authority of the Shakespearan text. Rather, I have sought to tease out trends within vernacular and commercial sonnet videos and to explore the political unconscious of these interventions, with a view to signalling the kind of responses to the the poems that we *could* encounter on YouTube, responses that are open to a queering of normative or traditional iterations. In other words, vernacular expression can profit from a greater sense of plenitude, and a recognition of difference within the *Sonnets*.

Shakespeare criticism has a role to play here, especially in terms of teaching approaches to the *Sonnets* (since these necessarily impact on how students come to understand the texts) and in fostering a keener sense of the relation between history and contemporary constructions of sexuality and desire.

Videos such as *Kirk/Spock* and *Nahrazuje* are important exemplars here, because, at the very least, they force us to ask questions about the figuring of love and desire in the *Sonnets*, in contrast to other productions that presume to know and name those expressions as heterosexual. The availability of these videos on YouTube, along with those using kinetic typography, do present interesting opportunities for students and enthusiasts of the *Sonnets* alike. On YouTube, we encounter the interplay of form and theme; indeed, the platform functions as a kind of *Wunderkabinet* of interpretations, adaptations and responses to the *Sonnets*. When video-makers turn to Shakespeare's *Sonnets* in the future, it is hoped that they might initiate more experimental modes of response. For now, however, the volume of sonnet videos on YouTube should not be taken as a sign of diversity, nor should it prevent scholars from noting how old blind spots, or transcendentalizing tendencies, can re-emerge. As we search, view and use sonnet videos on YouTube, a hermeneutics of suspicion seems both a necessary and useful starting point.

# 5

# The Teaching and Learning Tube: Challenges and Affordances

*Learning is but an adjunct to ourself,*
*And where we are, our learning likewise is.*
SHAKESPEARE, *LOVE'S LABOUR'S LOST* (IV.3)[1]

*The Internet as an 'always on' window of nearly*
*endless information acts both as a source of*
*opportunity and as a site of tremendous challenge,*
*particularly when it comes to determining the quality*
*and validity of that information.*
MARK A. GAMMON AND JOANNE WHITE[2]

*Shared online video is a unique form of learning that*
*will be interesting to monitor in the coming years. With*
*it, the world has become much more open for students*
*to learn, and share their learning with others.*
CURTIS BONK[3]

From a learning perspective, there is much reason to be excited about YouTube Shakespeare. As a technology providing access to an archive of past performances, as well as enabling vernacular production, YouTube's benefits for pedagogy and learning are immediately apparent. The site has its own niche space called YouTube-EDU and promotes itself as an educational and learning tool. Shakespearean institutions like the RSC, the Globe theatre and the Folger also use YouTube to promote their activities, with their channels showcasing outreach and educational initiatives. There is ample evidence on YouTube of the extent to which learners are using the site as a learning tool. Practices that are well established among the so-called 'digital natives' (such as online posting, remix and mashup) are being harnessed by educators in the interests of fostering various experiential, collaborative and peer-learning scenarios. Video-sharing technologies, as Curtis Bonk recognizes above, signal open forms of learning. They also signal asynchronous learning: 'where we are, our learning likewise is', to echo the aphoristic Berowne in *Love's Labour's Lost*. The platform provides learners with an array of Shakespeare content, which can potentially illuminate and deepen their understanding of the text and its diverse contexts. In making videos, learners can take responsibility for their own learning and contribute to the kind of Shakespeare that emerges in their classroom.[4] For educators, there is a ready-made archive of past performances in clip form, which can be easily embedded into learning materials, shared through other social media platforms, or played in a classroom setting. Suggesting new forms of interactive learning, as well as a contemporary Shakespeare, YouTube Shakespeare presents significant opportunities not only for learners, but also for the field of Shakespeare studies itself.

However, to learn through YouTube in a meaningful way requires that the learner and educator alike possess reasonable levels of media literacy skills, both in terms of participating and evaluating the 'always on window'. The platform also raises several anxieties associated with Web 2.0 learning and the habits of 'digital natives' more generally.[5] Of significance here are debates about the impact of Web 2.0 on human cognition, in particular the effects of a technology that not only mediates our experiences, but also provides for a vast store of information. As some critics have argued, such outsourcing fundamentally alters how and what we remember.[6] Out of the concern that the Web 2.0 culture diminishes human intellect – what one writer refers to as the 'googlization of memory' – flow more specific implications for learners, from concerns that Web 2.0 technologies involve a turn away from the text and close reading skills, to criticism that they produce reduced attention spans, which result in surface learning.[7] Moreover, Web 2.0 can also be said to advance a neo-liberal understanding of the student as an independent learner, thus foreshortening the responsibilities of structured and funded education. From this perspective, YouTube may not be the best space either to engage learners in Shakespeare or to remember the texts better. YouTube Shakespeare might also stand accused of fostering a Bardic-centric learning context, one that risks extracting Shakespeare from the period that he is so often taken as exemplary of.[8] Furthermore, as suggested in the previous chapters on race in YouTube Shakespeare and gender and sexuality in *Sonnet* uploads, the new platform can return old blind spots and stereotypes about Shakespeare texts.

There are important issues here that demonstrate the need for a critical, rather than celebratory, attitude to YouTube as a Shakespeare learning resource. To this end, as well as including suggestions for assignments that might enable teachers and students to further exploit the affordances of YouTube, this chapter addresses the potential pitfalls of use. In weighing up the affordances and limitations of YouTube, the chapter contends that it is a valuable learning resource, but one best regarded and utilized as a complement to, rather than a replacement for, more established modes of teaching and learning Shakespeare.

The discussion is informed by literature on Web 2.0 learning and recent considerations about Shakespeare pedagogy, but I also draw upon some of my own experiences and reflections as a teacher of Shakespeare at university. Consequently, the focus pertains largely to higher education, though hopefully there will be some useful insights for secondary-level teachers and learners.

# Shakespeare among the digital natives: YouTube and Web 2.0 learning

To consider YouTube in a pedagogic and learning context raises issues regarding the perception and suitability of Web 2.0 and social media networks, especially given their association with entertainment and leisure time.[9] The work of Michael Wesch and Alexandra Juhasz, already encountered in this book, provide contrasting evaluations as to YouTube's learning potential. Wesch and Juhasz have explored YouTube in theory and also praxis – both use the site extensively in their teaching. Whereas Wesch emphasizes YouTube's democratizing possibilities and its participatory culture[10], Juhasz identifies several limitations, from the unwieldy architecture of the site and the preponderance of 'bad content' to the acritical browsing produced by video surfing.[11] Juhasz does concede that in the area of specialist or niche tubes, the site can be efficacious.[12] Yet, a broader suspicion about Web 2.0 remains. As Louise Marshall and Will Slocombe note, educators may have reservations based on pedagogy ('Will this technology assist my students?') or a combination of the pedagogic and the personal ('Social networking has no place in a classroom'); furthermore, students themselves may react negatively to the 'pedagogic adoption of these technologies, especially those … that they perceive as "theirs"'.[13] If educators are to seriously address how YouTube might be used to enhance student learning, a good starting point is an open acknowledgement that students now habitually go online for research purposes, actively seeking out the resources of Web 2.0.[14]

Such an acknowledgement need not involve pandering to the lowest common denominator, nor should it be regarded as an admission of defeat on the part of the teacher. Professional scholars themselves now conduct much of their research online: as we access the latest databases, hypertexts, or the latest article via *Jstor* or *ProjectMuse*, 'we should be grateful', as Cathy N. Davidson puts it, 'that the humanities were not left behind in the massive project of synthesizing, aggregating, and archiving data' that the digital enabled.[15]

Confronting the new realities and contexts of student learning and information sourcing – in particular the noted tendency among the current generation of students to opt for the convenience and availability of online resources in place of traditional scholarly resources – allows us to address the ways in which we might guide learners in their use.[16] In the process, it also helps to focus on the development of important skills, including self-directed learning, media literacy and media responsibility.[17] However, the learning potential of open-access, social media resources also requires further consideration. The dichotomy of digital versus print-based pedagogy (which maps onto wider debates about online versus offline teaching, the predation of digital technologies and the future of the printed book) is not helpful, since it pits putative technophobes against apparent technophiles, preventing productive dialogue.[18] Furthermore, where the authority of the printed text is invoked, it can sometimes give rise to the notion of a pristine pre-digital pedagogy, imagined as inherently deep, engaging and successful. By the same token, however, Web 2.0 and social media networks should not be heralded as learning resources simply because they are new, or because students are increasingly learning within a digital context. Rather, technology 'should be utilized only where it can serve to enhance a learning environment'.[19]

Some recent literature on Web 2.0 learning has been celebratory. Appropriating the more positive aspects of the discourse on new media, it suggests that Web 2.0 marks a shift away from the 'banking concept' of learning, with its hierarchical relation of teacher as the depositor of knowledge, and the student as its receptacle, towards a student-centred model of learning.[20] Enabled by the culture of media participation associated with YouTube and other Web 2.0 platforms, learners are understood as having greater opportunities to intervene in the flow and consumption of information. 'Web 2.0 harnesses the collective intelligence of individuals to situate us in a time of endless information abundance – the participatory learning age.'[21] While Web 2.0 is regarded here as furthering the democratization of the classroom by empowering the learner, other critics have highlighted the challenges of this new learning landscape. In an overview of debates regarding the learning resource potential of Web 2.0 and social media, Marilyn Tadros importantly asks,

> How should the classroom respond to the overwhelming distractions of constant connectivity? Should the pedagogy change? Should faculty continue to compete for student attention and hang on to prevalent methods of teaching or should they learn the new media themselves and reinvent their teaching methodology?[22]

In posing these questions, Tadros is concerned not to alienate more traditional modes of teaching and learning, especially in terms of anxieties that to use social media is to sacrifice deep for surface learning. Social media platforms are 'tools to further education and not a goal in themselves'.[23] Pedagogy needs to accommodate itself to the Web 2.0 environment 'because digital natives think differently'.[24] There is, then, an onus on the educator to adapt to the habits and expectations of the 'net geners' or 'digital natives'.[25] Admittedly, these labels are generalizing and problematic – they can give the impression that students now are generically predisposed to, or skilled in the use of, online technologies, or that earlier generations, characterized as 'digital immigrants', are less capable of adapting to digital resources. Nonetheless, they capture changes in learner attitude and habit, which educators have been noticing over the past few years.

'The information-age mindset' is sometimes differentiated from previous generations in terms of a set of preferences, attributes and competencies. The information-age learner prefers 'doing rather than knowing', 'typing rather than handwriting' and 'staying connected'.[26] To these one can add the attributes of 'attentional deployment', or the capacity to multitask (which can involve the decision 'not to pay attention to things that don't interest them') and 'fast response time', or the capacity to respond quickly and to expect rapid responses.[27] The net generation learners are 'intuitive visual communicators', though their skills with visual images may come at the expense of less proficient text literacy than previous generations.[28] Generational particularities may also involve a move from deep to hyper-attention, although as Katherine N. Hayles suggests, rather than posit stark dichotomies between these poles of learning, there is much to be gained by pursuing the potential bridges between more traditional values of close reading and digital reading.[29] These developments are reflective, then, of a new learning culture. Indeed, one might go as far as to suggest that they reflect not just a mode of learning, but a way of being, or the 'ontology of the digital'.[30]

Placing a greater emphasis on the role of the user than on medium, Henry Jenkins draws upon his concept of participatory culture to capture the shifting information and learning context of Web 2.0. In a report for the MacArthur Foundation in the United States, Jenkins emphasizes the low barriers to engagement in Web 2.0 and the affordances of the digital in facilitating vernacular creation, contribution and connection. In order to negotiate this seemingly free flow of information, the Web 2.0 learner will require a suite of what Jenkins calls 'new literacies', which build on traditional skills of research and critical analysis.[31] The requisite skills include: play, or 'the capacity to experiment with one's surroundings as a form of problem-solving'; performance, or 'the ability to adopt alternative identities for the purpose of improvisation and discovery'; simulation, or 'the ability to interpret and

construct dynamic models of real-world processes'; appropriation, or 'the ability to meaningfully sample and remix media
content'; multitasking; distributed cognition, or 'the ability to
interact meaningfully with tools that expand mental capacities'; collective intelligence, or 'the ability to pool knowledge';
judgement, or 'the ability to evaluate the reliability and
credibility of different information sources'; and transmedia
navigation, or 'the ability to follow the flow of stories and
information across multiple modalities'.[32]

Some of these literacies, such as multitasking, overlap with
the skills and attributes of the Web 2.0 learner that have
already been noted. Others, such as simulation and transmedia
navigation, envisage forms of virtual and networked learning
that many students already undertake but that may take
on new levels of sophistication in the future. While Jenkins
runs the risk of overstating the democratizing properties of
participatory culture and while some of the desired media
literacies appear more suitable to a corporate rather than a
learning environment, his taxonomy encourages educators
and students alike to reflect on emerging learning patterns and
habits. At issue here is the ways learners go about acquiring,
utilizing and sharing information, and how they might do
so in the future. As Jenkins argues, stakeholders and policy-
makers in education need to recognize these new media skills
and to develop them in the interests of students now and in
the future.

For teachers, then, even this admittedly broad sense of the
continually shifting conditions of learning is of value, as we
consider how best to engage learners in Shakespeare's texts.
My purpose in outlining the profile of the Web 2.0 learner is
not to suggest that they are the antithesis to Shakespeare, or
to traditional forms of research and learning. Rather, it is to
focus attention on the predominant learning contexts within
which new students of Shakespeare (in the sense of a first-year
undergraduate taking an introductory Shakespeare course
at university) or returning students (in the sense of a undergraduate studying a new Shakespeare text) are operating. A

resource like YouTube can provide a bridge between these contexts and the texts. In other words, we need to consider harnessing both YouTube's participatory and archival dimensions, as well as the skills of the digital natives.

Learning Shakespeare has always presented its own set of challenges, from the specificities of the language and the depth of the critical heritage to the global reach of the texts' reception. At the same time, the ubiquity of Shakespeare within contemporary culture, as well as his valorized place within schools and universities, has helped to perpetuate the notion that the texts are immediately relevant and accessible to learners. For example, in the RSC's *Shakespeare: A Worldwide Classroom*, Tracy Irish writes:

> With around half the world's secondary school pupils likely to study at least something about him as part of their school curriculum, Shakespeare is probably education's most prescribed author. But millions of young people are also encountering a sneakier Shakespeare, one who has crept into popular culture through film, video, images and music, adapted and appropriated by the contemporary artists that young people feel readier to relate to.[33]

On the one hand, there is a much greater overlap between the two Shakespeares as they are imagined here. The institutionalized Shakespeare (perpetuated through the curricula of schools, colleges and universities, as well as through the activities of organizations like the RSC) circulates alongside 'sneakier' iterations of the plays, through either the use of a YouTube amateur performance in class or a more sustained examination of the remediation of Shakespeare in social media. Yet, on the other hand, as professional teachers of Shakespeare have discovered, among learners a perceptual gap between the early modern playwright and the Shakespeare of the popular cultural marketplace often exists, especially in terms of the language of the plays. For those students whose first encounter with Shakespeare might be through the medium of film, as Tiffany Stern notes, 'the reality of the text can disappoint rather than thrill them'.[34] In this sense, Shakespeare is something of a familiar stranger – recognizable and proximate, yet also unknown. As research conducted in secondary schools attests, Shakespeare is often perceived as intimidating, alienating or difficult.[35] What happens in first encounters with Shakespeare is crucial in determining subsequent levels of interest and engagement at third level. How learning occurs and at what pace can differ among any cohort of learners and, as educators have recognized, it is necessary to consider different learning strategies that adapt to learners and their expectations.

Within Shakespeare studies, a key teaching and learning strategy, and one that has grown in emphasis over recent years, is a performance-based approach to the text. This approach underwrites recent initiatives at the RSC, for example, to engage a younger demographic in Shakespeare, as part of its three-pronged strategy *Stand Up for Shakespeare* – 'do it on your feet', 'see it live', 'start it earlier' – and to energize teaching from primary schools upwards.[36] In schools and universities, the performance approach involves an 'actorly reading' of the text, or more dynamic methods, which encourage students to participate, collaborate and perform, as in 'learning "without chairs"'.[37] These initiatives are exciting and have proved effective, but they have resource implications in terms of delivery and assessment. As practical approaches to the text, they are also better suited to small-group teaching contexts than to large lectures, which present different challenges for learners and teachers alike. However, it is in the context of large groups that the possibilities of social media become evident. By providing students with structured learning pathways in the form of, say, problem-solving exercises, to be pursued after a lecture, social media platforms can compensate for the potentially reduced levels of face-to-face teaching, or the limits of synchronous teaching.

Web 2.0 and social media tools are already having an impact on Shakespeare teaching and learning, as these gradually become integrated with more established approaches to the texts.[38] Nonetheless, their use is still novel enough to attract coverage in the popular media, with such headlines as 'Teachers shake up Shakespeare with Digital Media',[39] 'Giving Literature Virtual Life', [40] and 'Twitter used to teach *Hamlet*'.[41] These headlines refer to initiatives underway across schools and colleges.[42] In one Canadian school, Twitter and blogs are used to introduce Grade 12 students to *Hamlet*; the students set up Twitter accounts under the characters' names, which enables a participative engagement with the play.[43] A similar technique is being deployed by the Globe theatre, where, as part of advance promotion for an upcoming production, a website gives visitors 'behind the scenes' access to the play, including blogs in the characters' own words.[44] Virtual reality or SecondLife is being used by Katherine Rowe to immerse students in the conditions of Shakespeare's theatre.[45] Other university teachers incorporate wikis into the design of their Shakespeare modules. One outcome of using this online editing tool, with its properties of hyperlinking and collaborative-knowledge or information gathering, is that it encourages students towards self-reliance and critical awareness.[46] Instructors also discovered that the creation of wikis had important discipline-specific outcomes, enabling students 'to witness first-hand some of the concealed postmodernist assumptions enmeshed in the creation of historical explanation or narrative'.[47] While tools such as wikis and Twitter can be used in isolation, they are much more effective as interlinked elements within the convergence culture of Web 2.0; for example, a blog, or a tweet, might embed a link to a video posted on YouTube.

The YouTube Shakespeare video is becoming ubiquitous in the classroom and with good reason. First, there is evidence to suggest that audiovisuals enable learning to occur, especially in large lectures, which position the learner in a passive role.[48] Evidence also suggests that students appreciate short illustrative clips in lectures, which they can review again later. [49] To be of value, however, the teacher must flag the relevance of a given video clip and the material itself must be critically evaluated. Second, YouTube is convenient – where teachers and lecturers have long used the film or performance clip to elucidate a point of interpretation, the video-sharing technology makes the Shakespeare clip easier to source and access, while also allowing for easy embedding (in multiple formats, from the lecture itself through to digital reading lists as posted on the Virtual Learning Environment (VLE) of a module).[50] Third, YouTube is current and appeals to the Web 2.0 learner. However, employing YouTube, or any other web-based technology, needs to be more than about invigorating the classroom or lecture hall with multimedia. Writing before the founding of YouTube, Roger Osche posed an important question about digital Shakespeare: 'How might we engage these new technologies while maintaining our traditional focus on Shakespeare's language? Will we abandon the more difficult study of the printed text in favour of the relatively passive viewing of motion picture?'[51] With these questions in mind and in the interests of prompting critical reflection on YouTube Shakespeare, I want to address the potential drawbacks of the site as a learning resource. I will then elaborate on its pedagogical value through detailed assignments that build on the skills of the Web 2.0 learner and also develop critical media literacy.

# Critical reflections on YouTube Shakespeare

## Shakespeare reduced

YouTube includes clips and excerpts from Shakespeare in performance and film, with full productions far less common. Rather than the 'two hours' traffic' of the stage, this is Shakespeare in fragments.[52] Considering YouTube's attention economy, there is the risk that the site promotes learning by surfing and thus militates against deep learning. However, as noted above, research on Web 2.0 learning suggests that the so-called 'net geners' are in fact engaging in forms of multi-tasking rather than surfing. As they navigate through the windows of the worldwide web, they also demonstrate an innate capacity to sort through a breath of information and data. The challenge for teachers of Shakespeare is to appeal to learners' familiarity with online resources, while at the same time developing traditional reading skills and research skills.

## YouTube unbounded

The range and diversity of content on YouTube – even within a Shakespeare search – is daunting. Faced with such an unbounded archive, a learner will have to surf through videos quite extensively, so as to filter out less impressive content (such as sponsored SparkNotes videos offering basic plot summaries) and to arrive at more interesting resources (such as a mashup that offers a new interpretation of the play, a vlog from the viewpoint of a character, an interview with a director, or a Shakespeare scholar discussing their work). The quantity of content on YouTube highlights the importance of developing and utilizing assignments that promote focused, critical and evaluative searching.

## YouTube can be unreliable

As a user-generated content platform, YouTube is an accidental archive and, as such, is unreliable. A tuber may delete content, or YouTube itself may do so where copyright infringement occurs. Since users tag content, the fundamental architecture of the site is also unreliable. Given the absence of any systematic forms of annotation, descriptions vary according to the user and may even be misleading. As Juhasz argues, 'the undisciplined nature of YouTube, its inability to provide structures, clear links, group spaces – really any kind of coherence – is its biggest fault, at least for online learning'.[53] The absence of such functionalities raises broader questions regarding YouTube's values, and indeed its politics. As Juhasz asks, 'why do they *not* want us to do these things' on the platform? 'Expanded functionality', she suggests, 'would serve to get in the way of the quick, fluid movement from video to video and page to page that defines YouTube viewing, besting older models of eyeball delivery' for advertisers.[54] The structural deficiencies of YouTube can also be a source of frustration for the researcher or learner, as they search and use its content. Thus, it may be necessary for YouTube 'to be complemented by more focused, communal, and expert-led sites of learning'.[55] Dedicated Shakespeare video archives, such as the 'Global Shakespeares' site, redress some of these deficiencies.[56] Including stage productions and films from across the globe, the site provides systematic description and annotation as well as multiple search filters. It suggests new possibilities for teaching and learning, including a broadening of our understanding of the transnational locations from where Shakespeare is produced, as well as realizing a deeper comparative approach than has hitherto been possible.[57] However, encouraging learners to set up a YouTube account can minimize the unreliability of the platform; learners can also be encouraged to develop consistent annotations of videos for themselves, perhaps using the 'Global Shakespeares' site as a template.[58]

# Screen-time, or video killed the Shakespearean reader

YouTube is an audio-visual medium, where clips present learners with diverse modes of appeal to the visual and aural senses. However, although YouTube offers learners insight into the different forms Shakespeare can take across media, there is a risk that learners will find the patience and concentration required for the printed text especially demanding by contrast. This issue highlights the need for the teacher to communicate the relevance of a video and to encourage learners to regard videos as offering 'an additional medium to be used alongside text'.[59] Assignments are thus important in encouraging learners to work from video content back to the text itself. Furthermore, while students can be encouraged and guided in their use of YouTube as a learning resource, the onus needs to be on them to complete the study of the play: 'put the choice of what to read and what to omit back on them', suggests one teacher; students 'need to understand the consequences to the parameters they are setting'.[60]

## YouTube is homogenizing

With content uploaded on YouTube acquiring a generic quality as it is encountered on the interface, the various forms Shakespeare can take – film, television, stage performance, documentaries – become undifferentiated. As Lauren Shohet has argued, YouTube 'homogenizes forms'.[61] The risk is that viewing Shakespeare via YouTube delimits attention to questions of genre and medium. The homogenizing effect has particular ramifications for stage, or embodied performances: while YouTube provides an archive of these 'live' performances, it also involves a blurring of distinctions between the live and the mediatized, taken to be the more general condition of cultural production within postmodernity.[62] In this regard, accessing Shakespeare performance on YouTube involves loss.[63] However, we need to be careful that a nostalgia for the live performance does not valorize it as some kind of pure iteration of the text, or one that is more stable than that offered by other media. With various forms presented in aggregate, YouTube also allows for the development of medium-awareness among students, as well as historical consciousness.[64] YouTube illustrates the concept of remediation and thus offers an entry point into thinking about the effect of medium on a Shakespearean story. Of particular value here are the four principles towards analysing Shakespeare and new media as suggested by Katherine Rowe: 'mine the scholarship specific to your medium', paying close attention to the history and conventions of a medium or format; 'distinguish media from display technologies'; '[r]eplay' or view closely and carefully; and '[r]ewind', or reflect on such terms as remediation and convergence in order to consider how they might illuminate understandings of Shakespeare.[65] Assignments using YouTube Shakespeare could include elements that encourage students to think about the medium of YouTube itself, both as a means towards promoting critical media literacy, but also so as to foster an awareness of form and its shaping force on narrative.

## Shakespeare and company

Using YouTube as a learning resource for Shakespeare involves encountering disparate content. As emphasized in Chapter 1, amateur and commercial content coincide and overlap; commercial interests inscribe the participatory culture of YouTube. To use or recommend YouTube as a learning resource is to bring the images of the marketplace – and the ideologies that form their base – into the classroom, be it in the form of sponsored links, pop-up adverts at the start of videos, or perhaps less obviously owing to its ubiquity, the corporate brand of YouTube itself. Arguably, there is nothing especially new at work here – Shakespeare has long circulated within different, but interconnecting spaces or markets, including mass media and education.[66] With its mix of vernacular and professional content, however, YouTube Shakespeare does present a new opportunity to think critically about how Shakespeare is produced, constituted and resourced within the culture industry. In using YouTube as a learning resource, then, there is both an opportunity and a necessity for learners to acquire critical media skills in order that they question – and not merely consume – media content. By extension, learners can become conscious of their own participation in the creation of Shakespeare and the determination of his cultural value. For instance, students might compare to what extent other Renaissance dramatists are represented on YouTube. Does the archive enable an understanding of Shakespeare-in-context, or is YouTube Bardic-centric?

## Digital divides

YouTube is as an example of the low entry-level for participation and publishing associated with Web 2.0. However, it cannot be assumed that all learners are predisposed to digital technologies and social media, or that they possess the elementary media skills to participate in these resources.[67] Educational theorists have drawn attention to the need to address how social networks reflect and also replicate divisions and inequities present in offline social interactions.[68] The use of Web 2.0 resources presents new challenges for the teacher, whose students may prove more tech-savvy, thus producing another type of digital divide.[69] Furthermore, not all learners have access to a computer, or a mobile computer device, and some may not have access to broadband outside of a school or college network. There are also issues about the availability of high-speed Internet in developing countries, which impacts negatively on access to educational resources.[70]

## Tube, teacher, decentred knowledge

The introduction of a resource like YouTube into a learning context has implications for the role of teacher. One effect of Web 2.0 is a decentring of knowledge and authority, which explains why new technologies are regarded as strong contributors to student-directed learning. Whether one agrees with the argument that traditional forms of authority and knowledge are being replaced by the intangible authority of the web search, the availability and proliferation of information does change the role of the teacher. He/she is less of a specialist and more of a navigator steering students in their searches through data. For those teachers of Shakespeare for whom the plays were taught through the lens of cultural materialism, with its Foucauldian emphasis on the circulation of knowledge and power, the democratizing possibilities of online learning might add a welcome dimension to the kind of Shakespeare they want to encourage their students to engage with. Yet, YouTube potentially delimits a learner's capacity to differentiate between forms of Shakespeare content. At stake here is the wider perception of YouTube as a catalyst for acritical, unfocused browsing.[71] This ushers in a postmodern relativism, where traditional distinctions between forms of cultural production, and the value attached to them, become blurred. However, it is important that students are afforded the opportunity to determine their own learning. Through trial and error, students might actively assess and critically evaluate content; Web 2.0 and social media offer good platforms for such experiential learning.

# Learning with YouTube Shakespeare: Affordances and responsibilities

In exploring YouTube's limitations, the value of the site as a learning resource also comes into focus. When viewed from another perspective, the unbounded nature of YouTube as an archive promotes a thickening of a learner's sense of Shakespeare, as they encounter multiple iterations of a play, scene or character. Yet, the issue as to whether time spent moving through the small screens of YouTube distracts – or *detracts* – from the experience of the text itself remains; indeed, in advocating the use of YouTube, the textual corpus risks being treated as remains, in the sense of being left behind.[72] I would argue that YouTube Shakespeare is a resource, not a substitute for a close reading of the text: in this sense, too, the text remains. Additionally, students need to be encouraged to search deeply and meaningfully.

There are three immediate pay-offs from using YouTube as a Shakespeare learning resource, each of which stem from its status as a video-share platform. First, video-sharing creates an archive that, notwithstanding its unreliability, provides learners with access to a wealth of Shakespeare content (the assignments below elaborate on how this material might be purposefully explored and embedded into learning outcomes). Second, the site's roots within participatory culture and the related vernacular forms (remix, mashup, vlogging) are appealing to the Web 2.0 student and, as such, exceed traditional Shakespeare pedagogies. Through YouTube culture, learners can be encouraged to adopt a participatory role in (re)making Shakespeare; there are certainly enough examples of responses to incentivize production. Students move from being consumers of data, or contributors to meaning, to active participants and revisers. As Osche argues, the task of making and recording a scene should not be seen in any way as remedial. Rather, it importantly builds on the Web 2.0 learner's propensity to think in visual terms and provides students with a structure: 'in the process of preparing, taping, editing, and reflecting upon a particular role or scene, they transform the role and become part of the text itself'.[73] Giving students creative licence may involve granting them the freedom to leave the text behind, though as Barbara Hodgdon has suggested, such a move invariably involves a return to it.[74] As students are encouraged to collaborate on a production, share content and offer constructive criticism, YouTube offers the potential for individual, as well as peer-based learning. Third, with its easily portable and spreadable URLs, YouTube allows for the embedded argument – learners can pinpoint a scene from a Shakespeare film, or an actor's performance, and embed the link into a document. This signals new forms of argument and writing that employ hyperlinks, allowing information to be sourced easily and precisely by subsequent readers.[75]

Of course, there are a host of issues regarding the veracity, provenance and evaluation of YouTube content. In order to unfold YouTube's learning potential, teachers will need to work with their students on what Mark Gammon and Joanne White refer to as the 'critical competencies necessary for assessing, analyzing, evaluating, and creating media content'.[76] In the new learning context of a 'world immersed in ubiquitous data', these media literacies are crucial – learners need to actively assess and double-check content, especially where its provenance may not be clear (as can be the case with an inadequate description for a YouTube video).[77] Moreover, 'the rise in decentralized opportunities for creation and sharing must be met with a concomitant recognition of the distributed responsibility for critical analysis and evaluation'.[78] As students' learning paths are rerouted and altered by new modes of content production within Web 2.0 – we are now dealing with a situation where students are making content as well as consuming and commenting on it – students themselves will need to partake in those roles of assessor and critic previously undertaken by traditional gatekeepers of information, such as teachers and librarians.

There may be some resistance among students to the introduction of critical analysis into the sphere of online video, on the basis that it removes the enjoyment or entertainment sought in the first instance. Yet, tubers are already adept at comment, critique and semiotic analysis, often noting the minute details of a video.[79] It is imperative that students acquire media literacy skills and learn to view video inquisitively and critically, so that responsibility and accountability are understood as integral to online expression, be it in the form of posting, production or commentary. The discussion in Chapter 3 of posts in terms of hatred-as-performance highlights the importance of educating students in reflective and ethical media use, in relation to both their immediate peers and a broader social network.

In order to maximize YouTube as a learning resource, teachers may find it useful to set up a channel for their Shakespeare course(s), with individual modules perhaps differentiated by playlists. A channel is a useful tool for teachers – for example, it allows students to collate their selected videos into thematic playlists. Creating a digital footprint for the professional and pedagogical activities of the Shakespeare teacher is also an important first step towards encouraging students to regard YouTube as a learning resource. It makes good sense not only to provide a link to the channel on the course website or VLE, but also to show the channel to students in the first class or meeting. Here, the instructor can establish how the channel relates to the module and to the learning outcomes. Additionally, learners may benefit from some guidance as to the educational uses and benefits of YouTube and Web 2.0; they are more likely to participate if they are provided with a clear understanding of how YouTube relates to their learning.

In the interests of creating a student-centred learning environment, students might be encouraged – though certainly not required – to set up a channel themselves. This will enable them to subscribe to the course or module channel and to access updates within it. Currently, channel subscriptions are the only form of group activity enabled by YouTube's architecture. Despite this, there are several advantages to students setting up their own YouTube channel. First, they can begin to shape their own learning and participate fully in the culture of YouTube Shakespeare (while at the same keeping it distinct from their use of YouTube as entertainment or social space). They can also use the email facility within YouTube to liaise with each other, or the wider YouTube community. Good starting activities include curating videos that relate to their learning into playlists and developing systematic forms of annotation. Second, a channel enables students to respond to videos, in the form of likes and posts. A third advantage of being signed into YouTube is that the algorithm will generate recommendations based on playlists and viewing history, thus enabling students to follow up on earlier searches. To anyone who already has a YouTube channel, what I am outlining here will invariably appear self-evident, but such fundamentals are important if we are to extend the use of YouTube as a learning resource beyond the practice of playing clips in class. It is about formalizing what might already constitute a subconscious habit for the Web 2.0 student.

Using YouTube as a learning resource has important implications for student privacy, peer-interaction and also the relationship between faculty and students. A case study on the use of Facebook as an educational resource provides some useful caveats and recommendations, which can be adapted to YouTube.[80] I offer the following suggestions. Student participation should be optional. In the interests of privacy, where a teacher already has a YouTube channel, they should create a separate one for teaching use only. Likewise, students should be advised to create a separate channel for their learning. They should also be advised that posts and other forms of communication that occur through YouTube must be relevant to the course material and avoid personal information. It is therefore recommended that teachers familiarize students with YouTube's community guidelines, as well as the privacy settings available on a YouTube channel. As noted above, in discussing content on the site and in engaging in online expression, students must learn to be responsible and to make ethical choices.

# Suggested assignments

Previous chapters have addressed some of the conceptual categories – online identity and expression, the semiotics of race, gender politics – through which YouTube Shakespeare can be examined. The assignments below deliberately suggest additional terms for investigation. They are intended to exploit YouTube as an archive of Shakespeare resources, to develop deep searching and to foster a critical use. In devising the exercises, several research questions have been crucial. How can the use of YouTube foster a Shakespeare that appeals to the Web 2.0 learner? How can the new literacies of the Web 2.0 learner (such as performance, appropriation, multitasking, collaboration, evaluation and cross-media navigation) be deployed? In what ways can we utilize YouTube's expression modes and genres to explore Shakespeare? What kind of meaningful searches could students undertake to assist them in approaching those aspects of Shakespeare that they find intimidating or difficult? How can YouTube-as-archive be used to enhance learning about key areas of Shakespeare studies, such as performance, adaptation and remediation?

I am also interested in the possibility of YouTube returning a Shakespeare that is incomplete as a body of knowledge. Of relevance here is a recent proposal for a model of engagement with Shakespeare based on participation rather than ownership: 'to think of Shakespeare as an issue to be addressed, rather than as a stable body of knowledge to be mastered, offers students and teachers the chance to explore the multiplicity of Shakespeares now available to us'.[81] From this viewpoint, students might recognize that there are multiple, though interconnecting, layers to Shakespeare as a subject of study (the performance history, the critical tradition, adaptations across media, to name just a few), a realization that can be daunting for a learner, but exciting too.[82]

The exercises that follow are presented as they might be on a schedule for a module and as part of the learning outcomes provided to a student. Thus, each assignment follows a template, with a brief description of the task, including the rationale behind it and the learning outcomes. While suggested links are provided in some instances, I have stopped short of giving examples of videos, since to do so would be contrary to the objectives of promoting discovery among learners and encouraging purposeful searches. Different teachers will most likely have different approaches and strategies (for example, the principles of enquiry-based learning inform some of the tasks below), but it is hoped that the suggestions will prove adaptable to a range of teaching and learning contexts. Learners should be given a clear sense of how the fulfilment on one task relates to their wider learning; as such, the tasks probably work best as part of formative assessment. Feedback on the completed assignments is also crucial, since it can encourage students to plan ahead for summative assessment (in the form of an exam or major essay).[83] Such measures are important if YouTube Shakespeare is to be more than a dynamic interface viewed quickly in class.

# 1. Can we learn from YouTube Shakespeare?

Just as studies of the Shakespeare film developed from questions about adaptation to interrogate the medium of cinema itself, attention is now turning to Shakespeare in a new media or Web 2.0 context. What are the implications of a medium like YouTube for the study of Shakespeare? What kind of Shakespeare is produced through YouTube, especially when we consider the site in terms of media convergence, with vernacular content coinciding with commercially produced content and also advertisements? Furthermore, YouTube might be described as Bardic-centric in the sense that it limits an understanding of the drama of Shakespeare's contemporaries. With these issues in mind, respond to one of the following tasks:

## Group A

YouTube is interested in establishing 'Shakespeare' as a subject category within the search category of 'Education'. Your remit is to provide a subset of descriptive search categories that YouTube could adapt into a user-friendly search filter. It should also be noted that YouTube have expressed some concern about those Shakespeare videos that infringe copyright.

Working within your assigned group, establish a set of discovery questions to formulate a response to the scenario.

Each group will present their findings in a short PowerPoint presentation in the next seminar.

## Group B

A Shakespeare research institute wishes to persuade YouTube to include 'Shakespeare' as a searchable category on the site. Your remit is to provide a subset of descriptive search categories that will meet the requirements of several constituencies of user (including scholars, secondary-level students, university students, theatregoers).

Working within your assigned group, establish a set of discovery questions to respond to the scenario outlined here. Each group will present their findings in a short PowerPoint presentation (to last no more than 5 minutes) in the next seminar.

## Learning outcomes

- *Knowledge and understanding:* To demonstrate a clear understanding of Shakespeare in a medium-specific context; to demonstrate an understanding of YouTube culture (and the constituencies and needs within it).

- *Intellectual skills:* Develop and strengthen critical analysis and media literacy.

- *Subject-specific skills:* Strengthen competence in identifying the relevance of medium specificity to Shakespearean adaptation; strengthen ability to identify a variety of ways that Shakespeare is produced within the culture industry; strengthen ability to critically evaluate medium and online culture.

- *Practical/transferable skills:* Strengthen ability to arrange and evaluate information; develop ability to problem-solve and identify gaps in knowledge; develop ability to collaborate as part of a group; develop oral expression and presentation skills; develop ability to deliver and accept feedback in a constructive manner.

### *Suggested links*

See videos on YouTube culture by Michael Wesch at
http://www.youtube.com/user/mwesch
and Alexandra Juhasz at http://www.youtube.com/user/
MediaPraxisme.

## 2. Your Shakespeare: Creating a YouTube Shakespeare channel

As part of this class, we strongly advise you set up your own channel on YouTube as a number of the continuous assessment exercises use the site. Supporting materials (including schedule, learning outcomes, details of assessment, bibliography) for this seminar are available on the module database, where you will also find the link to the module's Shakespeare channel. Through your own channel, you will be able to subscribe to the module channel and to respond to videos within it. We will review YouTube's Community Guidelines in the first class, so as to ensure that everyone is familiar with best practice. With your own channel, you might consider creating a playlist of relevant videos in order to organize resources in a way that best suits your learning (for instance, consider arranging playlists by text, character, learning outcome or theme). The objective of this optional exercise is to find resources on YouTube that will deepen your understanding of Shakespeare (and you can determine the context here: it might include areas like film adaptations, amateur culture, women in Shakespeare).

## *Learning outcomes*

- *Knowledge and understanding:* To demonstrate a clear understanding of Shakespeare in a medium-specific context; to demonstrate an understanding of YouTube's functionality as an archive.
- *Intellectual skills:* Develop and strengthen critical analysis and media literacy.
- *Subject-specific skills:* Strengthen competence in identifying and organizing Shakespeare resources; strengthen ability to critically assess resources.
- *Practical/transferable skills:* Strengthen ability to arrange and evaluate information; develop ability to structure and organize learning.

# 3. What's on stage?

Shakespeare's plays have a long theatrical history, but also a living one. Using YouTube to explore which Shakespeare plays are being produced in theatres, select 3 videos that showcase different productions from the past 6 months. You might find it useful to consider what you can discover about (i) production decisions and influences; (ii) the director's perspective on the play; (iii) how the actor(s) prepares; (iv) the kind of Shakespeare generated by the production and/or promotional material; (v) the degree of information available and how it is presented on YouTube; (vi) the extent to which a production incorporates other media. Write a short analysis (400 words) of your selected videos. These will be added to the class playlist for discussion in next week's seminar.[84]

## *Learning outcomes*

- *Knowledge and understanding:* To demonstrate a clear understanding of Shakespeare in performance; to demonstrate a clear understanding of a performance-based approach to Shakespeare.

- *Intellectual skills:* Develop and strengthen critical analysis.
- *Subject-specific skills:* Strengthen competence in identifying synchronic and diachronic approaches to performance contexts for Shakespeare; strengthen competence in critically evaluating performance contexts for Shakespeare.
- *Practical/transferable skills:* Strengthen competence in information retrieval and in evaluation of online resources; develop oral and written expression; develop ability to deliver and accept feedback in a constructive manner.

# 4. Shakespeare's language

The language of Shakespeare can sometimes be intimidating. As a consequence, there can be a temptation to ignore a play's verbal structure, or to separate it from consideration of character and theme. It is a commonplace that Shakespeare's language was written for performance, but what should Shakespeare sound like? How can we engage with Shakespeare's language, rather than ignore it?[85] YouTube provides us with an impressive archive of Shakespeare performances – exploring these could provide insight into such questions. The language of the plays both requires work and rewards it – for instance, an understanding of iambic pentameter and Shakespeare's use of it informs our sense of character, just as thematic concerns of a play are established and unfolded through metaphor.

Consider the following task. A theatre company is preparing for a production aimed at a group of college students. It wants to use three YouTube videos, which explain the language in an interesting way. The company is especially interested in

YouTube because of the range of performance styles available there and also because of the 'Like/Dislike' and comment feature, which provides feedback on videos. Working within your assigned group, establish a set of discovery questions to enable you to determine what resources will best suit the scenario presented. You will then need to select and evaluate your videos and discuss how you are going to present your findings in next week's seminar.

## Learning outcomes

- *Knowledge and understanding:* To demonstrate a clear understanding of Shakespeare's language; to demonstrate a clear understanding of the significance of language in relation to an analysis of character and theme.
- *Intellectual skills:* Develop and strengthen critical analysis.
- *Subject-specific skills:* Strengthen competence in identifying the language of Shakespearean drama and to critically evaluate it.
- *Practical/transferable skills:* Strengthen ability to arrange and evaluate information; develop ability to collaborate as part of a group; develop ability to problem-solve and identify gaps in knowledge; develop oral expression and presentation skills; develop ability to deliver and accept feedback in a constructive manner.

## Suggested links

Actor Ben Crytsal discusses Shakespeare's use of language at http://www.youtube.com/watch?v=0Qv-sjQHgZ8.

# 5. Video creation: Broadcast your Shakespeare

YouTube Shakespeare is more than an archive of clips from old media: it is also a platform for sharing do-it-yourself responses to the plays. As part of your response to Shakespeare, consider making a video for upload to the site. Some students may not wish to appear before the camera, let alone upload a video on YouTube; however, there are other ways to participate (as script editor, camera operator, director). In addition, YouTube culture involves multiple forms of expression that allow for more distanced modes of self-expression (the mashup, the video-essay, the movie-trailer parody). There is an exciting opportunity to undertake your own adaptation and to experiment with form, plot, character and language. You might find it helpful to first search through some creative responses to Shakespeare on YouTube.

This assignment on making your own content is informed by recent scholarship on experiential learning (or 'learning-by-doing'), which suggests the benefits for the learner themselves in becoming 'knowledge constructors'.[86] Web 2.0 is especially adept at enabling us all to contribute to the flow of information and, as such, has interesting implications for how we learn. Some of you may already be familiar with video creation and manipulation, others less so. There are useful 'how to' videos on YouTube. Video creation may be something you do as entertainment, or that you associate with fan culture, but it can be usefully extended to your coursework. Some opening questions include the following. How are you going to present your Shakespeare scene or character? How might you use form or medium to say something about the text? What is the objective of your textual intervention? You might choose to pursue concepts that we have been exploring in relation to Shakespeare, such as intertextuality, medium-specificity and remediation. However, we are not prescribing criteria for inclusion: this is intended to be a free-thinking creative exercise, which allows for personal responses to the texts.

## Learning outcomes

- *Knowledge and understanding:* To demonstrate a clear understanding of the processes involved in constructing a creative adaptation in the context of Shakespeare; to demonstrate, through experiential learning, an understanding of intertextuality, remediation, medium-specificity and form.
- *Intellectual skills:* Develop and strengthen textual analysis through adaptation; develop media production and media literacy.
- *Subject-specific skills:* Strengthen competence in identifying aesthetics and politics of adaptation; strengthen ability to respond creatively to the Shakespearean text.
- *Practical/transferable skills:* Strengthen ability to arrange and re-present information; develop ability to structure and organize learning; develop ability to collaborate as part of a group; develop oral expression and presentation skills; develop ability to deliver and accept feedback in a constructive manner.

## Suggested links

YouTube guide to use and functions: http://www.youtube.com/t/about_essentials.
And community: http://www.youtube.com/t/community_guidelines.
RSC Top Filming Tips:
http://www.rsc.org.uk/education/research-case-studies/our-projects/fighting-words.aspx.
Helpful tips for Web 2.0 editing resources and apps:

Bryan Alexander and Alan Levine, 'Web 2.0 Storytelling: Emergence of a New Genre', *EDUCAUSE Review* (2008): 41–56.

# 6. Analysing character

What informs our sense of a Shakespeare character? Characters can often be our first entry point into the world of the play; they can seem familiar and fully formed, as if in possession of a stable personhood. However, character is an effect of dramatic form (as the term 'dramatis personae' reminds us). Furthermore, conceptions and expectations of character are formed culturally and through the categories of class, race and gender. YouTube Shakespeare provides us with a databank of performances from across media that suggest different ways of approaching character and afford insight into how an actor makes meaning.[87]

Using YouTube, select and examine three different portrayals of two characters from the assigned text. Your sample of videos should include at least one theatre production, one film and one amateur performance. Write a short analysis (400 words) of your selected videos. These will be added to the class playlist for discussion in next week's seminar.

Alternatively, you can elect to make a character-study video. This might take the form of one of the following: a performance of a monologue; a video essay showcasing representations of a character; a character's vlog; a film short that focuses on a character. Your video will be added to the class playlist for discussion in next week's seminar.

Before you begin, you might find it helpful to use a word association exercise to establish your initial sense of character. Then, having looked at YouTube, perform the same exercise and compare the results. Did your search through the site change those initial impressions?

## *Learning outcomes*

- *Knowledge and understanding:* To demonstrate a clear understanding of character as an approach to Shakespeare; to demonstrate, through experiential learning and/or creative adaptation, an understanding of dramatic form.

- *Intellectual skills:* Develop and strengthen textual analysis through adaptation; develop media literacy and media production.

- *Subject-specific skills:* Strengthen ability to recognize different approaches to character and to Shakespearean performance; strengthen ability to respond creatively to the Shakespearean character.

- *Practical/transferable skills:* Strengthen ability to arrange and evaluate information; develop ability to structure and organize learning; develop oral expression and presentation skills; develop ability to deliver and accept feedback in a constructive manner.

# 7. Prop search and trace

Yorick's skull, Macbeth's dagger, Richard II's looking glass, Desdemona's handkerchief, Henry IV's hollow crown, Ophelia's dress – these are some of the shifting properties of Shakespeare performance, which we sometimes overlook in reading a play. They are called for by the text, but are subject to change in accordance with the choices of a particular production. As such, props provide us with visual cues that shape how a production conveys meaning: they can situate the play within a particular location, or alert an audience to the re-presentation of a historical past. In film, too, properties function as indexical signs through which an audience makes meaning. Close attention to costume choices, for example, reveals much about what a given production is attempting to say with or through Shakespeare, from questions about gender and class to the nature of political authority, both then and now. Costume, as Bridget Escolme reminds us in an important essay, is 'a material factor in the semiotic and phenomenological production of meaning in its own right'.[88] YouTube Shakespeare provides a vast databank for the exploration of the properties of Shakespearean theatre and film.

For this task, select two properties from the assigned Shakespeare text and examine how they have been used, or adopted, or altered across different theatre and/or film productions. In your search, you may find the following questions a helpful starting point:

- How do props specify a time period or setting?
- What do you consider as 'authentic' props for Shakespearean theatre?
- Do props specify only one time period, or several?
- Why would a director choose to suggest different historical references?
- How does a modern dress production deal with the charge of anachronism?
- Do you think modern dress productions succeed in using Shakespeare to comment on the present?
- Is there a risk that modern-dress Shakespeare simplifies the past or makes it a version of the present?

Write a short analysis (400 words) of your selected videos. These will be added to the class playlist for discussion in next week's seminar.

## Learning outcomes

- *Knowledge and understanding:* To demonstrate a clear understanding of theatrical properties in Shakespearean theatre; and their semiotic significance.

- *Intellectual skills:* Develop and strengthen critical analysis.
- *Subject-specific skills:* Strengthen competence in identifying and critically evaluating the materiality of Shakespearean drama.
- *Practical/transferable skills:* Strengthen ability to arrange and evaluate information; develop ability to collaborate as part of a group; develop oral expression and presentation skills; develop ability to deliver and accept feedback in a constructive manner.

## Suggested links

Folger Library video on stage combat and weapons: http://www.youtube.com/watch?v=X2MkD3bkPhk.

# 8. Find the specialists

YouTube Shakespeare provides us with an archive of Shakespeare performance, from stage and film to the various genres of vernacular culture. Critics and writers also have a presence on the site. For this assignment, search and select three videos, which include the following properties: (i) the video was made by, or features, a Shakespeare critic; (ii) the individual(s) featured in the video are included in the course bibliography.

Write a short review (400 words) of your selected videos. Your review should include a brief outline of the key points or arguments made, including what the author identified as their interest in or passion for Shakespeare, and a brief evaluation of the extent to which the videos contribute to the study of Shakespeare. The videos will be added to the class playlist for discussion in the next seminar.

## *Learning outcomes*

- *Knowledge and understanding:* To demonstrate a clear understanding of critical issues and debates within Shakespeare studies.
- *Intellectual skills:* Develop and strengthen critical analysis.
- *Subject-specific skills:* Strengthen competence in identifying critical issues and directions within Shakespeare studies; strengthen ability to critically evaluate current scholarship.
- *Practical/transferable skills:* Strengthen ability to arrange and evaluate information; develop oral and written expression; develop ability to deliver and accept feedback in a constructive manner.

# 9. Global Shakespeare

What we understand by Shakespeare is contingent on a range of factors and variables (including those of language, class, race, gender). Yet, the texts are understood as global in the double sense that they are performed and produced across the world and because they circulate within a global marketplace. With reference to a case study of a selected Shakespeare text, the purpose of this assignment is to use YouTube to critically examine the global reach of Shakespeare and/or Shakespeare in the context of globalization. To what extent can YouTube return a transnational Shakespeare? Does YouTube return a predominantly Anglophone Shakespeare? What is the significance of YouTube's regionalized search filters? How useful is the site in deepening our understanding of the local dimensions of the globally produced Bard?

Using a YouTube playlist, add and briefly annotate 8 videos that you think are exemplary of a global Shakespeare. Your playlist should also include a 150-word overview or headnote explaining your selection. The playlists will be reviewed and compared in class.

## *Learning outcomes*

- *Knowledge and understanding:* To demonstrate a clear understanding of critical issues and debates within Shakespeare studies.
- *Intellectual skills:* Develop and strengthen critical analysis; strengthen media literacy skills.
- *Subject-specific skills:* Strengthen competence in identifying the category of the global in relation to the reception of Shakespeare; strengthen ability to organize and critically evaluate resources.
- *Practical/transferable skills:* Strengthen ability to arrange and critically evaluate information, including attention to algorithmic search; develop written and also presentation skills; develop ability to deliver and accept feedback in a constructive manner.

## *Suggested links*

Channel of MIT Global Shakespeare project:
http://www.youtube.com/user/globalshakespeare

# 10. Mashup Shakespeare

Mashups are a generic feature of YouTube: tubers have proved adept at remixing media content, operating through a combined logic of copy, splice and repurpose. One effect of this repurposing is that it 'makes visible the degree to which all cultural expression builds on what has come before'.[89] Shakespeare's texts themselves involve the remixing of other texts, as in the chronicles of Halle and Holinshed in the history plays. Another effect is to provoke a re-evaluation of what is being cited or repurposed, challenging our conception of the original. However, through their appropriation, if this is the correct term, of existing media content, mashups often stand accused of copyright infringement; where a copyright holder pursues the matter, YouTube will remove the video.

For this in-class assignment, watch the mashup that has been assigned to your group and use the following questions to open the discussion:

- What Shakespeare text does the mashup use or reference?
- Are there any alterations (such as word order, redistribution of lines) made to the Shakespeare text(s)?
- Can you identify the different media that are cited in the video?
- To what extent, if any, is the remixing of Shakespeare with other media effective?
- Consider which of the following terms best describes the video: 'appropriation', 'adaptation', 'spin-off', 'surrogate', 'supplement'.
- How useful is it to consider Shakespeare's texts as mashups?
- To what extent, if any, did the mashup or remix focus your attention on intertextuality in Shakespeare?
- Does the mashup infringe copyright and if so, in what ways?

Each group will need to nominate a raconteur who will act as its spokesperson and report back to the wider class on your findings.

## *Learning outcomes*

- *Knowledge and understanding:* To demonstrate a clear understanding of medium and form; to demonstrate a clear understanding of textual issues with reference to Shakespeare.
- *Intellectual skills:* Develop and strengthen media literacy skills; develop and strengthen textual analysis.
- *Subject-specific skills:* Strengthen competence in addressing intertextuality in Shakespeare and Shakespeare adaptations; strengthen ability to critically evaluate different forms or media.
- *Practical/transferable skills:* Strengthen ability to critically evaluate information; develop oral communication and also presentation skills; develop ability to collaborate as part of a group; develop ability to deliver and accept feedback in a constructive manner.

# Coda

As we have seen, the implications of using YouTube and social media as learning resources are wide ranging, both in terms of confronting the association of such technologies with distraction and commercialization, as well as issues regarding access, privacy and veracity. These issues take on a more specific dimension in the context of higher education, where academics prize intellectual inquiry and the expansion of a field of knowledge, but do so within the context of a series of gatekeeping mechanisms (including archival research, peer review, scholarly referencing, institutional assertions of ownership over research, and library and database subscription services). There are good reasons for these mechanisms, which are intrinsic to the values of the academic profession. They also guard against the phenomenon of 'sharecropping', where someone else takes credit, or profit, for the time and insights of others.[90]

As Bryan Alexander asks, 'How can higher education respond, when it offers a complex, contradictory mix of openness and restriction, public engagement and cloistering?'[91] One response is that universities and academic culture need to be much more open to Web 2.0. Academics and teachers must now engage in a quid pro quo, whereby they do not simply make use of, say, a YouTube video embedded in a PowerPoint presentation, or posted on the course VLE, but consider how they might also participate in such platforms. Participation might take some of the forms suggested above, such as a YouTube channel for a specific module, with playlists for each lecture or seminar, but could also involve content production and uploading. Web 2.0 technologies offer significant possibilities for higher education, but only if, as Brian Lamb argues, educators and institutions prove accommodating to the culture of openness, access and reuse associated with such technologies: 'we might ask if the content we presently lock down could be made public with a license specifying reasonable terms of reuse'.[92] With reference to data mashups (here denoting a combination of 'the data and functionalities of two or more Web applications'), Lamb envisages a scenario of 'open and discoverable formats', 'open and transparent licensing' and 'open and remixable formats', which would enable educators to share, customize or adapt each other's materials.[93] In this scenario of acknowledged (re)use, educators might cooperate on learning strategies and at the same time disseminate their teaching and research specialism more widely.

However, the issue of how higher education avails itself of Web 2.0 also needs to be addressed from the perspective of online vernacular culture itself – what might be at stake for a vernacular production like a YouTube video when used in an academic context? To use YouTube videos in a class setting, or as learning resources, is to potentially delimit those qualities that make them attractive to students in the first instance, such as entertainment, individual creative engagement and the free play associated with online aliases. As educators increasingly turn to online platforms to engage students, harnessing the online properties of accessibility, connectivity and interactivity, they may unwittingly contribute to an institutionalizing of online vernacular expression and production. However, as noted in earlier chapters, amateur or vernacular expression overlaps with school or university culture, and tubers are themselves adept at negotiating different types of use in their online lives. On YouTube, a sharp distinction between different forms of expression does not necessarily pertain.

Hopefully, in the years to come, people will still be making their own Shakespeare monologue, creating a mashup, or uploading a film short, or will have developed different genres. Forms of vernacular creativity may become more established within assessment or fully integrated into the learning outcomes of a Shakespeare module. Video tagging and embedding may lead to new forms of essay and modes of argument. The field of Shakespeare studies has demonstrated an encouraging openness to new pedagogies, as evidenced by the incorporation of virtual worlds and Twitter into learning. Shakespeare journals available online are also beginning to recognize the benefits of embedding videos into articles or including hyperlinks.

There is still some way to go, however, not least in terms of Shakespearean scholars and teachers creating a greater presence on YouTube and other social media sites. Perhaps the next move could be for journals to set up a YouTube channel, with annotated playlists categorized by subject, to allow for a comparison of videos discussed across a set of articles. Scholars are only beginning to tap into the opportunities of YouTube as a site of knowledge exchange. There may be some reticence here, due in part to the nature of humanities academic research and publishing, where new research projects and arguments are closely guarded until publication.[94] Yet, YouTube should be regarded as a showcasing platform, where expertise in an area, or a new research project, can be broadcast to an immediate cohort of students (through a dedicated channel for a Shakespeare module, as in the example discussed above), or even to the wider network of YouTube users. In addition to the various functions that it has for learners – as an archive of past performance, as a platform for vernacular expression, as a space to stake a claim in the kind of Shakespeare that they learn – YouTube Shakespeare can also become a space where scholars share their work, integrate teaching and research activities and promote a sense of Shakespeare as a labile hermeneutic field. For YouTube to work in these ways will require a network of students and scholars to pursue its potentials, and to do so reflectively. It will also require bringing some of the skills of our field, such as a keen sense of critical analysis and deep research, to our media use.

Shakespeare studies moves through certain trends; to the suggestion that 'Shakespeare-in-a-broader-context seems to be where Shakespeare *is* – or where he is going', should be added adaptations across media.[95] As new media platforms variously alter, expand or challenge what constitutes Shakespeare, debates within the field regarding the cultural value attached to Shakespeare and its significance are now especially important. As I have argued throughout this book, the YouTube Shakespeare video can be many things, stretching the already pliable Bard in directions both new and familiar. Ironic and irreverent, parodic and celebratory too, ideologically conservative, yet also challenging, online video provides us with a frequently satisfying contemporary media edification of Shakespeare.

Videos are interpretations of the texts and as demonstrated by earlier chapters, frequently address those aspects of the plays that have previously energized criticism, but do so through new modes and genres. In undertaking close readings of these and other categories of video in Chapter 1, and in focusing in subsequent chapters on thematic concerns – online expression and agency with regard to *Hamlet*, race in *Othello* and *Romeo and Juliet*, gender and sexuality in the *Sonnets* – this book has argued that YouTube videos should be regarded as a form of Shakespeare criticism in, and of, the present. Viewed in such terms, we can begin to place videos in a productive dialogue with debates within the field and to take seriously the implications and politics of online creative expression and response. YouTube offers an expansion of what Shakespeare is understood to encompass. As such, YouTube Shakespeare videos are not parasitical fragments that reduce the plays and poems to remains, but the metadata that make up our newly networked Shakespeare. YouTube constitutes a vital site for the continuation of Shakespeare, in forms both recognizable, and as yet unimaginable.

# NOTES

## Introduction

1 Shakespeare, *Alls Well That End's Well*, ed. G. K. Hunter (London, 1967).

2 See http://www.youtube.com/yt/press/statistics.html (accessed 25 June 2013).

3 Richard Burt characterizes this phenomenon as 'loser criticism' in his Introduction to *Shakespeare after Mass Media* (New York, 2002), 1–32. See also Katherine Rowe, 'Crowd-Sourcing Shakespeare: Screen Work and Screen Play in Second Life', *SSt* 38 (2010): 58–67. The article is also available, with illustrations, at http://www.brynmawr.edu/english/Faculty_and_Staff/rowe/CrowdSourcing.html (accessed 25 June 2013). On the academy's vested interest in Shakespeare's cultural capital, see Terence Hawkes, *Meaning by Shakespeare* (London, 1992), 141–53; and Ivor Kamps, 'Alas, Poor Shakespeare! I Knew Him Well' in *Shakespeare and Appropriation*, ed. Christy Desmet and Robert Sawyer (London, 1999), 15–31.

4 http://www.youtube.com/results?search_query=Shakespeare&oq=Shakespeare&gs_l=youtube.3...136122.138059.0.138420.11.8.0.0.0.0.0.0...0.0...1ac.1.11.youtube (accessed 25 June 2013).

5 Luke McKernan's Bardbox, which closed in June 2013, remains online as a descriptive archive of 'the best examples' of Shakespeare online videos. http://bardbox.wordpress.com/ (accessed 25 June 2013). There have been several forays into YouTube Shakespeare. See: Christy Desmet, 'Paying Attention in Shakespeare Parody: From Tom Stoppard to YouTube', *SS* 61 (2008): 227–38; Lauren Shohet, 'YouTube, Use, and the Idea of the Archive', *SSt* 38 (2010): 68–76; Ayanna Thompson,

'Unmooring the Moor: Researching and Teaching on YouTube', *SQ* 61.3 (2010): 337–56, updated in the same author's *Passing Strange: Shakespeare, Race and Contemporary America* (Oxford, 2011), 145–67; and Barbara Hodgdon, '(You)Tube Travel: The 9:59 to Dover Beach, Stopping at Fair Verona and Elsinore', *Shakespeare Bulletin* 28.3 (2010): 313–30.

6 http://www.youtube.com/results?search_type=videos&search_query=shakespeare&search_sort=video_view_count (accessed 25 June 2013).

7 The Shakespeare episode was broadcast on 11 March 1999. The video is no longer available on YouTube.

8 http://www.youtube.com/watch?v=Mp_v_dP8s–8 (accessed 25 June 2013).

9 http://www.youtube.com/user/CSshakespeare?feature=watch (accessed 25 June 2013).

10 See: Jean Burgess and Joshua Green, *YouTube* (Cambridge, 2009); Pelle Snickars and Patrick Vonderau, eds, *The YouTube Reader* (Stockholm, 2009); Alexandra Juhasz, *Learning from YouTube*, http://vectors.usc.edu/projects/learningfromyoutube/# (accessed 25 June 2013); and Geert Lovink and Sabine Niederer, eds, *Video Vortex Reader: Responses to YouTube* (Amsterdam, 2008). Available at http://networkcultures.org/wpmu/portal/publications/inc-readers/videovortex/ (accessed 25 June 2013).

11 Kylie Jarrett, 'Beyond Broadcast Yourself™: The Future of You Tube', *Media International Australia* 126 (2008): 132–44.

12 Michael Strangelove, *Watching YouTube: Extraordinary Videos by Ordinary People* (Toronto, 2010); Anandan Kavoori, *Reading YouTube: The Critical Viewers Guide* (New York, 2011).

13 On Shakespeare's exemplarity, see John J. Joughin, 'Shakespeare's Genius: *Hamlet*, Adaptation and the Work of Following', in *The New Aestheticism*, ed. John J. Joughin and Simon Malpas (Manchester, 2003), 131–50.

14 Burt, *Shakespeare after Mass Media*, 1–32; and the same author's 'Shakespeare, More or Less? From Shakespeareccentricity to Shakespearecentricity and Back' in

*Shakespeares after Shakespeare: An Encylopedia of the Bard in Mass Media and Popular Culture*, ed. Richard Burt, 2 vols (Wesport, CT, 2007), 1–9. Burt notes generic distinctions between mass culture (imposed on 'the people') and popular culture (for and by 'the people') and suggests that they are far from discrete. Stuart Hall similarly observes the intersection of mass and popular culture in 'What is this "black" in Black Popular Culture' in *Stuart Hall: Critical Dialogues in Cultural Studies*, ed. David Morley and Kuan-Hsing Chen (New York, 1996), 465–75. The phrase 'eternal sameness' is from Theodor W. Adorno, *The Culture Industry: Selected Essays on Mass Culture* (London, 2001), 100. For an application of Adorno to Shakespeare, see Michael D. Bristol, *Big-Time Shakespeare* (London, 1996), 88–117.

15 Douglas Lanier, *Shakespeare and Modern Popular Culture* (Oxford, 2002); Robert Shaugnessy, ed., *The Cambridge Companion to Shakespeare and Popular Culture* (Cambridge, 2007).

16 The phrase is Stanley Cavell's, quoted in Joughin, 132. For a lively approach to the plays using contemporary culture, see Fran Teague, 'Using Shakespeare with Memes, Remixes and Fanfic', *SS* 64 (2011): 74–82. The categories employed to analyse Shakespeare's afterlives have been debated and compared extensively. See: Daniel Fischlin and Mark Fortier's introduction to *Adaptations of Shakespeare* (London, 2000), 1–24; Christy Desmet, Introduction in *Shakespeare and Appropriation*, 1–12; Julie Sanders, *Adpatation and Appropriation* (London, 2006); Margaret Kidnie, *Shakespeare and the Problem of Adaptation* (London, 2009); Marianne Novy, *Transforming Shakespeare: Contemporary Women's Re-Visions in Literature and Performance* (New York, 1999); and Christy Ruby Cohn, *Modern Shakespeare Offshoots* (Princeton, NJ, 1976).

17 Desmet, *Shakespeare and Appropriation*, 3.

18 Kidnie, 9.

19 Kiernan Ryan, *Shakespeare*, 3rd edn (Basingstoke, 2002), 175.

20 The reference here is to Jacques Derrida, *Specters of Marx*, trans. Peggy Kamuf (London, 1994), 18. See also: Joughin,

142–4; Sanders, 158–60; and Maurizio Calbi's study, *Spectral Shakespeares: Media Adaptations in the Twenty-First Century* (Basingstoke, 2013).

21 Fischlin and Fortier, 3.

22 Stig Hjarvard, *The Mediatization of Culture and Society* (New York, 2013), 27.

23 See Janet Wasko and Mary Erickson, 'The Political Economy of YouTube', in *The YouTube Reader*, 372–86.

24 Martin Lister et al., *New Media: A Critical Introduction* (London, 2009), 13.

25 Jay D. Bolter and Richard Grusin, *Remediation: Understanding New Media* (Cambridge, MA, 2000); Richard Grusin, 'YouTube at the End of New Media', in *The YouTube Reader*, 60–7; Geoffrey Whintrop Young, 'Hardware/Software/Wetware', in *Critical Terms for Media Studies*, ed. W. J. T. Mitchell and Mark B. Hansen (Chicago, 2010), 194. Kathernine N. Hayles favours the term 'intermediation' as a way of capturing 'interactions between systems of representations' from language and code and to analogue and digital as well as conveying those 'mediating interfaces connecting humans with intelligent machines' (*My Mother was a Computer: Digital Subjects and Literary Texts* (Chicago, 2010), 33).

26 Bolter and Grusin, 15.

27 Scott Lash and Celia Lurry, *Global Culture Industry: The Mediation of Things* (Cambridge, 2007), quoted in Sarah Kember and Joanna Zylinska, *Life after New Media: Mediation as Vital Process* (Cambridge, MA, 2012), 22.

28 Geert Lovink, *Networks Without a Cause* (London, 2011), 145.

29 Grusin, 65.

30 Mark B. Hansen, 'New Media', in *Critical Terms for Media Studies*, 184.

31 Henry Jenkins, *Convergence Culture* (New York, 2006), 1–24; Henry Jenkins, Sam Ford and Joshua Green, *Spreadable Media: Creating Value and Meaning in a Networked Culture* (New York, 2013).

32 Jenkins, *Convergence Culture*, 2.

33 Ibid., 3.

34 Michael Wesch, 'An Anthropological Introduction to YouTube', http://www.youtube.com/watch?v=TPAO-lZ4_ hU&feature=player_embedded (accessed 25 June 2013).

35 Kember and Zylinska, xiv, 3.

36 Ibid., 13–14. For supporting arguments about technogenesis, see Whintrop Young, 195–6; and Katherine N. Hayles, *How We Think: Digital Media and Contemporary Technogenesis* (Chicago, 2012), 1–21.

37 Hansen, 180.

38 Hawkes, *Meaning by Shakespeare*, 3.

39 Hansen, 181.

40 Kember and Zylinska, 1–28.

41 Mark B. Hansen, Introduction to Bernard Stiegler, 'Memory', in *Critical Terms for Media Studies*, 64.

42 Frank Kessler and Mirko Tobias Schafer, 'Navigating YouTube: Constituting a Hybrid Information Management System', in *The YouTube Reader*, 275–91.

43 Hansen, 'New Media', 173.

44 Ibid., 173.

45 See *Gen V Research Men 18–34 The On-Demand Video Consumer* (May 2012), available as a PDF at http://www. youtube.com/yt/advertise/research.html (accessed 25 June 2013).

46 Jonathan Alexander and Jacqueline Rhodes, 'Technologies of the Self in the Aftermath: Affect, Subjectivity, and Composition', *Rhetoric Review* 29.2 (2010): 145–64.

47 Consider China's TUDOU or Russia's RuTube.

48 Burgess and Green, 106. Comparable sites include DailyMotion and Vevo.

49 For instance, YouTube is the most shared content on Facebook. See *Gen V Research Men 18–34*.

50 See Robert Gehl, 'YouTube as Archive: Who will Curate this Digital Wunderkammer?', *International Journal of Cultural Studies* 12.1 (2009): 43–59.

51  John Hartley, 'Uses of You Tube: Digital Literacy and the
    Growth of Knowledge', in Burgess and Green, *YouTube*, 133.
    On the pleasures of storytelling in cyberspace, see Janet H.
    Murray's inventive study, *Hamlet on the Holodeck: The Future
    of Narrative in Cyberspace* (Cambridge, MA, 1997).

52  See Francesco Casetti, 'Back to the Motherland: the Film
    Theatre in the Postmedia Age', *Screen* 52.1 (2011): 1–12.

53  Burgess and Green, 60; Patricia G. Lange, 'Videos of Affinity',
    in *The YouTube Reader*, 70–88.

54  Michael Dobson, *Shakespeare and Amateur Performance: A
    Cultural History* (Cambridge, 2011).

55  See Craig Dionne, 'The Shatnerification of Shakespeare: *Star
    Trek* and the Commonplace Tradition', in *Shakespeare After
    Mass Media*, 173–91.

56  Douglas Bruster, *Quoting Shakespeare: Form and Culture in
    Early Modern Drama* (Lincoln, 2000), 23; see also Sanders,
    4–5.

57  Sinckars and Vonderau, 11.

58  See Wasko and Erickson, 372–86.

59  On Shakespeare's capital, see Kate Rumbold, 'Brand
    Shakespeare?', *SS* 64 (2011): 25–37.

60  To be fair to Jenkins, however, his broadly optimistic account
    of individual agency within mass media is punctuated by the
    acknowledgement that 'the constructs of capitalism will greatly
    shape the creation and circulation of most media texts for the
    foreseeable future and that most people do not (and cannot)
    opt out of commercial culture' (*Spreadable Media*, xii).

61  See Andrew Keen, *The Cult of the Amateur* (New York,
    2008); and Sharon O'Dair, '"Pretty Much How the Internet
    Works"; Or, Aiding and Abetting the Deprofessionalization of
    Shakespeare Studies', *SS* 64 (2011): 83–96.

62  The phrase 'highlighting' is from Kavoori, 12. On print and
    digital, see Hayles, *How We Think*, 1–21. On the use of the
    clip before the advent of YouTube, see Laurie Osborne, 'Clip
    Art: Theorizing the Shakespeare Film Clip', *SQ* 53:2 (2002):
    227–40.

63  Douglas Lanier, 'Post-Textual Shakespeare', *SS* 64 (2011): 146.

**64** Lanier, 161–2.

**65** Lovink, 50–62. The YouTube comment feature has a limit 500 words.

**66** Desmet, 237.

**67** Barbara Hodgdon, 'The Last Shakespeare Picture Show of Going to the Barricades', in *Teaching Shakespeare*, ed. Peter Skrebels and Sieta van de Hoeven (Kent Town, 2002), 105–20.

**68** Courtney Lehmann and Lisa Starks, eds, *Spectacular Shakespeare: Critical Theory and Popular Cinema* (Madison, NJ, 2002), 9.

**69** Anna Maria Cimitile and Katherine Rowe, 'Introduction: Overlapping Mediascapes in the Mind', Shakespeare in the Media: Old and New, special issue, *Anglistica* 15:2 (2011): ii. Available at http://www.anglistica.unior.it/content/shakespeare-media-old-and-new (accessed 25 June 2013).

**70** See Richard A. Lanham, *The Economics of Attention: Style and Substance in the Age of Information* (Chicago, 2007), 79–129.

**71** Douglas Lanier applies these terms in his essay, 'Recent Shakespeare Adaptation and the Mutations of Cultural Capital', *SSt* 38 (2010): 104–13.

**72** The key texts here are: Hugh Grady, *Shakespeare's Universal Wolf: Studies in Early Modern Reification* (Oxford, 1996); Terence Hawkes, *Shakespeare in the Present* (London, 2002); and Ewan Fernie, 'Shakespeare and the Prospect of Presentism', *SS* 58 (2005): 69–184. The reference to the time as out of joint is of course to Derrida, via *Hamlet*, on the masterpiece as 'the thing that haunts' (Derrida, *Specters of Marx*, 18). Fernie quotes the passage in his essay.

**73** Hawkes, 22.

**74** Jacques Derrida, *Of Grammatology*, trans. Gayatri Chakravorty Spivak (Baltimore, 1976), 70.

**75** Fernie, 179.

**76** On the relation between (new) historicism and presentism, see Grady, 1–25; and more recently, Lucy Munro, 'Shakespeare and the Uses of the Past: Critical Approaches and Current Debates', *Shakespeare* 7:1 (2011): 102–25. On presentism's conceptual limitations, see Adrian Streete, 'The Politics of

Ethical Presentism: Appropriation, Spirituality and the Case of *Antony and Cleopatra*', *Textual Practice* 22.3 (2008): 405–31.

77 Cary DiPietro and Hugh Grady, 'Presentism, Anachronism and the Case of *Titus Andronicus*', *Shakespeare* 8:1 (2012): 49. For a defence of historical inquiry, see Linda Charnes, 'Anticipating Nostalgia: Finding Temporal Logic in a Textual Anomaly', *Textual Cultures* 4:1 (2009): 72–83.

78 Fernie, 179; emphasis added.

79 Jan Kott, *Shakespeare Our Contemporary*, trans. Boleslaw Taborski (London, 1965).

80 Fernie, 183.

81 Cary DiPietro, 'Sex, Lies and Videotape: Representing the Past in *Shakespeare in Love*, Mapping a Future for Presentism', *Shakespeare* 3:1 (2007): 56.

82 On this call for a new aesthetic, see DiPietro, 19; and also Joughin and Malpas, 1–19.

83 Katherine Rowe, 'Shakespeare and Media History', in *New Cambridge Companion to Shakespeare*, ed. Margreta de Grazia and Stanley Wells (Cambridge, 2010), 306.

84 http://www.youtube.com/t/terms (accessed 25 June 2013).

85 The discussion is informed here by the Association of Internet Researchers' *Ethical Decision-Making and Internet Research: Recommendations from the AoIR Ethics Working Committee (Version 2.0)*, http://aoir.org/documents/ethics-guide/ (accessed 25 June 2013).

86 Ibid., 6; Lange, 171.

87 As in Thompson, *Passing Strange*, 148–50.

88 A standardized email was sent, via my YouTube channel, to the username attached to the video. The email requested permission to discuss the video as part of an academic monograph. It introduced the author (a link to my staff profile on the university homepage was included in order to verify the project) and the nature of the study. Correspondence entered into was conducted solely through the YouTube account and is only stored there (i.e., data has not been stored externally or downloaded). In those cases where no response was received, I have omitted the username and video URL. Similarly, in the

case of videos that feature minors (i.e., under 18 years of age), usernames and video URLs have been omitted.

89 Hansen, 178.

# Chapter one

1 Geert Lovink, *Networks Without a Cause* (London, 2011), 136.

2 Ken Hillis, Michael Petit and Kylie Jarrett, *Google and the Culture of Search* (London, 2013), 54.

3 Viewer post on The Geeky Blonde's *Twelfth Night*, http://www.youtube.com/watch?v=BrGvvXRRb08 (accessed 25 June 2013).

4 http://www.youtube.com/t/terms (accessed 25 June 2013). Two key requirements are that users do not post inappropriate material and do not infringe copyright.

5 Hillis, Petit and Jarrett, 53–76; and Tarleton Gillespie, 'The Relevance of Algorithms', http://culturedigitally.org/2012/11/the-relevance-of-algorithms/ (accessed 25 June 2013).

6 See Renjie Zhou, Samamon Khemmarat and Lixin Gao, 'The Impact of YouTube Recommendation System on Video Views', *Proceedings of the 10th ACM SIGCOMM Conference on Internet Measurement* (Melbourne, 2010), 404–10.

7 Frank Kessler and Mirko Tobias Schafer, 'Navigating YouTube: Constituting a Hybrid Information Management System', in *The YouTube Reader*, ed. Pelle Snickars and Patrick Vonderau (Stockholm, 2009), 275–91.

8 Key texts here include: Margaret Kidnie, *Shakespeare and the Problem of Adaptation* (London, 2009); Douglas Lanier, *Shakespeare and Modern Popular Culture* (Oxford, 2002); and Pascale Aebischer and Nigel Wheale, 'Introduction', in *Remaking Shakespeare: Performance Across Media, Genres and Cultures*, ed. Pascale Aebischer, Edward J. Esche and Nigel Wheale (Basingstoke, 2003), 1–17.

9 Richard Burt, 'Shakespeare, More or Less? From Shakespeareccentricity to Shakespearecentricity and Back', in

*Shakespeares after Shakespeare: An Encylopedia of the Bard in Mass Media and Popular Culture*, ed. Richard Burt, 2 vols (Wesport, CT, 2007), 5.

10  Lovink, 145.

11  http://www.youtube.com/results?search_query=Shakespeare %2C+%22As+You+Like+It%22&oq=Shakespeare%2C+%2 2As+You+Like+It%22&gs_l=youtube.3..0l5j0i5.810.3351.0 .3725.4.4.0.0.0.0.160.475.1j3.4.0...0.0...1ac.1.11.youtube. qwotkyD5u5M (accessed 14 May 2013).

12  Jay D. Bolter and Richard Grusin, *Remediation: Understanding New Media* (Cambridge, MA, 2000), 45.

13  Jean Burgess and Joshua Green, *YouTube* (Cambridge, 2009), 38–57. Various estimates have been made regarding the ratio of commercial to user-generated content. Burgess and Green note that 42 per cent of the sampled videos come from traditional media (45–6). However, this picture is complicated by findings that indicate the popularity of traditional media within the Most Viewed category, where content from traditional and broadcast media accounts for 66 per cent, and the Most Favourited category, where it accounts for 47 per cent, compared with 43 per cent for use-generated content. These figures suggest that for a significant number of users, YouTube is a distribution channel and a means to share favourite clips from TV and film. Other studies support Burgess and Green's findings. According to Gijs Kruitbosch and Frank Nack, user-generated content tends to feature less extensively in the most viewed videos: see their article, 'Broadcast Yourself on YouTube – Really?', in *Proceedings of the 3rd ACM International Workshop on Human-Centered Computing*, Vancouver, 2008. ACM (New York), 7–10. See also: Yuan Ding et al., 'Broadcast Yourself: Understanding YouTube Uploaders', *Proceedings of the 2011 ACM SIGCOMM Conference on Internet Measurement Conference* (Berlin, 2011), 361–70, http://doi. acm.org/10.1145/1462027.1462029 (accessed 25 June 2013).

14  Geoffrey V. Carter and Sarah J. Arroyo, 'Video and Participatory Cultures: Writing, Rhetoric, Performance, and the Tube', *Enculturation* 8 (2010): 1, http://enculturation.gmu. edu/8 (accessed 25 June 2013).

15 Burgess and Green, 57. On the continuum between producer and user, see Alex Bruns, *Blogs, Wikipedia, Second Life, and Beyond: From Production to Produsage* (New York, 2008).

16 On YouTube and copyright arrangements, see Chapter 2, 115–17.

17 Zhou, Khemmarat and Gao, 405.

18 Anandan Kavoori, *Reading YouTube* (New York, 2011), 6.

19 Richard Grusin, 'YouTube at the End of New Media', in *The YouTube Reader*, 60–7; Bolter and Grusin, 46.

20 Bolter and Grusin, 33.

21 Lev Manovich, *The Language of New Media* (Cambridge, MA, 2001), 128. Manovich remains instructive, but for a critique, see Alexander Galloway, *The Interface Effect* (Cambridge, 2012), 1–10.

22 Ibid., 128–29; Kruitbosh and Nack, 7.

23 Robert Gehl, 'YouTube as Archive: Who will Curate this Digital Wunderkammer?', *International Journal of Cultural Studies* 12.1 (2009): 54–5.

24 Ibid., 48.

25 Manovich, 77.

26 Ibid., 78.

27 Kavoori, 8.

28 Grusin, 60.

29 Lovink, 136.

30 The average viewing session of 28 minutes (based on 2007 data) is given in Meeyoung Cha et al., 'I Tube, You Tube, Everybody Tubes: Analyzing the World's Largest User Generated Content Video System', *Proceedings of the 7th ACM SIGCOMM Conference on Internet Measurement* (2007), 1–14. Lovink (136) cites a 15 minutes average, based on data for 2010.

31 Richard A. Lanham, *The Economics of Attention: Style and Substance in the Age of Information* (Chicago, 2007), 46.

32 Kavoori, 7.

33 Alexandra Juhasz, *Learning from YouTube* (Cambridge, MA, 2011), http://vectors.usc.edu/projects/learningfromyoutube/texteo.php?composite=85 (accessed 25 June 2013).

**34** Lovink, 137. See also Thomas Elsaesser, 'Tales of Epiphany and Entropy: Around the World in Eighty Clicks', in *The YouTube Reader*, 166–86.

**35** Lovink, 136.

**36** Burgess and Green, 70–2.

**37** Elsaesser, 186.

**38** Chris Anderson, 'The Long Tail', *Wired* 12.10 (2004), http://www.wired.com/wired/archive/12.10/tail. html?pg=2&topic=tail&topic_set= (accessed 25 June 2013).

**39** Juhasz, http://vectors.usc.edu/projects/learningfromyoutube/ texteo.php?composite=85 (accessed 25 June 2013).

**40** It is of course possible to open up YouTube in more than one window. By minimizing the windows on a desktop, a simultaneous comparison of two videos becomes possible. However, that these steps are necessary in the first instance illustrates the limitations of the current interface.

**41** Zhou, Khemmarat and Gao, 405.

**42** Galloway, 86.

**43** http://www.youtube.com/watch?v=BPc2fcxOUxE (accessed 25 June 2013).

**44** http://www.youtube.com/watch?v=ziXqEX6AwKA (accessed 25 June 2013).

**45** http://www.youtube.com/watch?v=9eYoorZaP-c (accessed 25 June 2013).

**46** *Google+: Tom*, uploaded 30 March 2012; 686,221 views, http://www.youtube.com/watch?v=BQDYt61yHdg (accessed 25 June 2013). In Google's vision of human memory, however, Jaques' entropic conclusion, on 'second childishness and mere oblivion' (II.7.166), is omitted.

**47** A search under 'Seven Ages of Man' returns 1,890 results; a search under 'All the World's a Stage' generates 1,460 results.

**48** Garber, *Shakespeare and Modern Culture*, xxii. See also *Shakespeare after all* (New York, 2004), 29–41 and *Shakespeare's Ghost Writers: Literature as Uncanny Causality*, Routledge Classics (London, 2010).

49 Douglas Lanier, 'Film Spin-offs and Citations', in *Shakespeares After Shakespeares: an Encyclopedia of the Bard in Mass Media and Popular Culture*, 2 vols, ed. Richard Burt (Westport, CT, 2006), 136.

50 Richard Burt, 'Shakespeare, More or Less? From Shakespeareccentricity to Shakespearecentricity and Back', 6.

51 As searched 29 June 2013, using double quotation marks for the lines in order to limit stop-words being included in results.

52 http://www.youtube.com/watch?v=y2a5Gar2uLE (accessed 25 June 2013). On Shakespeare and the commonplace tradition, see Douglas Bruster, *Quoting Shakespeare: Form and Culture in Early Modern Drama* (Lincoln, 2000), 13–51.

53 Garber, *Shakespeare After All*, 39.

54 The URL for this video has been omitted because the performers were minors at the time of its production.

55 For example, see *French Old People Fighting* (uploaded 27 February 2011; 36,942 views), http://www.youtube.com/watch?v=MrL4FC-JbCw (accessed 25 June 2013).

56 The practice of theatre companies uploading performance clips and promotional trailers raises a specific point about YouTube and labour. Do actors get paid for their work as it is remediated on YouTube? If clips are under a certain length (3 minutes), the actor may not get any additional payment. On the suggestion that YouTube's archive involves a new exchange value, see Gehl, 45–8. On the demographic of the on-demand video, see YouTube's own research available at http://www.youtube.com/yt/advertise/research.html.

57 See Kate Rumbold, 'From "Access" to "Creativity": Shakespeare Institutions, New Media, and the Language of Cultural Value', *SQ* 63.1 (2010): 313–36.

58 Ayanna Thompson, *Passing Strange: Shakespeare, Race and Contemporary America* (Oxford, 2011), 146.

59 Henry Jenkins, *Convergence Culture: Where Old and New Media Collide* (New York, 2006), 2.

60 Jenkins, *Convergence,* 290; Henry Jenkins, *Textual Poachers: Television Fans and Participatory Culture* (London, 1992); and, more recently, Henry Jenkins, Sam Ford and Joshua

Green, *Spreadable Media: Creating Value and Meaning in a Networked Culture* (New York, 2013).

61  Michael Dobson, *Shakespeare and Amateur Performance: A Cultural History* (Cambridge, 2011).

62  Jenkins, *Convergence*, 274.

63  Burgess and Green, 25; Jean Burgess, '"All your Chocolate Rain are belong to us?": Viral Video, YouTube and the Dynamics of Participatory Culture', in *Video Vortex Reader: Responses to YouTube*, ed. Geert Lovink and Sabine Niederer (Amsterdam, 2008), 101–9, http://networkcultures.org/wpmu/portal/publications/inc-readers/videovortex/ (accessed 25 June 2013).

64  John Hartley, 'Uses of You Tube: Digital Literacy and the Growth of Knowledge', in Burgess and Green, *YouTube*, 133.

65  For example, *Charlie Bit my Finger - Again* (uploaded 22 May 2007; 527,214,587 views), http://www.youtube.com/watch?v=_OBlgSz8sSM (accessed 25 June 2013). On this iconic video, see Michael Strangelove, *Watching YouTube: Extraordinary Videos by Ordinary People* (Toronto, 2010), 55–60; and Kavoori, 51–4.

66  Jose van Dijck, '"You" as in YouTube: Defining User Agency in Social Media', in *Managing Media Economy, Media Content and Technology in the Age of Digital Convergence*, ed. Zvezdan Vukanovic and Paulo Faustino (Lisbon, 2011), 303.

67  Burgess and Green, 57.

68  Jenkins, Ford and Green, 154.

69  Ibid., 155.

70  See 'Rights you licence' section of YouTube's Terms, http://www.youtube.com/t/terms (accessed 25 June 2013).

71  Research suggests 4 in every 10 videos on YouTube carry ads, http://www.marketingcharts.com/direct/more-youtube-videos-carry-ads–14907/ (accessed 25 June 2013).

72  http://www.youtube.com/watch?v=YZMQomUjQVs (accessed 25 June 2013). The film is made by Shelton Films.

73  On Shakespeare films and 'Bardic commodification', see Carolyn Jess-Cooke, 'Screening the McShakespeare in

Post-Millenial Shakespeare Cinema', in *Screening Shakespeare in the Twenty-First Century*, ed. Mark Thornton Burnett and Ramona Wray (Edinburgh, 2006), 163–84.

74 My thinking here is partly in response to concerns raised in Christy Desmet's paper, 'The Economics of (In)Attention in YouTube Shakespeare', for the seminar on 'Social Media Shakespeare', which Maurizio Calbi and I convened at the Shakespeare Association of America conference (Toronto, April 2013). Warm thanks to Christy for allowing me to cite it here.

75 http://www.youtube.com/channel/HCUiUSlb0hB9M (accessed 25 June 2013).

76 http://www.fastcompany.com/1715183/how-youtubes-global-platform-redefining-entertainment-business (accessed 25 June 2013).

77 See: Juhasz; Siva Vaidhyanathan, *The Googlization of Everything* (Berkeley, 2011); Frederic Jameson, 'Postmodernism, or the Cultural Logic of Late Capitalism', *New Left Review* I:146 (1984): 53–92.

78 Burgess and Green, 104–5; Janet Wasko and Mary Erickson ('The Political Economy of YouTube', in *The YouTube Reader*, 372–86) offer a bleaker assessment of YouTube's future, in which parent company Google increasingly supports corporate partners to the detriment of non-commercial users. In May 2013, YouTube announced plans to offer a premium subscription service. See Matthew Garrahan and Andrew Edgecliffe, 'Google set to unveil subscriptions for specialist YouTube videos', *Financial Times*, 5 May 2013, http://www.ft.com/cms/s/0/c27c9856-b3fd–11e2–b5a5–00144feabdc0.html#axzz2VYB2effp (accessed 25 June 2013).

79 See Kavoori, 29–49; Burgess, 101–9.

80 Burgess, 101; and Limor Shifman, 'Anatomy of a YouTube Meme', *New Media Society*,14:2 (2011): 187–203.

81 Jenkins, Ford and Green, 18–19. The availability of meme generator sites also lowers the entry level for participation. See http://meemsy.com/ and http://weknowmemes.com/ (accessed 25 June 2013).

82  http://www.youtube.com/watch?v=iCkYw3cRwLo (accessed 25 June 2013).

83  Emily Dugan and Louise Fitzgerald, 'A Brief History of the *Harlem Shake*', *The Independent*, 3 March 2013, http://www.independent.co.uk/arts-entertainment/theatre-dance/news/a-brief-history-of-the-harlem-shake–8518071.html (accessed 25 June 2013). On statistics for the *Harlem Shake* trend, see http://youtube-trends.blogspot.ie/search/label/Viral (accessed 25 June 2013).

84  When the videos that simply mention Shakespeare in their title are excluded, there are 54 videos that fuse Shakespeare with the *Harlem Shake* meme. The sample is taken from 14 February 2013 (the date when the first Harlem Shakespeare video was posted) until 16 April 2013.

85  http://www.youtube.com/watch?v=ZOdSVbJ_Tug (accessed 14 February 2013).

86  The URL for this and subsequent videos have been omitted so as to protect the identity of the participants who are minors.

87  See the case study in Patricía dias da Silva and José Luís Garcia, 'YouTubers as Satirists', *JeDEM* 4:1 (2012): 89–114.

88  *Downfall*, dir. Oliver Hirschbiegel (Constantin Film, 2004). A *Downfall* meme generator is available online at http://downfall.jfedor.org/create/.

89  http://www.youtube.com/watch?v=sfkDxF2kn1I (accessed 25 June 2013).

90  Shifman, 190. http://www.youtube.com/watch?v=fQ97CZU_7kA (accessed 25 June 2013).

91  da Silva and Garcia, 97.

92  http://www.youtube.com/watch?v=KwdHRbcWpvo (accessed 25 June 2013).

93  http://www.youtube.com/watch?v=8Pkioh8BHY8 (accessed 25 June 2013).

94  http://www.youtube.com/watch?v=Wl5L4oGCYkg (accessed 25 June 2013).

95  http://www.youtube.com/watch?v=10GtBHhG8sc (accessed 25 June 2013).

96  da Silva and Garcia, 106.

97  Quoted in Garber, *Shakespeare and Modern Culture*, 146. This is Adorno's qualification of his earlier observation that 'to write a poem after Auschwitz is barbaric'.

98  http://www.youtube.com/watch?v=10GtBHhG8sc (accessed 25 June 2013).

99  John Drakakis, 'Present Text: Editing *The Merchant of Venice*', in *Presentist Shakespeares*, ed. Hugh Grady and Terence Hawkes (London, 2007), 94.

100  Harold Bloom, *Shakespeare: The Invention of the Human* (London, 1999), 190.

101  Robert Conkie, 'Shakespeare Aftershocks: Shylock', *Shakespeare Bulletin* 27 (2009): 549.

102  Maria Jones, 'The Cultural Logic of "Correcting" *The Merchant of Venice*', in *World-Wide Shakespeares: Local Appropriations in Film and Performance*, ed. Sonia Massai (London, 2005), 123. On performance history, see *The Merchant of Venice*, ed. John Drakakis (London, 2012), 112–59. On the long history of sympathetic portrayals of Shylock, see John Gross, *Shylock: Four Hundred Years in the Life of a Legend* (London, 1992).

103  David Thacker, 'The Director's Cut: Interviews with David Thacker and Darko Tresnjak', in *The Merchant of Venice*, ed. Jonathan Bate and Eric Rasmussen (Basingstoke, 2010), 142.

104  Quoted in Jones, 125.

105  Ibid., 125.

106  Barbara Hodgdon, 'Afterword', in *World-Wide Shakespeares*, 159.

107  James O'Rourke, 'Racism and Homophobia in *The Merchant of Venice*', *ELH* 70 (2003): 376.

108  *Romeo + Juliet*, dir. Baz Luhrmann (Twentieth Century Fox, 1996).

109  http://www.youtube.com/watch?v=AU1zJofOY60 (accessed 25 June 2013). The release of Luhrmann's *Great Gatsby* (Warner Brothers, 2013), with DiCaprio in the title role, has generated new audiences for this video.

110 The track is from the album *Dangerous and Moving* (2005), http://www.tatugirls.com/#!featured (accessed 25 June 2013).

111 Jonathan Gray, *Show Sold Separately: Promos, Spoilers and other Media Paratexts* (New York, 2010), 143–74.

112 Matt Hills, *Fan Cultures* (London, 2002), 3–6.

113 Gray, 154.

114 *Heroes* aired from 2006 to 2010, http://www.imdb.com/title/tt0813715/ (accessed 25 June 2013).

115 Hills, 4.

116 My thinking is influenced here by Douglas Lanier's 'Recent Shakespeare Adaptation and the Mutations of Cultural Capital', *SSt* 38 (2010): 104–13. Lanier uses Deleuze to frame the relation between Shakespeare and recent Shakespeare films.

117 Gray, 159.

118 Uploaded 16 August 2011 by LionsgateFilmsUK, http://www.youtube.com/watch?v=bsYrGIQnmxo (accessed 25 June 2013).

119 Shakespeare, *Coriolanus*, ed. Peter Holland (London, 2013), 139.

120 The title sequence describes the location as 'A Place Calling Itself Rome', a reference to John Osborne's 1973 play based on *Coriolanus* (Holland, 135).

121 As such, the film continues what Douglas Lanier regards as the post-textual strain of Shakespeare movies of the past decade ('Recent Shakespeare Adaptation and the Mutations of Cultural Capital', 108).

122 http://www.youtube.com/watch?v=qBmpR1MSncA (accessed 25 June 2013).

123 http://www.youtube.com/watch?v=rIMNOq2ooaE (accessed 25 June 2013).

124 See Fionnuala O'Neill, 'Review of Shakespeare's *Coriolanus* (adapted for film and directed by Ralph Fiennes)', *Shakespeare* 8.4 (2012): 456–60; and Holland, 133–40.

125 See Coppelia Kahn, *Roman Shakespeare: Warriors, Wounds, and Women* (London, 1997), 144–59; and Janet Adelman, *Suffocating Mothers: Fantasies of Maternal Origin in*

*Shakespeare's Plays,* Hamlet *to* The Tempest (New York, 1992), 130–64.

126 http://www.youtube.com/channel/UC5tqpsbHaiG5YPVElgMby3g (accessed 25 June 2013). The Geeky Blonde also appears on another YouTube channel which features Shakespeare, http://www.youtube.com/user/ExeuntPursuedByABear (accessed 25 June 2013).

127 The productions can be added to the long history of female performances of Shakespeare. See Tony Howard, *Women as Hamlet: Performance and Interpretation in Theatre, Film, and Fiction* (Cambridge, 2007).

128 http://www.youtube.com/watch?v=5qofKucG3oE (accessed 25 June 2013).

129 Consider the use of marionettes in George Bernard Shaw's *Shakes versus Shav* to dramatize creative rivalries between himself and the Bard. See Cary di Pietro, 'George Bernard Shaw and the Politics of Bardoloatry', in *Shakespeare and the Irish Writer*, ed. Janet Clare and Stephen O'Neill (Dublin, 2010), 106–22.

130 Christy Desmet, 'Paying Attention in Shakespeare Parody: From Tom Stoppard to YouTube', *SS* 61 (2008): 227–38.

131 http://www.youtube.com/watch?v=WEV4_7a_p_k (accessed 25 June 2013).

132 http://www.youtube.com/watch?v=1mHQ8te8Rfk (accessed 25 June 2013).

133 On slash, see Chapter 4, 184.

134 http://www.youtube.com/watch?v=B1Hw9SGJg8c (accessed 25 June 2013).

135 http://www.youtube.com/watch?v=BrGvvXRRb08 (accessed 25 June 2013).

136 Simon Dentith, *Parody* (London, 2000), 9.

137 Jameson, 53–92; Linda Hutcheon, *A Poetics of Postmodernism* (London, 1988), 1–21.

138 Jameson, 56, 65.

139 Ibid., 60.

140 Linda Hutcheon, *A Theory of Parody* (London, 1985), 6.

141  Ibid., 60.

142  Dentith, 162.

143  See Valerie Traub, *Desire and Anxiety: Circulations of Sexuality in Shakespearean Drama* (London, 1992), 117–44.

144  http://www.youtube.com/watch?v=4DAKoc9BGzo (accessed 25 June 2013).

145  See R. W. Maslen, *Shakespeare and Comedy* (London, 2006).

146  Post on *Macbeth* performance, http://www.youtube.com/watch?v=5qofKucG3oE (accessed 25 June 2013).

147  Post on *Twelfth Night*, http://www.youtube.com/watch?v=BrGvvXRRb08 (accessed 25 June 2013).

148  Stephen Purcell, *Popular Shakespeare: Simulation and Subversion on the Modern Stage* (Basingstoke, 2009), 96.

149  Ibid., 96.

150  http://www.youtube.com/watch?v=dJwU-BhbBUY (accessed 25 June 2013).

151  See Courtney Lehmann, *Shakespeare Remains: Theatre to Film, Early Modern to Postmodern* (Ithaca, 2002); Maurizio Calbi, 'Shakespeare in the Extreme: Addiction, Ghosts and (Re)Mediation in Alexander Fodor's *Hamlet*', *Literature Film Quarterly* 39.2 (2011): 85–98.

152  Lanier, *Shakespeare and Modern Popular Culture*, 115. As Lanier notes, *Shakespeare in Love*, dir. John Madden (Miramax, 1998) exemplifies this pop culture response to authorship (124).

153  http://www.youtube.com/watch?v=lwfCIn66E–8 (accessed 25 June 2013).

154  http://www.youtube.com/user/MrShakespeareReads (accessed 25 June 2013).

155  See Lanier, *Shakespeare and Modern Popular Culture*, 132–41.

156  See Diana E. Henderson, 'Shakespeare: The Theme Park', in *Shakespeare after Mass Media*, ed. Richard Burt (New York, 2002), 107–26.

157  http://www.youtube.com/user/WannabeComedian3721?feature=watch (accessed 25 June 2013). The doll is from the Little Thinkers series; see http://www.philosophersguild.com/Dolls/.

158 http://www.youtube.com/watch?v=zKViLn--Zxs (accessed 25 June 2013).

159 Graham Holderness, '"Author! Author!": Shakespeare and Biography', *Shakespeare* 5:1 (2013): 122–31.

160 http://www.youtube.com/watch?v=FzRWckuHWmY (accessed 25 June 2013).

161 Garber, *Shakespeare's Ghost Writers*, 70.

162 Burgess and Green, 83.

163 See Craig Dionne and Parmita Kapadia, eds, *Native Shakespeares: Indigenous Appropriations on a Global Stage* (Aldershot, 2008).

164 Sonia Massai, 'Defining Local Shakespeares', in *World-Wide Shakespeares*, 3–11.

165 Massai, 4; Houlahan, 'Hekepia? The *Mana* of the Maori *Merchant*', in *World-Wide Shakespeares*, 141.

166 Alexander Huang, *Chinese Shakespeares: Two Centuries of Cultural Exchange* (New York, 2009), 31.

167 Mark Thornton Burnett, *Shakespeare and World Cinema* (Cambridge, 2012).

168 An MIT project, the database is available on open access. It provides a systematic form of annotation that YouTube videos lack. See Alexander Huang, 'Global Shakespeare 2.0 and the Task of the Performance Archive', *SS* 64 (2011): 38–51.

169 Consider Google President Eric Schmidt's claim that 'YouTube is emerging as the first global TV station … The living room for the world.' Quoted in http://www.fastcompany.com/1715183/how-youtubes-global-platform-redefining-entertainment-business (accessed 25 June 2013).

170 Toby Miller, 'Cybertarians of the World Unite: You Have Nothing to Lose but Your Tubes', in *The YouTube Reader*, 427.

171 http://www.youtube.com/yt/press/statistics.html (accessed 25 June 2013). Other samples of geographic distribution support YouTube's figures. Ding et al. (363–4) found that the US accounts for 31.1 per cent of the total YouTube uploaders, with Britain, Germany, France, Spain, Canada, Mexico,

Italy and the Netherlands accounting for 43.7 per cent. The countries accounting for the remaining 25.2 per cent of uploaders are not specified in the study.

172 On national IP addresses as 'digital enclosures', see Lovink, 20–2.

173 Burgess and Green, 86.

174 Ibid., 85.

175 Gillespie, 25.

176 Hillis, Petit and Jarrett, 54.

177 Ibid., 67.

178 Miller, 437.

179 See http://bufvc.ac.uk/shakespeare/ (accessed 25 June 2013).

180 Gillespie, 12.

181 Burnett, 13.

182 See the playlist Shakespeare and World Cinema on my YouTube channel, http://www.youtube.com/user/ Shakespeareonutube?feature=guide (accessed 25 June 2013). Of the 17 titles unavailable on YouTube, several are available on comparable video-sharing platforms like Dailymotion.

183 Prior to my active searching of these titles, they did not appear within results for a generic search of a play.

184 *Gedebe*, dir. Nam Ron (2002), http://www.youtube.com/ watch?v=Y8PxFNmbPJ8 (accessed 25 June 2013).

185 *Amar te Duele/Love Hurts*, dir. Fernando Sariñana (Altavista Films, 2002). As far as I can determine, there are only 2 fan-made videos of *Amar te Duele* on YouTube.

186 Burnett, 233–5.

187 Ibid., 234.

188 *Chicken Rice War*, dir. Chee Kong Cheah (Mediacorp Raintree, 2000). See Huang, *Chinese Shakespeares*, 12; Burnett, 135–9.

189 *Hamlet*, dir. Michael Almereyda (Miramax, 2000). See Richard Burt, 'Shakespeare and Asia in PostDiasporic Cinemas', in *Shakespeare: The Movie II*, ed. Richard Burt and Lynda E. Boose (London, 2003), 265–303. On the Irish subtexts, see Mark Thornton Burnett, 'Writing Shakespeare in the Global Economy', *SS* 58 (2005): 185–98.

190  *Prince of the Himalayas*, dir. Sherwood Hu (Shanghai Film Studios, 2006).

191  *The Banquet*, dir. Xiaogong Feng (Media Asia Films, 2006). Huang, *Chinese Shakespeares*, 230. See also Richard Burt, 'Mobilizing Foreign Shakespeares in Media', in *Shakespeare in Hollywood, Asia and Cyberspace*, ed. Alexander C. Huang and Charles S. Ross (West Lafayette, 2009), 231–8.

192  Huang, 'Global Shakespeare 2.0 and the Task of the Performance Archive', 51.

193  http://www.youtube.com/watch?v=4651gGaXTpE.

194  The film is directed by Ing K and Manit Sriwanichpoom. See http://www.shakespearemustdie.com/ (accessed 25 June 2013).

195  http://asiancorrespondent.com/79666/thai-macbeth-movie-banned/ (accessed 25 June 2013).

196  http://www.youtube.com/watch?v=vd6JEk6Imco (accessed 25 June 2013).

197  Manovich, 217.

# Chapter two

1  Shakespeare, *Hamlet*, ed. Ann Thompson and Neil Taylor (London, 2006).

2  Xelanderthomas, http://www.youtube.com/watch?v=LzHjIj3fpR8 (accessed 25 June 2013).

3  Joshje777, http://www.youtube.com/watch?v=ijrJ07BMubY (accessed 25 June 2013).

4  Kenneth Dinkins, http://www.youtube.com/watch?v=iBvVr8pWN28 (accessed 25 June 2013).

5  Heiner Müller, 'Hamletmachine', in *Adaptations of Shakespeare,* ed. Daniel Fischlin and Mark Fortier (London, 2000).

6  My thanks to the author of this short story, Liam O'Dowd, and to the class of EN220: After Shakespeare, for their creative responses.

7  Issac Asimov, 'The Immortal Bard', in *After Shakespeare*, ed. John Gross (Oxford, 2002), 327–9; *2001: A Space Odyssey*, dir. Stanley Kubrick (MGM, 1968).

8  http://www.youtube.com/watch?v=DbK1eCt97ag (accessed 25 June 2013). The video was originally made for a DVD, *God Hates Cartoons*. See www.brightredrocket.com (accessed 25 June 2013).

9  See Richard Halpern, *Shakespeare among the Moderns* (Ithaca, NY, 1997), 227–88.

10  Ibid., 228.

11  Margreta de Grazia, *Hamlet without* 'Hamlet' (London, 2007), 170.

12  http://www.youtube.com/results?search_query=Shakespeare%2 C+Hamlet&oq=Shakespeare%2C+Hamlet&gs_l=youtube.3... 21042.22263.0.22465.7.6.0.0.0.0.0.0..0.0...0.0...1ac.1.11. youtube (accessed 25 June 2013).

13  I owe this insight to Christy Desmet's 'Paying Attention in Shakespeare Parody: From Tom Stoppard to YouTube', *SS* 61 (2008): 237.

14  See Henry Jenkins, *Convergence Culture: Where Old and New Media Collide* (New York, 2006).

15  Alexandra Juhasz, *Learning from YouTube* (Cambridge, MA, 2011), http://vectors.usc.edu/projects/learningfromyoutube/# (accessed 25 June 2013).

16  http://www.youtube.com/results?search_query=Hamlet%2 C+%22To+be+or+not+to+be%22&oq=Hamlet%2C+%22 To+be+or+not+to+be%22&gs_l=youtube.12..0l10.5734.1 1279.0.13237.4.4.0.0.0.0.170.612.0j4.4.0...0.0...1ac.1.11. youtube.095V6em6www (accessed 25 June 2013). Placing 'To be or not to be' in quotation marks is important so as to avoid results including stop words.

17  See Peter Donaldson, '"All Which It Inherit": Shakespeare, Globes and Global Media', SS 52 (1999): 183–200; Katherine Rowe and Thomas Cartelli, *New Wave Shakespeare on Screen* (London, 2007), 55–68. On the use of 'old' technologies in Almereyda's *Hamlet*, see Mark Thornton Burnett, '"To Hear and See the Matter": Communicating Technology in Michael

Almereyda's *Hamlet*', *Cinema Journal* 42.3 (2003): 48–69; and Katherine Rowe, '"Remember me": Technologies of Memory in Michael Almereyda's *Hamlet*', in *Shakespeare: the Movie II*, ed. Richard Burt and Lynda E. Boose (London, 2003), 37–55. On Fodor's *Hamlet*, see Maurizio Calbi, 'Shakespeare in the Extreme: Addiction, Ghosts and (Re)-Mediation in Alexander Fodor's *Hamlet*', *Literature Film Quarterly* 39.2 (2011): 85–98.

18  Martin Lister et al., *New Media: A Critical Introduction* (London, 2009), 228.

19  Lawrence Lessig, *Remix: Making Art and Commerce Thrive in the Hybrid Economy* (London, 2008). Available at http://www.scribd.com/doc/47089238/Remix (accessed 25 June 2013); and John Shiga, 'Copy-and-Persist: the Logic of Mashup Culture', *Critical Studies in Media Communication* 24.2 (2007): 93–114.

20  http://www.youtube.com/watch?v=T8Hdhrd-dPI (accessed 25 June 2013).

21  Virginia Kuhn, 'The Rhetoric of Remix', *TWC* 9 (2012), doi:10.3983/twc.2012.0358. (accessed 25 June 2013).

22  Paul Booth, 'Mashup as Temporal Amalgam: Time, Taste, and Textuality', *Transformative Works and Cultures* 9 (2012), doi:10.3983/twc.2012.0297. (accessed 25 June 2013).

23  Ibid.

24  http://www.youtube.com/watch?v=p9nw9u7F8RI. On this YouTuber, see http://www.johndishwasher.org/works.html (accessed 25 June 2013).

25  http://www.youtube.com/watch?v=Tlw6dCfk0Wo (accessed 25 June 2013).

26  See http://mashable.com/2010/10/05/lady-gaga-justin-bieber-youtube/ (accessed 25 June 2013).

27  Marjorie Garber, *Shakespeare and Modern Culture* (New York, 2009), xviii.

28  Paul Prescott, 'Shakespeare and Popular Culture', in *New Cambridge Companion to Shakespeare*, ed. Margreta de Grazia and Stanley Wells (Cambridge, 2010), 282.

**29** On the possibilities of using Lady Gaga to teach Shakespeare, see Sarah Olive, 'Shakespeare and Lady Gaga', *Alluvium* 1.1 (2012), http://www.alluvium-journal.org/2012/06/01/shakespeare-and-lady-gaga-2/ (accessed 25 June 2013).

**30** For a professional remix of 'Bad Romance' as a homage to the suffragette movement, see http://www.youtube.com/watch?v=IYQhRCs9IHM (accessed 25 June 2013).

**31** On rap, see Adam Hansen, *Shakespeare and Popular Music* (London, 2010), 66–74. On *Renaissance Man*, dir. Penny Marshall (Touchstone, 1994), see Richard Burt, 'Slammin' Shakespeare In Acc(id)ents Yet Unknown: Liveness, Cinem(edi)a, and Racial Dis-Integration', *SQ* 53 (2002): 201–26.

**32** Prescott, 280. See also Kevin J. Wetmore, 'Big Willie Style: Staging HipHop Shakespeare and Being Down with the Bard', in *Alternative Shakespeares*, Vol. 3, ed. Diana E. Henderson (London, 2008), 147–69.

**33** The URL for this video has been omitted because the performers were minors at the time of its production.

**34** The sketch was first performed as part of Comic Relief on BBC TV, http://www.youtube.com/watch?v=qjMKBCyf2pQ (accessed 25 June 2013). For a brief discussion, see Desmet, 'Paying Attention in Shakespeare Parody', 227–38.

**35** Jenkins, *Convergence Culture*, 282.

**36** The URL for this video has been omitted because the performer was a minor at the time of its production.

**37** See Courtney Lehmann, *Shakespeare Remains: Theatre to Film, Early Modern to Postmodern* (Ithaca, NY, 2002), 89–129.

**38** Jacques Derrida, *Specters of Marx*, trans. Peggy Kamuf (London, 1994), 22.

**39** Margaret Kidnie, *Shakespeare and the Problem of Adaptation* (London, 2009), 1–2.

**40** http://www.youtube.com/watch?v=F7gvq2cGA7E&feature=mfu_in_order&list=UL (accessed 25 June 2013).

**41** Halpern, 231.

42 Sarah Kember and Joanna Zylinska, *Life After New Media: Mediation as Vital Process* (Cambridge, MA, 2012),194.

43 http://www.youtube.com/watch?v=ZCmcCtB1Wco (accessed 25 June 2013).

44 http://www.youtube.com/watch?v=4arbX9AiBmA (accessed 25 June 2013).

45 http://www.digitalspy.ie/movies/news/a253165/ruffalo-incredible-hulk-is-like-hamlet.html (accessed 25 June 2013).

46 Juhasz, http://vectors.usc.edu/projects/learningfromyoutube/# (accessed 25 June 2013).

47 http://www.youtube.com/watch?v=ecqpCnJyhbc (accessed 25 June 2013).

48 Other non-diegetic elements in the video include Lou Reed's 'Heroin' and a quote from Kurt Vonnegut on smoking as a form of delayed self-annihilation.

49 Rowe, '"Remember me"', 46. See also Peter Donaldson, 'Hamlet among the Pixelvisionaries: Video Art, Authenticity and 'Wisdom' in Almereyda's *Hamlet*', in *A Concise Companion to Shakespeare on Screen*, ed. Diana E. Henderson (Oxford, 2006), 216–37.

50 Jay D. Bolter and Richard Grusin, *Remediation: Understanding New Media* (Cambridge, MA, 2000), 46.

51 On the vlog as a specific example of 'vernacular creativity', see Jean Burgess and Joshua Green, *YouTube* (Cambridge, 2009), 25–6. On Sadie Benning, see Donaldson, 'Hamlet among the Pixelvisionaries', 219–21. On the gender politics of the webcam, see Theresa M. Senft, *Camgirls: Celebrity and Community in the Age of Social Networks* (New York, 2008).

52 Juhasz, http://vectors.usc.edu/projects/learningfromyoutube/# (accessed 25 June 2013).

53 Wesch, 'An Anthropological Introduction to YouTube', http://www.youtube.com/watch?v=TPAO-lZ4_hU&feature=player_embedded (accessed 25 June 2013).

54 See Douglas Wolk, 'The Complete and Utter History of Numa Numa', http://www.youtube.com/watch?v=dRUy0It0wJ4 (accessed 25 June 2013).

55  http://www.youtube.com/watch?v=LzHjIj3fpR8 (accessed 25 June 2013).

56  http://www.youtube.com/watch?v=LzHjIj3fpR8 (accessed 25 June 2013).

57  The URL for this video has been omitted because at the time of uploading, the performer was a minor.

58  Michael Dobson, *Shakespeare and Amateur Performance: A Cultural History* (Cambridge, 2011), 2.

59  http://www.youtube.com/watch?v=TYXFFhP7aq8 (accessed 25 June 2013).

60  Thompson and Taylor, 5.

61  See Marvin Carlson, *The Haunted Stage: The Theatre as Memory Machine* (Ann Arbor, MI, 2001).

62  http://www.youtube.com/watch?v=C5E6K6ihtcI (accessed 25 June 2013).

63  Philip Auslander, *Liveness: Performance in a Mediatized Culture* (London, 1999), 7. For a counter-argument regarding the non-reproducibility of live performance, see Peggy Phelan, *Unmarked: the Politics of Performance* (London and New York, 1993).

64  See Burgess and Green, 27–30; and also Senft, 29–30.

65  http://www.youtube.com/user/shaktim (accessed 25 June 2013).

66  Quoted from description to 'Hamlet 365' playlist, http://www.youtube.com/playlist?list=PL510D29B806E46832 (accessed 25 June 2013).

67  http://www.youtube.com/watch?v=myutNk0FrN0 (accessed 25 June 2013).

68  http://www.youtube.com/watch?v=iBvVr8pWN28 (accessed 25 June 2013).

69  https://www.youtube.com/watch?v=ijrJ07BMubY (accessed 25 June 2013).

70  The URL for this video has been omitted because at the time of uploading, the performer was a minor. Chris Barrett is credited as the director. My thanks to him for providing background details about the piece.

71 Other videos include Hamlet's first encounter with the Ghost, where Hamlet is played as if possessed, and also Aaron's final monologue from *Titus Andronicus*.

72 On 'street' Shakespeare as deployed in recent Shakespeare films, see Thomas Cartelli, 'Shakespeare and the Street: Pacino's *Looking for Richard*, Bedford's *Street King*, and the Common Understanding', in *Shakespeare: the Movie II*, 186–99.

73 http://www.youtube.com/watch?v=eetJxqiR11w 7 (accessed 25 June 2013).

74 http://www.youtube.com/watch?v=tEPVEZ2m6Ok (accessed 25 June 2013).

75 Kathrin Peters and Andrea Seier, 'Home Dance: Mediacy and Aesthetics of the Self on You Tube', in *The YouTube Reader*, ed. Pelle Snickars and Patrick Vonderau (Stockholm, 2009), 201.

76 Linda Charnes, *Hamlet's Heirs: Shakespeare and the Politics of a New Millennium* (London, 2006), 65.

77 Lee Edelman, 'Against Survival: Queerness in a Time That's Out of Joint', *SQ* 62.2 (2011): 166.

78 For example, Edelman interprets Old Hamlet's demands on his son in terms of the preservation of normativity (see 164–9).

79 Charnes, 98.

80 See Kylie Jarrett, 'Beyond Broadcast Yourself™: The Future of YouTube', *Media International Australia* 126 (2008): 132–44.

81 Wesch, http://www.youtube.com/watch?v=TPAO-lZ4_hU&feature=player_embedded (accessed 25 June 2013).

82 See the example of actor Henry Dinkins, http://www.youtube.com/user/kenjr79/videos (accessed 25 June 2013).

83 Lisa Nakamura, *Cybertypes: Race, Ethnicity and Identity on the Internet* (London, 2001), 11.

84 See Fredric Jameson, *Postmodernism, or, The Cultural Logic of Late Capitalism* (Durham, NC, 1991).

85 Andy Grundberg, *Crisis of the Real: Writings on Photography, 1974–1989* (New York, 1990), 2.

**86** The phrase is Thomas Healy's in his 'Past and Present Shakespeares', in *Shakespeare and National Culture*, ed. John J. Joughin (Manchester, 1997), 214.

**87** De Grazia, 22.

**88** Jean Baudrillard, 'Simulacra and Simulations', in *Jean Baudrillard: Selected Writings*, ed. Mark Poster (London, 2001), 174.

**89** Lehmann, 1–24.

**90** See Tony Howard, *Women as Hamlet: Performance and Interpretation in Theatre, Film, and Fiction* (Cambridge, 2007).

**91** http://www.youtube.com/results?search_ query=Ophelia&page=6 (accessed 25 June 2013).

**92** There is an entire website (curated by Alan Young) featuring creative responses to Ophelia. See http://www. opheliapopularculture.com/ (accessed 25 June 2013).

**93** See Kaara L. Peterson and Deanne Williams, eds, *The Afterlife of Ophelia* (Basingstoke, 2012). The classic treatment remains Elaine Showalter's essay 'Representing Ophelia: Women, Madness, and the Responsibilities of Feminist Criticism', in *Shakespeare and the Question of Theory*, ed. Geoffrey Hartman and Patricia Parker (London, 1985), 77–94.

**94** Magda Romanska, 'NercOphelia: Death, Femininity and the Making of Modern Aesthetics', *Performance Research* 10.3 (2005): 35–53.

**95** Arthur Rimbaud, 'Ophélie' (1870). The original is reprinted, with prose translation, in *After Shakespeare*, 150–2.

**96** Mary Pipher, *Reviving Ophelia: Saving the Selves of Adolescent Girls* (New York, 1994). Sara Shandler credits Pipher's book as the impetus for her collection, *Ophelia Speaks: Adolescent Girls Write about their Search for Self* (New York, 1999). On Pipher and the cultural meanings of Ophelia, see Jennifer Hulbert, '"Adolescence, Thy Name is Ophelia!": The Ophelia-ization of the Contemporary Teenage Girl', in Kevin Wetmore, Jennifer Hulbert and Robert York, *Shakespeare and Youth Culture* (New York, 2006), 199–220.

**97** Christy Desmet and Sujata Iyengar, 'Rebooting Ophelia: Social Media and the Rhetorics of Adaptation', in *The Afterlife of Ophelia*, 61, 68.

98 http://www.youtube.com/watch?v=sjY_o2shG0I (accessed 25 June 2013).

99 See Marnina Gonick, 'Between "Girl Power" and "Reviving Ophelia": Constituting the Neoliberal Girl Subject', *NWSA* 18.2 (2006): 1–23.

100 Quoted in Hulbert, 205.

101 Quoted in Gonick, 12.

102 Gonick, 13.

103 http://www.youtube.com/watch?v=OrRtJY28ps8 (accessed 25 June 2013).

104 References in music videos to Ophelia that are influenced by Millais rather than Shakespeare include Kylie Minogue and Nick Cave, 'Where the Wild Roses Grow'; and more recently, 'Flower' (dir. Kylie Minogue, 2012).

105 http://www.youtube.com/watch?v=rGLWzjQz0JM (accessed 25 June 2013).

106 Essentially, the video is a PowerPoint presentation converted into a movie using Microsoft AVI.

107 A link to iTunes is provided below the video, one of the ways that amateur culture is intertwined with commercial media.

108 Bolter and Grusin, 59.

109 Ibid., 60.

110 Desmet and Iyengar, 62.

111 Judith Halberstam, *In a Queer Time and Place: Transgender Bodies, Subcultural Lives* (New York, 2005), 16.

112 Cathy Caruth, ed., *Trauma: Explorations in Memory* (Baltimore, 1995), vii.

113 Another response to joshje777 is *25a Rassegna Internz. dell' Acqua - Iris Selke Performance*, http://www.youtube.com/watch?v=0u__0zBr9Eg (accessed 25 June 2013).

114 At the time of writing, teen suicide is a high-profile issue in Ireland. See Jennifer O'Connell, 'We need to talk about suicide, but it's not a social-media conversation', *Irish Times*, 15 November 2012, http://www.irishtimes.com/newspaper/features/2012/1107/1224326229036.html (accessed 25 June 2013).

**115** Peterson and Williams, 3.

**116** Romanska, 37.

**117** Ibid., 39, 43.

**118** Gonick, 15.

**119** http://www.youtube.com/watch?v=Ty1aJ-wKLFU (accessed 25 June 2013).

**120** The URL for this video has been omitted because at the time of uploading, the performer was a minor.

**121** Romanska, 47.

**122** http://www.youtube.com/watch?v=2qsPSKoL4eo (accessed 25 June 2013).

**123** Carol Chillington Rutter, *Enter the Body: Women and Representation on Shakespeare's Stage* (London, 2001), 52–5.

**124** Ibid., 53.

**125** Coppelia Kahn, 'Afterword: Ophelia Then, Now, Hereafter', in *The Afterlife of Ophelia*, 232.

**126** Ibid., 237.

**127** Ibid., 235.

**128** Rutter, 27; see Katherine McLuskie, 'The Patriarchal Bard: Feminist Criticism and Shakespeare: *King Lear* and *Measure for Measure*', in *Political Shakespeare: Essays in Cultural Materialism*, ed. Jonathan Dollimore and Alan Sinfield (Manchester, 1994). For an overview of feminist readings of Shakespeare, see Phyllis Rackin, *Shakespeare and Women* (Oxford, 2005). For the claim that Shakespeare's plays critique contemporary early modern discourses of misogyny and patriarchy, see Juliet Dusinberre, *Shakespeare and the Nature of Women*, 3rd edn (Basingstoke, 2003).

**129** Kahn, 241.

**130** The video was entered into YouTube Play, a competition for creative video run by YouTube and the Guggenheim, http://www.guggenheim.org/new-york/press-room/releases/3515-ytprelease (accessed 25 June 2013).

**131** Millais had his model Elizabeth Siddall pose in a bathtub, kept warm only by oil lamps that had been placed underneath.

132 See Judith Butler, *Gender Trouble* (London, 1990), 186–93.

133 Bernadette Wegenstein, *Getting Under the Skin: The Body and Media Theory* (Cambridge, 2006), 63.

134 http://www.youtube.com/watch?v=ZDlgJMNhKdE (accessed 25 June 2013).

135 http://www.youtube.com/watch?v=L4PRLuiiKnM&list=PLF52 57F62099CE211&index=3 (accessed 25 June 2013).

136 http://www.youtube.com/watch?v=LhA9TkCEG0c (accessed 25 June 2013).

137 http://www.youtube.com/watch?v=av1DiVin960&feature =endscreen&NR=1 (accessed 25 June 2013). As no human subjects are identifiable in the video, the URL has been supplied.

138 *Final Destination* (dir. James Wong, 2000).

139 Jacqueline Urla and Alan C. Swedlund, 'The Anthropometry of Barbie: Unsettling Ideals of the Feminine Body in Popular Culture', in *A Reader in Promoting Public Health: Challenges and Controversy*, ed. Jenny Douglas et al. (London, 2007), 130.

140 Virginia Woolf, quoted in Sandra M. Gilbert and Susan Gubar, *The Madwoman in the Attic: The Woman Writer and the Nineteenth-Century Literary Imagination* (New York, 2000), 17.

141 Kim Toffoletti, *Cyborgs and Barbie Dolls: Feminism, Popular Culture and the Posthuman Body* (London, 2007), 59.

142 Ibid., p. 79.

143 http://www.youtube.com/watch?v=iT5H_-vIcJw (accessed 25 June 2013).

144 http://www.youtube.com/watch?v=d6Opie1eDcA (accessed 25 June 2013).

145 http://www.youtube.com/user/Opheliasays (accessed 25 June 2013).

146 http://www.youtube.com/user/OpheliaSaysWhaaaa (accessed 25 June 2013).

147 Gonick, 2.

148 Ibid., 18.

149  Senft, 43.

150  The websites YouTomb (http://youtomb.mit.edu)
     and WaybackMachine (http://archive.org/web/web.php)
     archive content removed from video-sharing sites due to
     copyright violation.

151  http://www.youtube.com/watch?v=qs0m9dGI5zQ&feature=ch
     annel&list=UL (accessed 25 June 2013).

152  Virginia Kuhn, 'The YouTube Gaze: Permission to Create?',
     *Enculturation* 7 (2010), http://enculturation.gmu.edu/
     the-youtube-gaze (accessed 25 June 2013).

153  Jenkins, 173.

154  Kuhn, 'The YouTube Gaze' (accessed 25 June 2013).

155  http://www.youtube.com/t/copyright_education (accessed 25
     June 2013).

156  For a discussion of these issues using the example of Anime,
     see Jenkins, 160–5.

157  http://www.youtube.com/watch?v=AZm4gRBzY20 (accessed
     25 June 2013).

158  http://www.youtube.com/watch?v=Vn_XwVRg8Rg (accessed
     25 June 2013).

159  http://www.youtube.com/watch?v=BdgjAZtIXvI (accessed 25
     June 2013).

160  Peter Holbrook, *Shakespeare's Individualism* (Cambridge,
     2010), 39.

# Chapter three

1  Paul Gilroy, *Against Race: Imagining Politcal Change beyond
   the Colour Line* (Cambridge, MA, 2000), 42.

2  Viewer comment, http://www.youtube.com/
   watch?v=WrWhnKUwb2g (accessed 25 June 2013).

3  Stuart Hall, 'New Ethnicities', in *Stuart Hall: Critical
   Dialogues in Cultural Studies*, ed. David Morley and
   Kuan-Hsing Chen (New York, 1996), 443.

4   Ayanna Thompson, *Passing Strange: Shakespeare, Race and Contemporary America* (Oxford, 2011), 3.

5   Jonathan Gil Harris, 'Shakespeare and Race', in *New Cambridge Companion to Shakespeare*, ed. Margreta de Grazia and Stanley Wells (Cambridge, 2010), 201.

6   Frantz Fanon, *Black Skin, White Masks*, trans. Charles Lam Markham (London, 1986), 112. The persistence of epidermal thinking in postmodern culture is pursued in Gilroy, *Against Race*, ch. 1.

7   Toni Morrison, 'Home', in *The House that Race Built*, ed. Wahneema Lubiano (New York, 1998), 5.

8   Consider the remarks by Toni Morrison about the election of Obama as a 'curious moment' because so much has been damaged already, yet there is the possibility of a 'reclamation of what America believed about itself'. Quoted in Sam Tanenhaus, 'A Conversation with Toni Morrison', *New York Times* YouTube channel, 1 December 2008, http://www.youtube.com/watch?v=Q5D5PLI7kvc (accessed 25 June 2013). See also Stephanie Li, *Signifying without Specifying: Racial Discourse in the Age of Obama* (New Brunswick, 2012), 1–23, where she considers Morrison's earlier claim that Bill Clinton had been America's 'First Black President'. For a critique of neo-liberal claims of a post-racial America, see Tim Wise, *Colorblind: The Rise of Post-Racial Politics and the Retreat from Racial Equality* (San Francisco, 2010).

9   Gilroy, *Against Race*, 52.

10  Lisa Nakamura, *Cybertypes: Race, Ethnicity and Identity on the Internet* (London, 2001); and *Digitizing Race: Visual Cultures of the Internet* (Minneapolis, 2008).

11  Nakamura, *Digitizing Race*, 204, 206.

12  Ibid., 208.

13  Nakamura, *Cybertypes*, 11, 13–14.

14  Michael Wesch, 'An Anthropological Introduction to YouTube', http://www.youtube.com/watch?v=TPAO-lZ4_hU&feature=player_embedded (accessed 25 June 2013).

15  http://www.youtube.com/watch?v=EwTZ2xpQwpA.

**16** See their *Halloween Responsibly PSA* (uploaded 2 October 2012), where they address stereotypes of Indian identity and also blackface, http://www.youtube.com/watch?v=tc_UxduE5lE (accessed 25 June 2013). My thanks to Padraig Kirwan for this reference.

**17** Anandan Kavoori, *Reading YouTube: The Critical Viewers Guide* (New York, 2011), 111.

**18** http://vectors.usc.edu/projects/learningfromyoutube/texteo.php?composite=159 (accessed 25 June 2013).

**19** Ibid.

**20** See Ania Loomba, *Shakespeare, Race and Colonialism* (Oxford, 2002), 22–44; and Sujata Iyengar, *Shades of Difference: Mythologies of Skin Colour in Early Modern England* (Philadelphia, 2005).

**21** Quoted in Marjorie Garber, *Profiling Shakespeare* (New York, 2008), 117.

**22** Loomba, *Shakespeare, Race and Colonialism*, 5.

**23** Thompson, *Passing Strange*, 146.

**24** http://www.youtube.com/watch?v=F96DlM3N5KQ (accessed 25 June 2013).

**25** http://www.youtube.com/watch?v=-DF7YQrC7HM (accessed 25 June 2013).

**26** http://www.youtube.com/watch?v=aTNe3wzWdJ8 (accessed 25 June 2013).

**27** Thompson, 6.

**28** In quoting from viewer posts, online aliases have been removed but comments can be easily sourced on YouTube through the links to individual videos.

**29** The URL for this video has been omitted because the performers were minors at the time of its production.

**30** On the genealogy of quoting Shakespeare, see Garber, *Profiling Shakespeare* (New York, 2008), 278–301.

**31** Michael Neill, 'Postcolonial Shakespeare? Writing away from the Centre', in *Postcolonial Shakespeares*, ed. Ania Loomba and Martin Orkin (London, 1998), 185.

**32** Harris, 'Shakespeare and Race', 204.

33 Celia R. Daileader, 'Casting Black Actors: beyond Othellophilia', in *Shakespeare and Race*, ed. Catherine M. S. Alexander and Stanley Wells (Cambridge, 2000), 180.

34 Margo Hendricks; 'Surveying "Race" in Shakespeare', in *Shakespeare and Race*, 1.

35 One could add Cleopatra to this triad, or the *Sonnets*, with their binaristic discourses of fairness and blackness. See Kim F. Hall, '"These bastard signs of fair": Literary Whiteness in Shakespeare's *Sonnets*', in *Postcolonial Shakespeares*, 64–83; and Carol Chillington Rutter, *Enter the Body: Women and Representation on Shakespeare's Stage* (London, 2001), 57–103.

36 Barbara Hodgdon, 'Race-ing *Othello*, Re-engendering White-Out, II', in *Shakespeare: The Movie II*, ed. Richard Burt and Lynda E. Boose (London, 2003), 98.

37 Gary Taylor, *Buying Whiteness: Race, Culture, and Identity from Columbus to Hip-hop* (New York, 2005), 354.

38 Richard Dyer, 'The Matter of Whiteness', in *Theories of Race and Racism*, ed. Les Black and John Solomos (New York, 2000), 539, 540.

39 Thompson, *Passing Strange*, 172.

40 Richard Burt, 'Slammin' Shakespeare In Acc(id)ents Yet Unknown: Liveness, Cinem(edi)a, and Racial Dis-Integration', *SQ* 53 (2002): 206.

41 Stuart Hall, 'What is this "Black" in Black Popular Culture', in *Stuart Hall: Critical Dialogues in Cultural Studies*, 468.

42 The impersonation of a person of colour by a white actor has been termed 'racebending'; see http://www.racebending.com/v4/about/what-is-racebending/. The site archives examples from Western media of the exclusion of non-white people.

43 Thompson, *Passing Strange*, 77.

44 For an excellent overview of the issues and debates, see Ayanna Thompson's Introduction in *Colorblind Shakespeare: New Perspectives on Race and Performance*, ed. Ayanna Thompson (London, 2006), 1–24; and Angela Pao, *No Safe Spaces: Re-casting Race, Ethnicity, and Nationality in American Theatre* (Ann Arbor, MI, 2011), 42–63.

45 Quoted in Pao, 46.

46 See Richard Burt, 'CivicShakesPR: Middlebrow Multiculturalism, White Television, and the Colour Bind', in *Colorblind Shakespeare*, 157–85.

47 Christy Burns, 'Suturing over Racial Differences: Problems for a Colorblind Approach in Visual Culture', *Discourse* 22.1 (2000): 70–91.

48 Ayanna Thompson, 'To Notice or Not To Notice: Shakespeare, Black Actors, and Performance', *Borrowers and Lenders* 4.1 (2008), http://www.borrowers.uga.edu/cocoon/borrowers/issue?id=7157 (accessed 25 June 2013).

49 Quoted in Thompson, *Passing Strange*, 102.

50 Lisa M. Anderson, 'When Race Matters: Reading Race in *Richard III* and *Macbeth*', in *Colourblind Shakespeare*, 101.

51 Ibid., 91.

52 Ibid.

53 K. Anthony Appiah, 'Racial Identity and Racial Identification', in *Theories of Race and Racism*, 610.

54 Kobena Mercer, 'Busy in the Ruins of Wretched Phantasia', in *Mirage: Enigmas of Race, Difference and Desire* (London, 1995), 26.

55 http://www.youtube.com/watch?v=8DAm8t8JAns (accessed 25 June 2013).

56 The Shylock video within Sykes' series is something of an exception here – a number of comments were made when the video was first uploaded and several connected Sykes' race to what was regarded as an empathetic portrayal of Shylock. The original video was removed and the comments deleted with it. Sykes has made the video available once more, but no comments have been posted on it.

57 The issue of audience identification with Othello is addressed in Elise Marks, 'Othello/me: Racial Drag and the Pleasures of Boundary-Crossing with *Othello*', *Comparative Drama* 35.1 (2001): 101–23.

58 http://www.youtube.com/watch?v=WrWhnKUwb2g (accessed 25 June 2013).

59 Errol Hill quoted in Burt, 'Slammin' Shakespeare In Acc(id) ents Yet Unknown', 219. For an incisive reading of Robeson, see Peter Erickson, *Citing Shakespeare: The Reinterpretation of Race in Contemporary Literature and Art* (New York, 2007), 77–101.

60 Burt, 'Slammin' Shakespeare In Acc(id)ents Yet Unknown', 202.

61 Marcus Sykes, by email via YouTube, 9 June 2011.

62 Quoted in Joyce Green MacDonald, 'Black Ram, White Ewe: Shakespeare, Race, and Women', in *A Feminist Companion to Shakespeare*, ed. Dympna Callaghan (Oxford, 2000), 199.

63 Daileader, 177–202. In *Racism, Misogyny and the 'Othello' Myth: Inter-Racial Couples from Shakespeare to Spike Lee* (Cambridge, 2005) Daileader broadens the term 'Othellophilia' to register the curious cultural obsession with (white) female sexuality in relation to interracial couplings.

64 Gary Younge, 'Who Thinks About the Consquences of Online Racism?', *Guardian*, 12 July 2012, http://www.guardian.co.uk/commentisfree/2012/jul/12/consequences-of-online-racism (accessed 25 June 2013).

65 Nakamura, *Cybertypes*, 11, 13–14.

66 Michael Wesch, 'An Anthropological Introduction to YouTube', http://www.youtube.com/watch?v=TPAO-lZ4_hU&feature=player_embedded (accessed 25 June 2013).

67 http://vectors.usc.edu/projects/learningfromyoutube/texteo.php?composite=110&tour=18&tag=6 (accessed 25 June 2013).

68 Thompson, *Passing Strange*, 160. On the Iago-effect and its relation to racism in the play, see Michael Neill, 'Unproper Beds: Race, Adultery, and the Hideous in *Othello*', *SQ* 40 (1989): 383–412.

69 On racial slurs, see Jane H. Hill, *Everday Language of White Racism* (Hoboken, NJ, 2009), 49–87.

70 http://www.youtube.com/watch?v=6ggNUtg38J4 (accessed 25 June 2013).

71 See Emily Bartels, 'Making More of the Moor: Aaron, Othello and Renaissance Refashionings of Race', *SQ* 41 (1990): 433–54.

72  Loomba, 79.

73  Younge, 'Who Thinks About the Consquences of Online
    Racism?'.

74  Juhasz, http://vectors.usc.edu/projects/learningfromyoutube/
    texteo.php?composite=85 (accessed 25 June 2013).

75  Thompson, *Passing Strange*, 146.

76  http://www.youtube.com/watch?v=qQP7J5jYrzE (accessed 25
    June 2013).

77  *Othello*, dir. Stuart Burge (Eagle Films, 1965); *Yes Sir, Mr
    Bones*, dir. Ron Ormond (Spartan, 1951).

78  The video is particular to *Othello*, but blackface does occur in
    films, either in the interests of historical accuracy, as in *Stage
    Beauty*, dir. Richard Eyre (Lionsgate, 2004), or with ironic
    treatment, as in *Tropic Thunder*, dir. Ben Stiller (Dreamworks,
    2008). See Richard Burt, 'Backstage Pass(ing): *Stage Beauty*,
    *Othello* and the Make-Up of Race', in *Screening Shakespeare
    in the Twenty First-Century*, ed. Mark Thornton Burnett and
    Ramona Wray (Edinburgh, 2006), 53–71.

79  In 2005, the Royal Opera in the UK announced that they
    would discontinue blacking up. See http://www.guardian.
    co.uk/uk/2005/nov/20/race.arts (accessed 25 June 2013).

80  Dympna Callaghan, '"Othello was a white man": Properties
    of Race on Shakespeare's Stage', in *Alternative Shakespeares*,
    Vol. 2, ed. Terence Hakwes (London, 1996), 196.

81  Karin H. deGravelles, 'You Be Othello: Interrogating
    Identification in the Classroom', *Pedagogy* 11.1 (2011): 161.

82  Quoted in deGravelles, 160.

83  Hugh Macrae Richmond, 'The Audience's Role in *Othello*', in
    *Othello: New Critical Essays*, ed. Philip C. Kolin (New York,
    2002), 96.

84  Quoted in Thompson, *Passing Strange*, 99.

85  MacDonald, 198; see also Ian Smith, 'Barbarian Errors:
    Performing Race in Early Modern England', *SQ*, 49.2 (1998):
    168–86.

86  Quoted in deGravelles, 161. A simillar case is made in Marks,
    101–23.

87 Thompson, *Passing Strange*, 97–117.

88 Virginia Mason Vaughan, 'Review of Ayanna Thompson, *Passing Strange*', *SQ* 63:2 (2012): 244–6.

89 Thompson, *Passing Strange*, 103, 117.

90 deGravelles, 172.

91 Ibid., 168.

92 The summary draws from Jane Gallop, 'Lacan's "Mirror Stage": Where to Begin', *SubStance* 11.12 (1982–83): 118–28.

93 This reading of Othello is richly explored in Djanet Sears' play *Harlem Duet*, available in *Adaptations of Shakespeare*, ed. Daniel Fischlin and Mark Fortier (London, 2000).

94 Fanon, 112.

95 Shannon Winnubust, 'Is the Mirror Racist? Interrogating the Space of Whiteness', *Philosophy Social Criticism* 30 (2004): 39.

96 Mercer, 28.

97 On the exclusionary politics of race and gender impersonation, see Callaghan, especially on 195–8, 210–12.

98 The URL for this video has been omitted as no reply to the request to discuss the video was received.

99 See Kevin J. Wetmore, 'Big Willie Style: Staging HipHop Shakespeare and Being Down with the Bard', in *Alternative Shakespeares*, Vol. 3, ed. Diana E. Henderson (London, 2008), 147–69. On the ubiquity of rap in modern Shakespeare performance, see Yu Jin Ko, 'Honolulu Theatre for Youth's Rap *Othello*', *Borrowers and Lenders* 2.1 (2006), http://www.borrowers.uga.edu/cocoon/borrowers/issue?id=7150 (accessed 25 June 2013).

100 http://www.youtube.com/watch?v=UC-f0drvdmM&feature=related (accessed 25 June 2013).

101 The work of Reduced Shakespeare has been regarded as producing simplistic equations between blackness and rap. See Wetmore, 151–2; and Douglas Lanier, *Shakespeare and Modern Popular Culture* (Oxford, 2002), 102–6.

102 The gag may play off associations of 'chocolate' in urban slang, where it refers to black people, often with a

connotation of sexual desire. See http://www.urbandictionary. com/define.php?term=sexual%20chocolate (accessed 25 June 2013).

103 I am appropriating a term here that has been used to denote a phase within race relations in America following the election of its first black president – see Li, *Signifying without Specifying*, 3.

104 On minstrelsy in nineteenth-century America and the role of Irish migrants, see Robert Nowatzki, 'Paddy Jumps Jim Crow: Irish-Americans and Blackface Minstrelsy', *Éire-Ireland* 41.3/4 (2007): 162–84.

105 See Dyer, 'The Matter of Whiteness', 539–48.

106 http://www.youtube.com/watch?v=szBg5uBmeDM (accessed 25 June 2013).

107 Philip Auslander, *Liveness: Performance in a Mediatized Culture* (London, 1999).

108 Mega64 have produced several comedy sketches and pilots. See http://mega64.wikia.com/wiki/Mega64e.

109 This video bears comparison with *All the Small Things* by American pop-rock group Blink 182.

110 Viewing statistics indicate that males in the 18–24 age demographic constitute the primary audience.

111 *O*, dir. Time Blake Nelson (Lionsgate, 2001); *Romeo + Juliet*, dir. Baz Luhrmann (Twentieth Century Fox, 1996).

112 Julie Sanders, *Shakespeare and Music: Afterlives and Borrowings* (Cambridge, 2007), 160.

113 Stephen Purcell, *Popular Shakespeare: Simulation and Subversion on the Modern Stage* (Basingstoke, 2009), 107–12.

114 Ibid., 111.

115 Linda Hutcheon, *A Theory of Parody* (London, 1985), 92.

116 Kavoori, *Reading YouTube*, 11, 112.

117 http://vectors.usc.edu/projects/learningfromyoutube/texteo. php?composite=23 (accessed 25 June 2013).

118 Gilroy, 181–4, 213–14; see also Lester K. Spence, *Stare in the Darkness: The Limits of Hip-hop and Black Politics* (Minneapolis, 2011).

119 Daileader, *Racism, Misogyny and the* 'Othello' *Myth*, 10.

120 On the representation of Desdemona, see Karen Newman, '"And Wash the Ethiop White": Femininity and the Monstrous in *Othello*', in her *Essaying Shakespeare* (Minneapolis, 2009), 37–58; and Edward Pechter, "Too Much Violence": Murdering Wives in *Othello*', in *Othello*, Norton Critical Edition, ed. Edward Pechter (New York, 2004), 366–87.

121 The URL for this video has been omitted as the participants may be minors.

122 http://www.youtube.com/watch?v=uBYyiNzcnH8 (accessed 25 June 2013). As with *The Story of Othello*, viewing statistics reveal that the video appeals to a predominantly male demographic.

123 See Lynda E. Boose, '"Let it be hid": The Pornographic Aesthetic of Shakespeare's *Othello*', in Othello, *Contemporary Critical Essays*, ed. Lena Cowen Orlin (London, 2003), 22–48.

124 Neill, 'Unproper Beds', 315.

125 Callaghan, 210.

126 MacDonald, 197.

127 http://www.youtube.com/watch?v=LKttq6EUqbE (accessed 25 June 2013).

128 There is an *Othello* connection here, since two years before Laurence Fishburne starred in *Othello*, dir. Oliver Parker (Castle Rock, 1995), he played Ike Turner in *What's Love Got to Do With It*, dir. Brian Gibson (Touchstone, 1993). Barbara Hodgdon notes that Fishburne's portrayal of one abusive black man may serve to further associations of *Othello* with the O. J. Simpson case, except that Fishburne plays Othello 'against such stereotypes of black masculinity' ('Race-ing *Othello*', 90).

129 Marjorie Garber, *Shakespeare and Modern Culture* (New York, 2009), 58.

130 Ibid., 46.

131 For a counter-reading, see Margo Hendricks, 'Gestures of Performance: Rethinking Race in Contempoary Shakespeare', in *Colorblind Shakespeare*, 187–203.

132 See Mark Burnett, *Shakespeare and World Cinema* (Cambridge, 2013), 195–231.

133 http://www.youtube.com/watch?v=_bcnxIJmy2g (accessed 25 June 2013). The film was directed by Terresa Dowell Vest and uploaded onto YouTube by CliffWilliamsTV, the actor who plays John, the film's Romeo figure. A potential influence for the film is Lou Reed's song 'Romeo had Juliette' from his album *New York* (1989). The song suggests an interracial theme in its lyrics about Romeo Rodriguez and Juliet Bell.

134 The name may allude to Luhrmann's film, where the singer Des'ree appears, her song 'Kissing You' acting as a theme tune to Romeo and Juliet's iconic love-at-first-sight moment.

135 See Stephen Buhler, 'Reviving Juliet, Repackaging Romeo: Transformations of Character in Pop and Post-Pop Music', in *Shakespeare after Mass Media*, ed. Richard Burt (New York, 2002), 245.

136 Sanders, 159.

137 http://www.youtube.com/watch?v=Gp45JprGwKA (accessed 25 June 2013). The video is available on YouTube (both in lyric form and as a full music video), and in comments, viewers express thanks for its renewed availability. It was produced in 1998. On the group, see http://www.euro-rap.com/start.htm?http://www.euro-rap.com/artists/poetrynmotion/poetrynmotion.htm (accessed 25 June 2013).

138 Burt, 'CivicShakesPR: Middlebrow Multiculturalism, White Television, and the Colour Bind', in *Colourblind Shakespeare*, 181.

139 Hall, 'New Ethnicities', 3.

# Chapter four

1 George Steevens, as quoted in Edmond Malone's gloss on Sonnet 20 in *The Plays and Poems of William Shakespeare*, ed. Edmond Malone (London, 1821), vol. 20, 241.

2 http://www.youtube.com/watch?v=H-_QlzUJBbU (accessed 25 June 2013).

3  *Shakespeare's Sonnets*, ed. Katherine Duncan-Jones (London, 1997).

4  See Introduction, note 5. A search under 'Shakespeare's Sonnets' returns 6,510 results, http://www.youtube.com/results?search_query=Shakespeare%27s+Sonnets&oq=Shakespe are%27s+Sonnets&gs_l.

5  This association is challenged in Patrick Cheney, *Shakespeare, National Poet-Playwright* (Cambridge, 2004).

6  *Shakespeare's Sonnets*. dir. Samuel Parker (2005); the film short appears on the DVD *Boys Briefs 3* (Picture This, 2006) and is available on YouTube; *Dead Poet's Society*, dir. Peter Weir (Touchstone Pictures, 1989); *Sense and Sensibility*, dir. Ang Lee (Columbia Pictures, 1995); *Venus*, dir. Roger Mitchell (Miramax, 2006). The citation in Lee's film is anachronistic for in terms of the 1811 setting, no such edition existed (Duncan-Jones, 78). The *Sonnets* make a cameo in *Did you hear about the Morgans?*, dir. Marc Lawrence (Columbia Pictures, 2009), where Sonnet 116 is included in a character's wedding vows.

7  Don Patterson, 'Shakespeare's *Sonnets*', *Guardian*, 16 October 2010, http://www.guardian.co.uk/books/2010/oct/16/shakespeare-sonnets-don-paterson (accessed 25 June 2013).

8  Stephen Booth, *An Essay on Shakespeare's* 'Sonnets' (New Haven, CT, 1969), 29.

9  An observation made to me by the playwright and poet Frank McGuinness; my thanks to Frank for allowing me to quote it here.

10  On the global reach of the *Sonnets*, see the impressive collection *William Shakespeare's* 'Sonnets' *for the First Time Globally Reprinted: A Quatercentenary Anthology 1609–2009*, with a DVD, ed. Manfred Pfister and Jürgen Gutsch (Dozwil, Switzerland, 2009).

11  http://www.youtube.com/watch?v=0Y8gM9vrLhw (accessed 25 June 2013).

12  The phrase is from Margreta de Grazia, 'The Scandal of Shakespeare's *Sonnets*', *SS* 46 (1994): 35–49; Jonathan Bate, 'Shakespeare was Straight', *Sunday Telegraph*, 28 September 1997; see also Bate's remarks in his Introduction, *Sonnets*

*and Other Poems*, ed. Jonathan Bate and Eric Rasmussen (Basingstoke, 2009), 12.

13  Madhavi Menon, 'Introduction: Queer Shakes', in *Shakesqueer: A Queer Companion to the Complete Works of Shakespeare*, ed. Madhavi Menon (Durham, 2011), 4.

14  Ibid., 24. As Will Stockton notes, however, Menon's provocative contention does tend to cast aside earlier queer scholarship. See his 'Shakespeare and Queer Theory', *SQ* 63.2 (2012): 224–35. See also the Introduction to *Queer Renaissance Historiography: Backward Gaze*, ed. Stephen Guy-Bray, Vin Nardizzi and Will Stockton (Farnham, Surrey, 2009), 1–10.

15  Jeffrey Masten, 'More or Less Queer', in Menon, *Shakesqueer*, 310.

16  Ramona Wray, 'Communicating Differences: Gender, Feminism, and Queer Studies in the Changing Shakespeare Curriculum', in *Teaching Shakespeare*, ed. G. B. Shand, (Chichester, 2009), 159.

17  Richard Halpern, *Shakespeare's Perfume: Sodomy and Sublimity in the* 'Sonnets' (Philadelphia, 2002), 3.

18  See Goran Stanivuković, 'Beyond Sodomy: What is Still Queer about Early Modern Queer Studies', in *Queer Renaissance Historiography*, 42–65.

19  Adena Rosmarin, 'Hermeneutics versus Erotics: Shakespeare's *Sonnets* and Interpretative History', *PMLA* 100 (1985): 24.

20  Jay D. Bolter and Richard Grusin, *Remediation: Understanding New Media* (Cambridge, MA, 2000), 34.

21  Ibid., 33.

22  On theatrical images, see Patrick Cheney, '"O, Let my Books Be ... Dumb presagers": Poetry and Theatre in Shakespeare's *Sonnets*', *SQ* 52.2 (2001): 222–54.

23  Marshall McLuhan, *Understanding Media* (London, 1964).

24  http://www.youtube.com/watch?v=–1OMKzTXIM0&feature=related (accessed 25 June 2013).

25  Anne Cranny-Francis, *Multimedia: Texts and Contexts* (London, 2005), 12.

26  Anandan Kavoori, *Reading YouTube* (New York, 2011), 8.

27 Ibid., 8.

28 John Ellis, 'The Literary Adaptation', *Screen* 23.1 (1982): 4.

29 Freely available YouTube productions compare favourably with the *Sonnets* for iPad app (http://www.touchpress.com/titles/shakespeares-sonnets/). Although impressive in its design and detail, the app does not incorporate visual treatments.

30 http://www.youtube.com/watch?v=k-kJyL_oeFs&feature=related (accessed 25 June 2013).

31 Duncan-Jones, 12.

32 Booth, *Essay*, 1, 78.

33 Roberto Simanowski, *Digital Art and Meaning: Reading Kinetic Poetry, Text Machines, Mapping Art and Interactive Installations* (Minneapolis, 2011); and Emelia Noronha, 'The Poetics of "Videopoetry" and Video Blogs', 2012 International Conference on Language, Medias and Culture, *IPEDR* 33 (2012): 109–13, www.ipedr.com/vol33/vol33-ICLMC2012-Contents.pdf (accessed 25 June 2013).

34 Jay Bolter, *Writing Space*, quoted in Simanowski, 63.

35 N. Katherine Hayles, *My Mother was a Computer: Digital Subjects and Literary Texts* (Chicago, 2010), 31.

36 Simanowski, 58–69; Jeneen Naji, 'Interactive Poetry: New Content for New Technologies', in *Managing Media Economy, Media Content and Technology in the Age of Digital Convergence*, ed. Zvezdan Vukanovic and Paulo Faustino (Lisbon, 2011), 471–96.

37 Simanowski, 71.

38 Ibid., 62.

39 Ibid.

40 Janez Strehovec, 'Text as Loop/On the Digital Poetry', *Proceedings of the Fifth International Digital Arts and Culture Conference,* RMIT, Melbourne, Australia, 19–23 May 2003, http://hypertext.rmit.edu.au/dac/papers/n.pdf (accessed 25 June 2013).

41 http://www.youtube.com/watch?v=HX8I6P9mLEc (accessed 25 June 2013).

42 See Arthur Marotti, *Manuscript, Print and the English Renaissance Lyric* (Cornell, NY, 1995).

43  Bolter and Grusin, 42.

44  Lauren Shohet, 'YouTube, Use, and the Idea of the Archive', *SQ* 38 (2010): 71.

45  See Booth, 12; Alan Sinfield, *Shakespeare, Authority and Sexuality: Unfinished Business in Cultural Materialism* (London, 2006), 163.

46  Kathyrn Schwarz, 'Will in overplus: Recasting Misogyny in Shakespeare's *Sonnets*', *ELH* 75.3 (2008): 758.

47  See http://www.youtube.com/user/TheSonnetProject (accessed 25 June 2013).

    A similar project has been undertaken at http://www.youtube.com/user/bernardshakespeare. The full text of the *Sonnets* is also available from CC Poems at http://www.youtube.com/course?list=ECBD1864B000E6F368 (accessed 25 June 2013).

48  Julian Yates, 'More Life: Shakespeare's Sonnet Machines', in *Shakesqueer*, 334.

49  Arayne Fradenburg, 'Momma's Boys', in *Shakesqueer*, 321.

50  Ibid., 326.

51  Ibid., 319.

52  Sinfield, 180. Both Fradenburg and Sinfield implicitly revert to Roland Barthes' notion of textual pleasures, of reading and writing as themselves erotic. See Roland Barthes, *The Pleasures of the Text*, trans. Richard Miller (New York, 1975).

53  Stephen Booth, 'I, You, He, She, and We: On the Sexual Politics of Shakespeare's *Sonnets*', in *Shakespeare's* 'Sonnets': *Critical Essays*, ed. James Schiffer (New York, 1999), 417. See also Josephine A. Roberts, '"Thou maist have thy Will": The Sonnets of Shakespeare and his Stepsisters', *SQ* 47.4 (1996): 412–15.

54  See Marianne Novy, *Engaging with Shakespeare: Responses of George Eliot and Other Women Novelists* (Iowa City, 1998).

55  http://www.youtube.com/watch?v=XOCL_NEgf0g (accessed 25 June 2013).

56  de Grazia, 35–49; Peter Stallybrass, 'Editing as Cultural Formation: The Sexing of Shakespeare's *Sonnets*', *MLQ* 54.1 (1993): 91–103.

57  Valerie Traub, 'Sex without Issue: Sodomy, Reproduction,

and Signification in Shakespeare's *Sonnets*', in *Shakespeare's 'Sonnets': Critical Essays*, 441.

58 Judith Butler, *Gender Trouble* (London, 1990), 24.

59 de Grazia, 43.

60 See Kim F. Hall, '"These bastard signs of fair": Literary Whiteness in Shakespeare's Sonnets', in *Postcolonial Shakespeares*, ed. Ania Loomba and Martin Orkin (London, 1998), 64–83.

61 http://www.youtube.com/watch?v=X6FFtq5CEoM (accessed 25 June 2013).

62 http://www.youtube.com/user/BilgeAndTyrone?feature=watch (accessed 25 June 2013).

63 These videos were uploaded between 15 and 16 December 2011. The channel also includes sonnets addressed to the so-called dark lady, which have been deselected from the sample. As these videos take the form of slide-show presentations or montages, and do not feature the creators themseleves, video URLs are provided in the notes below.

64 Sample from http://www.youtube.com/user/CarpenterAPEnglish?feature=watch (videos uploaded January 2011). The channel also includes a video for Sonnet 130, but as this sonnet is not addressed to the young man, it was not included in the sample.

65 http://www.youtube.com/watch?v=THGXkHYNbEo (accessed 25 June 2013).

66 http://www.youtube.com/watch?v=HB7y6jyL8Wo (accessed 25 June 2013).

67 http://www.youtube.com/watch?feature=endscreen&NR=1&v=THGXkHYNbEo (accessed 25 June 2013).

68 http://www.youtube.com/watch?v=XeSttqzPJCQ (accessed 25 June 2013).

69 http://www.youtube.com/watch?v=U–2Va7l6ZAI (accessed 25 June 2013).

70 http://www.youtube.com/watch?v=O5KQ_E-tfXc (accessed 25 June 2013).

71 http://www.youtube.com/watch?v=FnMDj1K0gks (accessed 25 June 2013). A similar move is evident on the YouTube

channel of SpokenVerse. See http://www.youtube.com/
watch?v=IVlOx1yGutc (accessed 25 June 2013).

72 http://www.youtube.com/watch?v=H-_QlzUJBbU (accessed 25
June 2013).

73 Burgess and Green, 25.

74 Judith Halberstam, *In a Queer Time and Place: Transgender
Bodies, Subcultural Lives* (New York, 2005), 19.

75 Lisa Duggan, *The Twilight of Equality: Neo-Liberalism,
Cultural Politics and the Attack on Democracy* (Boston, 2003),
quoted in Halberstam, 19.

76 See Lisa Nakamura, *Cybertypes: Race, Ethnicity and Identity
on the Internet* (London, 2001), 13–14.

77 On homosociality, see Eve Kosofsky Sedgwick, *Between Men:
English Literature and Male Homosocial Desire* (New York,
1985), 28–48; and Traub, 431–52.

78 Sedgwick, 28.

79 Halberstam, 2.

80 http://www.youtube.com/watch?v=X6FFtq5CEoM&gl=US
(accessed 25 June 2013).

81 http://www.youtube.com/watch?v=vtcRM8_uMMU (accessed
25 June 2013).

82 http://www.youtube.com/watch?v=M5Yv7y0Aa00 (accessed 25
June 2013).

83 See Craig Dionne, 'The Shatnerification of Shakespeare: *Star
Trek* and the Commonplace Tradition', in *Shakespeare After
Mass Media*, ed. Richard Burt (New York, 2002), 173–91.

84 Henry Jenkins, *Textual Poachers: Television Fans and
Participatory Culture* (London, 1992), 186.

85 Ibid., 191.

86 The URL for this video has been omitted because it features
performers who were minors at the time of its production.

87 http://www.youtube.com/watch?v=xyU-GetgFnM (accessed 25
June 2013). As this video is a montage of images and therefore
does not feature any individuals, the URL is provided.

**88** http://www.youtube.com/watch?v=AitTUJ9-bBk (accessed 25 June 2013).

# Chapter five

**1** Shakespeare, *Love's Labour's Lost*. (The lines form part of Berowne's long reflection on love, a speech that appears to have gone through several revisions. See Appendix 1 in H. R. Woudhuysen's Arden edition.)

**2** Mark Gammon and Joanne White, '(Social) Media Literacy: Challenges and Opportunities for Higher Education', in *Cutting-Edge Technologies in Higher Education*, ed. Charles Wankel, 3 vols (Bingley, 2011), Vol. 1, 333.

**3** Curtis Bonk, *The World is Open: How Web Technology is Revolutionizing Education* (Hoboken, NJ, 2009), 225.

**4** See Christy Desmet, 'Teaching Shakespeare with YouTube', *English Journal* 99.1 (2009): 65–70.

**5** Andrew Keen, *The Cult of the Amateur* (New York, 2008).

**6** Nicholas Carr, 'Is Google Making us Stupid?', *Atlantic Magazine* (July 2008), http://www.theatlantic.com/magazine/archive/2008/07/is-google-making-us-stupid/306868/ (accessed 25 June 2013), and the same author's *The Shallows: What the Internet is Doing to out Brains* (New York, 2011). For a more informed approach, see Katherine N. Hayes, *How We Think: Digital Media and Contemporary Technogenesis* (Chicago, 2012), 62–68; and Mark B. N. Hansen, 'New Media', in *Critical Terms for Media Studies*, ed. W. J. T Mitchell and Mark B. N. Hansen (Chicago, 2010), 172–85.

**7** Siva Vaidhyanathan, *The Googlization of Everything* (Berkeley, 2011), 174.

**8** I am conscious here of important calls for an expansion of the literary Renaissance. See Jane Grogan, 'Paradise Regained? Teaching the Multicultural Renaissance', in *Teaching the Early Modern Period*, ed. Derval Conroy and Danielle Clarke (Basingstoke, 2011), 124–45.

9   See: Neil Selwyn, 'Faceworking: Exploring Students'
    Education-Related Use of Facebook', *Learning, Media and
    Technology* 34.2 (2009): 157–74; R. Junco, G. Heibergert
    and E. Loken, 'The Effect of Twitter on College Student
    Engagement and Grades', *Journal of Computer Assisted
    Learning* 27.2 (2011): 119–32; and Ajjan Haya and Richard
    Hartshorne, 'Investigating Faculty Decisions to Adopt Web 2.0
    Technologies: Theory and Empirical Tests', *The Internet and
    Higher Education* 11.2 (2008): 71–80.

10  Michael Wesch, 'An Anthropological Introduction to
    YouTube', http://www.youtube.com/watch?v=TPAO-lZ4_
    hU&feature=player_embedded (accessed 25 June 2013).

11  Alexandra Juhasz, *Learning from YouTube* (Cambridge, MA,
    2011), http://vectors.usc.edu/projects/learningfromyoutube/
    texteo.php?composite=53&tag=10 (accessed 25 June 2013).

    See also Juhasz, 'Why Not (to) Teach on YouTube', in *Video
    Vortex Reader: Responses to YouTube*, ed. Geert Lovink
    and Sabine Niederer (Amsterdam, 2008), 133–140. http://
    networkcultures.org/wpmu/portal/publications/inc-readers/
    videovortex/ (accessed 26 June 2013).

12  For example, Juhasz discusses the role of YouTube in
    educational campaigns on AIDS.

13  Louise Marshall and Will Slocombe, 'From Passive to Active
    Voices: Technology, Community, and Literary Studies', in
    *Teaching Literature at a Distance: Open, Online and Blended
    Learning*, ed. Takis Kayalis and Anatasia Natsina (London,
    2010), 102.

14  For an imaginative account of the Web 2.0 student, see
    Cameron Barnes and Belinda Tynan, 'The Adventures of
    Miranda in the Brave New World: Learning in a Web 2.0
    Millennium', *ALT-J, Research in Learning Technology*
    15.3 (2007): 189–200. On data revealing student attitudes
    to Web 2.0, see the discussion about the 'googlization' of
    higher education students in Vaidhyanathan, 189–92; and
    the study conducted in the UK for the Joint Information
    Systems Committee, *Great Expectations of ICT: How
    Higher Education Institutions are Measuring Up* (June
    2008), http://www.jisc.ac.uk/media/documents/publications/

jiscgreatexpectationsfinalreportjune08.pdf (accessed 25 June 2013).

15 Cathy N. Davidson, 'Humanities 2.0: Promise, Perils, and Predictions', *PMLA* 123.3 (2008): 709.

16 See Katheryn Giglio and John Venecek, 'The Radical Historicity of Everything: Exploring Shakespearean Identity with Web 2.0', *DHQ* 3.3 (2009), http://www.digitalhumanities.org/dhq/vol/3/3/000063/000063.html (accessed 25 June 2013).

   See also Susan G. Ziegler, 'The (mis)education of Generation M', *Learning, Media and Technology* 32.1 (2007): 69–81.

17 Gammon and White, 329–45.

18 For an overview of the issues, see Hayles, *How We Think*, 23–54.

19 Marshall and Slocombe, 101. See also *Higher Education in a Web 2.0 World: Report of an independent Committee of Inquiry into the impact on higher education of students' widespread use of Web 2.0 technologies* (March 2009). Available at: http://www.jisc.ac.uk/media/ documents/publications/heweb20rptv1.pdf (accessed 25 June 2013).

20 The 'banking concept' of learning is outlined and critiqued in Paulo Freire, *The Pedagogy of the Oppressed*, trans. Myra Bergmna Ramos (London, 1972).

21 Bonk, 205.

22 Marilyn Tadros, 'A Social Media Approach to Higher Education', in *Educating Educators with Social Media*, 85.

23 Ibid., 86.

24 Ibid., 102.

25 See Don Tapscott, *Grown Up Digital: How the Net Generation is Changing Your World* (New York, 2009); and Marc Prensky, 'Digital Natives, Digital Immigrants', *On the Horizon* 9.5 (2001), http://www.marcprensky.com/writing/ (accessed 25 June 2013).

26 Jason L. Frand, 'The Information-Age Mindset: Changes in Students and Implications for Higher Education', *EDUCAUSE* (2000): 18–24.

27 Diana G. Oblinger and James L. Oblinger, 'Is it an Age or

IT: First Steps Toward Understanding the Net Generation',
in *Educating the Net Generation*, ed. Diana G. Oblinger and
James L. Oblinger (Washington, DC, 2005), 4.

28 Ibid.

29 See Katherine N. Hayles, 'Hyper and Deep Attention: The
Generational Divide in Cognitive Modes', *Profession* (2007):
187–99; and *How We Think*, 55–79.

30 Aden Evens, 'Web 2.0 and the Ontology of the Digital',
*DHQ* 6.2 (2012), http://www.digitalhumanities.org/dhq/
vol/6/2/000120/000120.html (accessed 25 June 2013).

31 Henry Jenkins, with Katie Clinton, Ravi Purushotma, Alice
J. Robison and Margaret Weigel, *Confronting the Challenges
of Participatory Culture: Media Education for the 21st
Century* (Chicago, 2006), http://www.nwp.org/cs/public/print/
resource/2713 (accessed 25 June 2013).

32 Ibid., 4.

33 *Shakespeare: A Worldwide Classroom* was a research project
funded by the British Council. See http://www.rsc.org.uk/
education/research-case-studies/how-the-world-teaches-
shakespeare/worldwide-classroom.aspx (accessed 25 June
2013).

34 Tiffany Stern, 'Teaching Shakespeare in Higher Education', in
*Shakespeare in Education*, ed. Martin Blocksidge (London,
2005), 122.

35 See Sheila Galloway and Steve Strand, *Creating a Community
of Practice: Final Report to the Royal Shakespeare Company's
Learning and Performance Network*, Research and
Development Programme for the evaluation of the RSC's
Learning and Performance Network (LPN), 2007–2009
(Centre for Educational Development Appraisal and Research,
University of Warwick, 2010). The survey was commissioned by
the RSC. It investigated attitudes to Shakespeare in the context
of evaluating the impact of the RSC's Learning and Performance
Network. As the authors summarize, 'the majority of students
held negative attitudes to Shakespeare: only 18 per cent
agreed that "Shakespeare is fun" (and 50 per cent disagreed);
Almost half (46 per cent) agreed with the statement "Studying
Shakespeare is boring"; Only 30 per cent agreed with the

statement "I would be happy to watch a Shakespeare play/film in my own time" (and 51 per cent disagreed)' (Galloway and Strand, 21). The survey was conducted across ten UK secondary schools participating in the LPN in 2007 and repeated in the same schools in 2009.

36 The manifesto is available at http://www.rsc.org.uk/education/sufs/ (accessed 25 June 2013).

37 G. B. Shand, quoted in Nicholas Monk, Carol Rutter and Jonathan Neelands, *Open Space Learning* (London, 2011), 29. For a discussion of practical and non-practical teaching approaches to Shakespeare, see *Open Space Learning*, 10–32, 57–91. On the value of reading the plays theatrically, see Anthony B. Dawson, 'Teaching the Script', in *Teaching Shakespeare: Passing it On*, ed. G. B. Shand (Chichester, 2009), 75–90.

38 Research conducted by Neil Thew across 51 third-level institutions in the UK revealed that among teachers of Shakespeare, 68 per cent indicated that they use electronic resources (including Internet resources/text databases) for teaching and 88 per cent used film and video. See *Teaching Shakespeare: A Survey of the Undergraduate Level in Higher Education* (The Higher Education Academy, 2006), 17–18.

39 http://www.edutopia.org/teaching-shakespeare-digital-media (accessed 25 June 2013).

40 Patricia Cohen, 'Giving Literature Virtual Life', *New York Times*, 22 March 2011, http://www.nytimes.com/2011/03/22/books/digital-humanities-boots-up-on-some-campuses.html?pagewanted=all&_r=0 (accessed 25 June 2013).

41 http://www.torontosun.com/2012/03/25/to-tweet-or-not-to-tweet-that-is-the-question (accessed 25 June 2013).

42 See also the outreach activities of the Folger Institute, where the language and logic of remix is used to teach Shakespeare in elementary schools, http://www.folger.edu/template.cfm?cid=2614 (accessed 25 June 2013).

43 Danika Barker (a teacher at Central Elgin Collegiate Institute, Toronto) outlines her approach at http://live.classroom20.com/1/post/2012/08/teaching-shakespeare-with-twitter.html (accessed 25 June 2013).

44 http://2012.playingshakespeare.org/ (accessed 25 June 2013). For a fascinating analysis of the live and the mediatized at the Globe, see Catherine Silverstone, 'Shakespeare Live: Reproducing Shakespeare at the "new" Globe', *Textual Practice* 19.1 (2005): 31–50.

45 See Katherine Rowe, 'Crowd-Sourcing Shakespeare: Screen Work and Screen Play in Second Life', *SSt* 38 (2010): 58–67. The article is also available, with illustrations, at http://www. brynmawr.edu/english/Faculty_and_Staff/rowe/CrowdSourcing. html (accessed 25 June 2013).

46 Wikis and Facebook have been deployed to teach *Romeo and Juliet* – see Hayles, *How We Think*, 73–4. The wiki is available at http://english149-w2008.pbworks.com/w/page/19011402/ Romeo%20and%20Juliet%3A%20A%20Facebook%20 Tragedy (accessed 25 June 2013).

47 Giglio and Venecek, 3.

48 See Richard E. Mayer, 'Applying the Science of Learning: Evidence-Based Principles for the Design of Multimedia Instruction', *American Psychologist* (2008): 760–9; and Troy Jones and Kristen Cuthrell, 'YouTube: Educational Potentials and Pitfalls', *Computers in the Schools* 28.1 (2011): 75–85.

49 Barbara Mitra, Jenny Lewin Jones, Heather Barrett and Stella Williamson, 'The Use of Video to enable Deep Learning', *Research in Post-Compulsory Education* 15.4 (2010): 405–14.

50 See Laurie E. Osborne, 'Clip Art: Theorizing the Shakespeare Film Clip', *SQ* 53.2 (2002): 227–40.

51 Roger Osche, 'Digital Shakespeare: Integrating Texts and Technology', in *For all Time? Critical Issues in Teaching Shakespeare*, ed. Peter Skrebels and Sieta van de Hoeven (Kent Town, 2002), 44.

52 Shakespeare, *Romeo and Juliet*, Prologue, 12. The similarities between the contemporary tendency to digest nuggets of information and the early modern tradition of the commonplace book have not gone unnoticed. See Neil Rhodes and Jonathan Sawday's Introduction to *The Renaissance Computer: Knowledge Technology in the First Age of Print* (London, 2000), 1–16; and Danielle Clarke, 'Renaissance Teaching and Learning: Humanist Pedagogy in the Digital Age

and What it Might Teach Us', in *Teaching the Early Modern Period*, 27–49.

53 Juhasz, http://vectors.usc.edu/projects/learningfromyoutube/texteo.php?composite=107&tour=9& (accessed 25 June 2013).

54 Juhasz, 'Why Not (to) Teach on YouTube', 135.

55 Juhasz, http://vectors.usc.edu/projects/learningfromyoutube/texteo.php?composite=18&tour=9& (accessed 25 June 2013).

56 This is a collaborative research project, directed by Professor Peter Donaldson of MIT, http://globalshakespeares.mit.edu/# (accessed 25 June 2013).

57 See Alexander Huang, 'Global Shakespeare 2.0 and the Task of the Performance Archive', *SS* 64 (2011): 38–51.

58 'Global Shakespeares' has a channel on YouTube, http://www.youtube.com/user/globalshakespeare (accessed 25 June 2013).

59 Mitra et al., 410.

60 Ceri Sullivan, 'The Importance of Boredom in Learning about The Early Modern', in *Teaching the Early Modern Period*, 223.

61 Lauren Shohet, 'YouTube, Use, and the Idea of the Archive', *SSt* 38 (2010): 69.

62 See Philip Auslander, *Liveness: Performance in a Mediatized Culture* (London, 1999), 7.

63 Shohet, 70.

64 Ibid., 70–1.

65 Katherine Rowe, 'Shakespeare and Media History', in *New Cambridge Companion to Shakespeare*, ed. Margreta de Grazia and Stanley Wells (Cambridge, 2010), 318–20.

66 See Michael D. Bristol, *Big-Time Shakespeare* (London, 1996).

67 Bryan Alexander and Alan Levine, 'Web 2.0 Storytelling: Emergence of a New Genre', *EDUCAUSE Review* (2008): 41–56.

68 See Guy Merchant, 'Unravelling the Social Network: Theory and Research', *Learning, Media and Technology* 37.1 (2012): 4–19.

69 See report cited above, note 19.

70  See Malik Aleem Ahmed, 'Social Media for Higher Education
    in Developing Countries – an Intercultural Perspective',
    in *Educating Educators with Social Media*, 59–80; and
    Laura Czerniewicz and Cheryl Brown, 'The Habitus of
    Digital "Strangers" in Higher Education', *British Journal of
    Educational Technology* 44.1 (2013): 44–53.

71  Juhasz, http://vectors.usc.edu/projects/learningfromyoutube/
    texteo.php?composite=53&tag=10 (accessed 25 June 2013).

72  On Shakespeare's spectrality, see Courtney Lehmann,
    *Shakespeare Remains: Theatre to Film, Early Modern to
    Postmodern* (Ithaca, NY, 2002).

73  Osche, 48.

74  Barbara Hodgdon, 'The Last Shakespeare Picture Show of
    Going to the Barricades', in *Teaching Shakespeare*, 116–17.

75  I have been influenced here by Katherine Rowe's comments,
    made in a short interview available on the Folger's YouTube
    channel, about the possibilities of the digital for Shakespeare
    studies. See http://www.youtube.com/watch?v=Aofsh1kBM
    1g&list=PL1F9AE3B7EBF9ADEC (accessed 25 June 2013).
    Equally, however, I am thinking of assignments and final essays
    by students in my Contemporary Shakespeare seminar: the
    students embedded video links into their work as merely a
    sensible thing to do.

76  Gammon and White, 333.

77  Tadros, 92.

78  Gammon and White, 335.

79  Desmet, 'Teaching Shakespeare with YouTube', 65.

80  See Terri L. Toner and Caroline Lego Munoz, 'Facebook
    and Education: A Classroom Connection', in *Cutting-Edge
    Technologies in Higher Education*, 33–57.

81  Jennifer Clement, 'Against Ownership', *Teaching Shakespeare* 2
    (2012): 14.

82  See Kate McLuskie, 'Dancing and Thinking: Teaching
    "Shakespeare" in the Twenty-First Century', in *Teaching
    Shakespeare*, 138.

83  I recommend requiring students to submit the assignment

electronically – this way, the teacher has time to review the videos selected by the students and to add them to a playlist, which can be used in the following week's class for group discussion. There are advantages here for the student too, since it allows them to watch and review videos in their own time.

84 From my own experience, using a playlist of student selections in the seminar can promote critical peer learning; students can often be critical of each other's selections (for instance, where a SparkNotes tutorial had been included).

85 See Russ MacDonald, 'Planned Obsolescence or Working at the Words', in *Teaching Shakespeare*, 35.

86 Giglio and Venecek, 15. See also Paul Skrebels, 'Shakespeare Reworked: Textual Intervention Strategies in the University Writing Classroom', in *For all Time?*, 55–67.

87 See Miriam Gilbert, 'A Test of Character', in *Teaching Shakespeare*, 91–104.

88 Bridget Escolme, 'Costume', in *Shakespeare and the Making of Theatre*, ed. Stuart Hampton-Reeves and Bridget Escolme (Basingstoke, 2012), 130.

89 Jenkins et al., 32.

90 Nicholas Carr, 'Sharecropping the Long Tail', available at http://www.roughtype.com/?p=634 (accessed 25 June 2013).

91 Bryan Alexander, 'Web 2.0: A New Wave of Innovation for Teaching and Learning?', *EDUCAUSE* 41.2 (2006): 32–44; Barnes and Tynan, 196.

92 Brian Lamb, 'Dr Mashup; or, Why Educators Should Learn to Stop Worrying and Love the Remix', *EDUCAUSE* 42.4 (2007): 13–24.

93 Ibid., 17–18.

94 The academic networking site academia.edu may be changing this somewhat, as scholars upload papers in advance of publication, or use the site to promote and disseminate work already published.

95 Stern, 139.

# BIBLIOGRAPHY

(Where an author/s has multiple titles to their credit, these are arranged in date order (earliest first). The exception are the plays and sonnets of Shakespeare, which are arranged alphabetically by title.)

Adelman, Janet, *Suffocating Mothers: Fantasies of Maternal Origin in Shakespeare's Plays,* 'Hamlet' *to* 'The Tempest' (New York, 1992).

Adorno, Theodor W, *The Culture Industry: Selected Essays on Mass Culture* (London, 2001).

Ahmed, Malik Aleem, 'Social Media for Higher Education in Developing Countries – an Intercultural Perspective', in *Cutting-Edge Technologies in Higher Education* ed. Charles Wankel, 3 vols (Bingley, 2011), Vol. 1, 59–80.

Alexander, Bryan, 'Web 2.0: A New Wave of Innovation for Teaching and Learning?', *EDUCAUSE* 41.2 (2006): 32–44.

Alexander, Bryan and Alan Levine, 'Web 2.0 Storytelling: Emergence of a New Genre', *EDUCAUSE Review* (2008): 41–56.

Alexander, Jonathan and Jacqueline Rhodes, 'Technologies of the Self in the Aftermath: Affect, Subjectivity, and Composition', *Rhetoric Review* 29.2 (2010): 145–64.

*Amar te Duele / Love Hurts*, dir. Fernando Sariñana (Altavista Films, 2002).

Anderson, Chris, 'The Long Tail', *Wired* 12.10 (2004), http://www.wired.com/wired/archive/12.10/tail. html?pg=2&topic=tail&topic_set= (accessed 25 June 2013).

Anderson, Lisa M., 'When Race Matters: Reading Race in *Richard III* and *Macbeth*', in *Colorblind Shakespeare: New Perspectives on Race and Performance*, ed. Ayanna Thompson (London, 2006), 89–102.

Appiah, Anthony K., 'Racial Identity and Racial Identification', in *Theories of Race and Racism*, ed. Les Black and John Solomos (New York, 2000), 607–15.

Asimov, Issac, 'The Immortal Bard', in *After Shakespeare*, ed. John Gross (Oxford, 2002), 327–9.

Association of Internet Researchers, *Ethical Decision-Making and Internet Research: Recommendations from the AoIR Ethics Working Committee (Version 2.0)*, http://aoir.org/documents/ethics-guide/ (accessed 25 June 2013).

Auslander, Philip, *Liveness: Performance in a Mediatized Culture* (London, 1999).

*The Banquet*, dir. Xiaogong Feng (Media Asia Films, 2006).

Barnes, Cameron and Belinda Tynan, 'The Adventures of Miranda in the Brave New World: Learning in a Web 2.0 Millennium', *ALT-J, Research in Learning Technology* 15.3 (2007): 189–200.

Bartels, Emily, 'Making More of the Moor: Aaron, Othello and Renaissance Refashionings of Race', *SQ* 41 (1990): 433–54.

Barthes, Roland, *The Pleasures of the Text*, trans. Richard Miller (New York, 1975).

Baudrillard, Jean, 'Simulacra and Simulations', in *Jean Baudrillard: Selected Writings*, ed. Mark Poster (London, 2001), 169–87.

Bloom, Harold, *Shakespeare: The Invention of the Human* (London, 1999).

Bolter, Jay D. and Richard Grusin, *Remediation: Understanding New Media* (Cambridge, MA, 2000).

Bonk, Curtis, *The World is Open: How Web Technology is Revolutionizing Education* (Hoboken, NJ, 2009).

Boose, Lynda E., '"Let it be hid": The Pornographic Aesthetic of Shakespeare's *Othello*', in *Othello*, Contemporary Critical Essays, ed. Lena Cowen Orlin (London, 2003), 22–48.

Booth, Paul, 'Mashup as Temporal Amalgam: Time, Taste, and Textuality', *TWC* 9 (2012), doi:10.3983/twc.2012.0297 (accessed 25 June 2013).

Booth, Stephen, *An Essay on Shakespeare's 'Sonnets'* (New Haven, CT, 1969).

—, 'I, You, He, She, and We: On the Sexual Politics of Shakespeare's *Sonnets*', in *Shakespeare's 'Sonnets': Critical Essays*, ed. James Schiffer (New York, 1999), 411–29.

Bristol, Michael D., *Big-Time Shakespeare* (London, 1996).

Bruster, Douglas, *Quoting Shakespeare: Form and Culture in Early Modern Drama* (Lincoln, 2000).

Buhler, Stephen, 'Reviving Juliet, Repackaging Romeo: Transformations of Character in Pop and Post-Pop Music', in

*Shakespeare after Mass Media*, ed. Richard Burt (New York, 2002), 243–64.

Burgess, Jean, '"All your Chocolate Rain are belong to us?": Viral Video, YouTube and the Dynamics of Participatory Culture', in *Video Vortex Reader: Responses to YouTube*, 101–9.

Burgess, Jean and Joshua Green, *YouTube* (Cambridge, 2009).

Burnett, Mark Thornton, '"To Hear and See the Matter": Communicating Technology in Michael Almereyda's *Hamlet*', *Cinema Journal* 42.3 (2003): 48–69.

—, 'Writing Shakespeare in the Global Economy', *SS* 58 (2005): 185–98.

—, *Shakespeare and World Cinema* (Cambridge, 2012).

Burns, Christy, 'Suturing over Racial Differences: Problems for a Colorblind Approach in Visual Culture', *Discourse* 22.1 (2000): 70–91.

Burt, Richard, 'Slammin' Shakespeare In Acc(id)ents Yet Unknown: Liveness, Cinem(edi)a, and Racial Dis-Integration', *SQ* 53 (2002): 201–26.

—, 'Backstage Pass(ing): *Stage Beauty*, *Othello* and the Make-Up of Race', in *Screening Shakespeare in the Twenty First-Century*, ed. Mark Thornton Burnett and Ramona Wray (Edinburgh, 2006), 53–71.

—, 'CivicShakesPR: Middlebrow Multiculturalism, White Television, and the Color Bind', in *Colorblind Shakespeare* (2006), 157–85.

—, 'Shakespeare, More or Less? From Shakespeareccentricity to Shakespearecentricity and Back', in *Shakespeares after Shakespeare: An Encylopedia of the Bard in Mass Media and Popular Culture*, ed. Richard Burt, 2 vols (Westport, CT, 2007), 1–9.

—, 'Mobilizing Foreign Shakespeares in Media', in *Shakespeare in Hollywood, Asia and Cyberspace*, ed. Alexander C. Huang and Charles S. Ross (West Lafayette, 2009), 231–8.

Butler, Judith, *Gender Trouble* (London, 1990).

Calbi, Maurizio, 'Shakespeare in the Extreme: Addiction, Ghosts and (Re)Mediation in Alexander Fodor's *Hamlet*', *Literature Film Quarterly* 39.2 (2011): 85–98.

Callaghan, Dympna, '"Othello was a white man": Properties of Race on Shakespeare's Stage', in *Alternative Shakespeares*, Vol. 2, ed. Terence Hakwes (London, 1996), 192–215.

Carlson, Marvin, *The Haunted Stage: The Theatre as Memory Machine* (Ann Arbor, MI, 2001).

Carr, Nicholas, 'Is Google Making us Stupid?', *Atlantic Magazine* (July 2008), http://www.theatlantic.com/magazine/ archive/2008/07/is-google-making-us-stupid/306868/ (accessed 25 June 2013).

—, *The Shallows: What the Internet is Doing to out Brains* (New York, 2011).

Cartelli, Thomas, 'Shakespeare and the Street: Pacino's *Looking for Richard*, Bedford's *Street King*, and the Common Understanding', in *Shakespeare: The Movie II*, ed. Richard Burt and Lynda E. Boose (London, 2003), 186–99.

Carter, Geoffrey V. and Sarah J. Arroyo, 'Video and Participatory Cultures: Writing, Rhetoric, Performance, and the Tube', *Enculturation* 8 (2010), http://enculturation.gmu.edu/8 (accessed 25 June 2013).

Caruth, Cathy, ed., *Trauma: Explorations in Memory* (Baltimore, 1995).

Casetti, Francesco, 'Back to the Motherland: The Film Theatre in the Postmedia Age', *Screen* 52.1 (2011): 1–12.

Cha, Meeyoung et al., 'I Tube, You Tube, Everybody Tubes: Analysing the World's Largest User Generated Content Video System', *Proceedings of the 7th ACM SIGCOMM Conference on Internet Measurement* (2007), 1–14.

Charnes, Linda, *Hamlet's Heirs: Shakespeare and the Politics of a New Millennium* (London, 2006).

—, 'Anticipating Nostalgia: Finding Temporal Logic in a Textual Anomaly', *Textual Cultures* 4.1 (2009): 72–83.

Cheney, Patrick, '"O, Let my Books Be … Dumb presagers": Poetry and Theatre in Shakespeare's *Sonnets*', *SQ* 52.2 (2001): 222–54.

—, *Shakespeare, National Poet-Playwright* (Cambridge, 2004).

*Chicken Rice War*, dir. Chee Kong Cheah (Mediacorp Raintree, 2000).

Cimitile, Anna Maria and Katherine Rowe, 'Introduction: Overlapping Mediascapes in the Mind', Shakespeare in the Media: Old and New, special issue, *Anglistica* 15.2 (2011): ii, http://www.anglistica.unior.it/content/shakespeare-media-old-and-new (accessed 25 June 2013).

Clarke, Danielle, 'Renaissance Teaching and Learning: Humanist Pedagogy in the Digital Age and What it Might Teach Us', in

*Teaching the Early Modern Period*, ed. Derval Conroy and
Danielle Clarke (Basingstoke, 2011), 27–49.

Clement, Jennifer, 'Against Ownership', *Teaching Shakespeare* 2
(2012): 14.

Cohen, Patricia, 'Giving Literature Virtual Life', *New York
Times*, 22 March 2011, http://www.nytimes.com/2011/03/22/
books/digital-humanities-boots-up-on-some-campuses.
html?pagewanted=all&_r=0 (accessed 25 June 2013).

Cohn, Ruby, *Modern Shakespeare Offshoots* (Princeton, NJ, 1976).

Conkie, Robert, 'Shakespeare Aftershocks: Shylock', *Shakespeare
Bulletin* 27 (2009): 549–66.

*Coriolanus*, dir. Ralph Fiennes (Lionsgate, 2012).

Cranny-Francis, Anne, *Multimedia: Texts and Contexts* (London,
2005).

Czerniewicz, Laura and Cheryl Brown, 'The Habitus of Digital
"Strangers" in Higher Education', *British Journal of Educational
Technology* 44.1 (2013): 44–53.

Daileader, Celia R., 'Casting Black Actors: beyond Othellophilia',
in *Shakespeare and Race*, ed. Catherine M. S. Alexander and
Stanley Wells (Cambridge, 2000), 177–202.

—, *Racism, Misogyny and the 'Othello' Myth: Inter-Racial Couples
from Shakespeare to Spike Lee* (Cambridge, 2005).

da Silva, Patrícia Dias and José Luís Garcia, 'YouTubers as
Satirists', *JeDEM* 4.1 (2012): 89–114.

Davidson, Cathy N., 'Humanities 2.0: Promise, Perils, and
Predictions', *PMLA* 123.3 (2008): 707–17.

Dawson, Anthony B., 'Teaching the Script', in *Teaching
Shakespeare: Passing it On*, ed. G. B. Shand (Chichester, 2009),
75–90.

deGravelles, Karin H., 'You Be Othello: Interrogating Identification
in the Classroom', *Pedagogy* 11.1 (2011): 153–75.

de Grazia, Margreta, 'The Scandal of Shakespeare's *Sonnets*',
*Shakespeare Survey* 46 (1994): 35–49.

—, *Hamlet without 'Hamlet'* (London, 2007).

Dentith, Simon, *Parody* (London, 2000).

Derrida, Jacques, *Of Grammatology*, trans. Gayatri Chakravorty
Spivak (Baltimore, 1976).

—, *Specters of Marx*, trans. Peggy Kamuf (London, 1994).

Desmet, Christy, 'Introduction', in *Shakespeare and Appropriation*,
ed. Christy Desmet and Robert Sawyer (London, 1999), 1–12.

—, 'Paying Attention in Shakespeare Parody: From Tom Stoppard to YouTube', *SS* 61 (2008): 227–38.

—, 'Teaching Shakespeare with YouTube', *English Journal* 99.1 (2009): 65–70.

Desmet, Christy and Sujata Iyengar, 'Rebooting Ophelia: Social Media and the Rhetorics of Adaptation', in *The Afterlife of Ophelia*, ed. Kaara L. Peterson and Deanne Williams (Basingstoke, 2012), 59–78.

Ding, Yuan et al., 'Broadcast Yourself: Understanding YouTube Uploaders', *Proceedings of the 2011 ACM SIGCOMM Conference on Internet Measurement Conference* (Berlin, 2011), 361–70, http://doi.acm.org/10.1145/2068816.2068850 (accessed 25 June 2013).

Dionne, Craig and Parmita Kapadia, eds, *Native Shakespeares: Indigenous Appropriations on a Global Stage* (Aldershot, 2008).

DiPietro, Cary, 'Sex, Lies and Videotape: Representing the Past in *Shakespeare in Love*, Mapping a Future for Presentism', *Shakespeare* 3.1 (2007): 40–62.

DiPietro, Cary and Hugh Grady, 'Presentism, Anachronism and the Case of *Titus Andronicus*', *Shakespeare* 8.1 (2012): 44–73.

Dobson, Michael, *Shakespeare and Amateur Performance: A Cultural History* (Cambridge, 2011).

Donaldson, Peter, '"All Which It Inherit": Shakespeare, Globes and Global Media', *SS* 52 (1999): 183–200.

—, 'Hamlet among the Pixelvisionaries: Video Art, Authenticity and "Wisdom" in Almereyda's *Hamlet*', in *A Concise Companion to Shakespeare on Screen*, ed. Diana E. Henderson (Oxford, 2006), 216–37.

*Downfall*, dir. Oliver Hirschbiegel (Constantin Film, 2004).

Drakakis, John, 'Present Text: Editing *The Merchant of Venice*', in *Presentist Shakespeares*, ed. Hugh Grady and Terence Hawkes (London, 2007), 75–95.

Dugan, Emily and Louise Fitzgerald, 'A Brief History of the *Harlem Shake*', *Independent*, 3 March 2013, http://www.independent. co.uk/arts-entertainment/theatre-dance/news/a-brief-history-of-the-harlem-shake–8518071.html (accessed 25 June 2013).

Dyer, Richard, 'The Matter of Whiteness', in *Theories of Race and Racism*, ed. Les Black and John Solomos (New York, 2000), 539–48.

Edelman, Lee, 'Against Survival: Queerness in a Time That's Out of Joint', *SQ* 62.2 (2011): 148–69.

Ellis, John, 'The Literary Adaptation', *Screen* 23.1 (1982): 3–5.

Elsaesser, Thomas, 'Tales of Epiphany and Entropy: Around the World in Eighty Clicks', in *The YouTube Reader*, 166–86.

Erickson, Peter, *Citing Shakespeare: The Reinterpretation of Race in Contemporary Literature and Art* (New York, 2007).

Escolme, Bridget, 'Costume', in *Shakespeare and the Making of Theatre*, ed. Stuart Hampton-Reeves and Bridget Escolme (Basingstoke, 2012), 128–45.

Evens, Aden, 'Web 2.0 and the Ontology of the Digital', *DHQ* 6.2 (2012), http://www.digitalhumanities.org/dhq/vol/6/2/000120/000120.html (accessed 25 June 2013).

Fanon, Frantz, *Black Skin, White Masks*, trans. Charles Lam Markham (London, 1986).

Fernie, Ewan, 'Shakespeare and the Prospect of Presentism', *SS* 58 (2005): 69–184.

*Final Destination*, dir. James Wong (New Line Cinema, 2000).

Fischlin, Daniel and Mark Fortier, eds, *Adaptations of Shakespeare: A Critical Anthology of Plays from the Seventeenth Century to the Present* (London, 2000).

Fradenburg, Arayne, 'Momma's Boys', in *Shakesqueer: A Queer Companion to the Complete Works of Shakespeare*, ed. Madhavi Menon (Durham, NC, 2011), 319–27.

Frand, Jason L., 'The Information-Age Mindset: Changes in Students and Implications for Higher Education', *EDUCAUSE* 35.5 (2000): 18–24.

Freire, Paulo, *The Pedagogy of the Oppressed*, trans. Myra Bergmna Ramos (London, 1972).

Gallop, Jane, 'Lacan's "Mirror Stage": Where to Begin', *SubStance* 11/12 (1982–83): 118–28.

Galloway, Alexander, *The Interface Effect* (Cambridge, 2012)

Galloway, Sheila and Steve Strand, *Creating a Community of Practice: Final Report to the Royal Shakespeare Company's Learning and Performance Network* (Centre for Educational Development Appraisal and Research, University of Warwick, 2010).

Gammon, Mark and Joanne White, '(Social) Media Literacy: Challenges and Opportunities for Higher Education', in *Cutting-Edge Technologies in Higher Education*, 329–46.

Garber, Marjorie, *Shakespeare After All* (New York, 2004).

—, *Profiling Shakespeare* (New York, 2008).

—, *Shakespeare and Modern Culture* (New York, 2009).

—, *Shakespeare's Ghost Writers: Literature as Uncanny Causality*, Routledge Classics (London, 2010).

*Gedebe*, dir. Nam Ron (Pustaka Cipta Sdn Bhd, 2002).

Gehl, Robert, 'YouTube as Archive: Who will Curate this Digital Wunderkammer?', *International Journal of Cultural Studies* 12.1 (2009): 43–59.

Giglio, Katheryn and John Venecek, 'The Radical Historicity of Everything: Exploring Shakespearean Identity with Web 2.0', *DHQ* 3.3 (2009), http://www.digitalhumanities.org/dhq/vol/3/3/000063/000063.html (accessed 25 June 2013).

Gilbert, Miriam, 'A Test of Character', in *Teaching Shakespeare: Passing It On*, 91–104.

Gil Harris, Jonathan, 'Shakespeare and Race', in *New Cambridge Companion to Shakespeare*, ed. Margreta de Grazia and Stanley Wells (Cambridge, 2010).

Gilroy, Paul, *Against Race: Imagining Politcal Change Beyond the Color Line* (Cambridge, MA, 2000).

Gonick, Marnina, 'Between "Girl Power" and "Reviving Ophelia": Constituting the Neoliberal Girl Subject', *NWSA* 18.2 (2006): 1–23.

Grady, Hugh, *Shakespeare's Universal Wolf: Studies in Early Modern Reification* (Oxford, 1996).

Gray, Jonathan, *Show Sold Separately: Promos, Spoilers and Other Media Paratexts* (New York, 2010).

Grogan, Jane, 'Paradise Regained? Teaching the Multicultural Renaissance', in *Teaching the Early Modern Period*, 124–45.

Grundberg, Andy, *Crisis of the Real: Writings on Photography, 1974–1989* (New York, 1990).

Grusin, Richard, 'YouTube at the End of New Media', in *The YouTube Reader*, ed. Pelle Snickars and Patrick Vonderau (Stockholm, 2009), 60–7.

Halberstam, Judith, *In a Queer Time and Place: Transgender Bodies, Subcultural Lives* (New York, 2005).

Hall, Kim F., '"These bastard signs of fair": Literary Whiteness in Shakespeare's *Sonnets*', in *Postcolonial Shakespeares*, ed. Ania Loomba and Martin Orkin (London, 1998), 64–83.

Hall, Stuart, 'New Ethnicities', in *Stuart Hall: Critical Dialogues in Cultural Studies*, ed. David Morley and Kuan-Hsing Chen (New York, 1996), 441–9.

Hall, Stuart, 'What is this "Black" in Black Popular Culture', in *Stuart Hall: Critical Dialogues in Cultural Studies*, 465–75.

Halpern, Richard, *Shakespeare among the Moderns* (Ithaca, NY, 1997).

—, *Shakespeare's Perfume: Sodomy and Sublimity in the* 'Sonnets' (Philadelphia, 2002).

*Hamlet*, dir. Michael Almereyda (Miramax, 2000).

Hansen, Adam, *Shakespeare and Popular Music* (London, 2010).

Hansen, Mark B. N., Introduction to Bernard Stiegler, 'Memory', in *Critical Terms for Media Studies*, ed. W. J. T Mitchell and Mark B. N. Hansen (Chicago, 2010), 64–6.

Hansen, Mark B. N., 'New Media', in *Critical Terms for Media Studies*, 172–85.

Hartley, John, 'Uses of You Tube: Digital Literacy and the Growth of Knowledge', in Burgess and Green, *YouTube,* 126–43.

Hawkes, Terence, *Meaning by Shakespeare* (London, 1992).

—, *Shakespeare in the Present* (London, 2002).

Haya, Ajjan and Richard Hartshorne, 'Investigating Faculty Decisions to Adopt Web 2.0 Technologies: Theory and Empirical Tests', *The Internet and Higher Education* 11.2 (2008): 71–80.

Hayles, Katherine N., 'Hyper and Deep Attention: The Generational Divide in Cognitive Modes', *Profession* (2007): 187–99.

—, *My Mother was a Computer: Digital Subjects and Literary Texts* (Chicago, 2010).

—, *How We Think: Digital Media and Contemporary Technogenesis* (Chicago, 2012).

Healy, Thomas, 'Past and Present Shakespeares', in *Shakespeare and National Culture*, ed. John J. Joughin (Manchester, 1997), 206–32.

Hebdidge, Dick, *Subcultures: The Meaning of Style* (London, 1979).

Henderson, Diana E., 'Shakespeare: The Theme Park', in *Shakespeare after Mass Media*, 107–26.

Hendricks, Margo; 'Surveying "Race" in Shakespeare', in *Shakespeare and Race*, 1–22.

—, 'Gestures of Performance: Rethinking Race in Contempoary Shakespeare', in *Colorblind Shakespeare* (2006), 187–203.

Hill, Jane H., *Everday Language of White Racism* (Hoboken, NJ, 2009), 49–87.

Hillis, Ken, Michael Petit and Kylie Jarrett, *Google and the Culture of Search* (London, 2013).

Hills, Matt, *Fan Cultures* (London, 2002).

Hjarvard, Stig, *The Mediatization of Culture and Society* (New York, 2013).

Hodgdon, Barbara, 'Race-ing *Othello*, Re-engendering White-Out, II', in *Shakespeare: The Movie II* (2003), 89–104.

—, 'Afterword', in *World-Wide Shakespeares: Local Appropriations in Film and Performance*, ed. Sonia Massai (London, 2005), 157–60.

—, 'The Last Shakespeare Picture Show of Going to the Barricades', in *Teaching Shakespeare: Passing it On* (2009), 105–20.

Holbrook, Peter, *Shakespeare's Individualism* (Cambridge, 2010).

Holderness, Graham, '"Author! Author!": Shakespeare and Biography', *Shakespeare* 5.1 (2013): 122–33.

Holland, Peter, 'Performing Shakespeare for the Web Community', in *Shakespeare in Hollywood, Asia and Cyberspace*, ed. Alexander C. Y. Huang and Charles Stanley Ross (West Lafayette, IN, 2009), 252–64.

Houlahan, Mark, 'Hekepia? The *Mana* of the Maori *Merchant*', in *World-Wide Shakespeares*, 141–8.

Howard, Tony, *Women as Hamlet: Performance and Interpretation in Theatre, Film, and Fiction* (Cambridge, 2007).

Huang, Alexander, *Chinese Shakespeares: Two Centuries of Cultural Exchange* (New York, 2009).

—, 'Global Shakespeare 2.0 and the Task of the Performance Archive', *SS* 64 (2011): 38–51.

Hulbert, Jennifer, '"Adolescence, Thy Name is Ophelia!": The Ophelia-ization of the Contemporary Teenage Girl', in Kevin Wetmore, Jennifer Hulbert, and Robert York, *Shakespeare and Youth Culture* (New York, 2006), 199–220.

Hutcheon, Linda, *A Theory of Parody* (London, 1985).

Iyengar, Sujata, *Shades of Difference: Mythologies of Skin Colour in Early Modern England* (Philadelphia, 2005).

Jameson, Frederic, 'Postmodernism, or the Cultural Logic of Late Capitalism', *New Left Review* 1.146 (1984): 53–92.

—, *Postmodernism, or, The Cultural Logic of Late Capitalism* (Durham, NC, 1991).

Jarrett, Kylie, 'Beyond Broadcast Yourself ™: The Future of YouTube', *Media International Australia* 126 (2008): 132–44.

Jenkins, Henry, *Textual Poachers: Television Fans and Participatory Culture* (London, 1992).

—, *Convergence Culture: Where Old and New Media Collide* (New York, 2006).

—, 'What happened before YouTube,' in Burgess and Green, *YouTube* (2009), 109–25.

Jenkins, Henry, with Katie Clinton, Ravi Purushotma, Alice J. Robison and Margaret Weigel, *Confronting the Challenges of Participatory Culture: Media Education for the 21st Century* (Chicago, 2006), http://www.nwp.org/cs/public/print/resource/2713 (accessed 25 June 2013).

Jenkins, Henry, Sam Ford and Joshua Green, *Spreadable Media: Creating Value and Meaning in a Networked Culture* (New York, 2013).

Jess-Cooke, Carolyn, 'Screening the McShakespeare in Post-Millennial Shakespeare Cinema', in *Screening Shakespeare in the Twenty-First Century*, 163–84.

Jones, Maria, 'The Cultural Logic of "Correcting" *The Merchant of Venice*', in *World-Wide Shakespeares*, 122–31.

Jones, Troy and Kristen Cuthrell, 'YouTube: Educational Potentials and Pitfalls', *Computers in the Schools* 28.1 (2011): 75–85.

Joughin, John J., 'Shakespeare's Genius: *Hamlet*, Adaptation and the Work of Following', in *The New Aestheticism*, ed. John J. Joughin and Simon Malpas (Manchester, 2003), 131–50.

Juhasz, Alexandra, 'Why Not (to) Teach on YouTube', in *Video Vortex Reader: Responses to YouTube*, ed. Geert Lovink and Sabine Niederer (Amsterdam, 2008), 133–40, http://networkcultures.org/wpmu/portal/publications/inc-readers/videovortex/ (accessed 25 June 2013).

—, *Learning from YouTube* (Cambridge, MA, 2011), http://vectors.usc.edu/projects/learningfromyoutube/# (accessed 25 June 2013).

Junco, R., G. Heibergert and E. Loken, 'The Effect of Twitter on College Student Engagement and Grades', *Journal of Computer Assisted Learning* 27.2 (2011): 119–32.

Kahn, Coppelia, *Roman Shakespeare: Warriors, Wounds, and Women* (London, 1997).

—, 'Afterword: Ophelia Then, Now, Hereafter', in *The Afterlife of Ophelia* (2012), 231–44.

Kamps, Ivor, 'Alas, Poor Shakespeare! I Knew Him Well', in *Shakespeare and Appropriation*, 15–31.

Kavoori, Anandan, *Reading YouTube* (New York, 2011).

Keen, Andrew, *The Cult of the Amateur* (New York, 2008).

Kember, Sarah and Joanna Zylinska, *Life after New Media: Mediation as Vital Process* (Cambridge, MA, 2012).

Kessler, Frank and Mirko Tobias Schafer, 'Navigating YouTube: Constituting a Hybrid Information Management System', in *The YouTube Reader*, 275–91.

Kidnie, Margaret, *Shakespeare and the Problem of Adaptation* (London, 2009).

Ko, Yu Jin, 'Honolulu Theatre for Youth's Rap *Othello*', *Borrowers and Lenders* 2.1 (2006), http://www.borrowers.uga.edu/783083/display (accessed 25 June 2013).

Kott, Jan, *Shakespeare Our Contemporary*, trans. Boleslaw Taborski (London, 1965).

Kruitbosch, Gijs and Frank Nack, 'Broadcast Yourself on YouTube – Really?', *Proceedings of the 3rd ACM International Workshop on Human-Centered Computing* (Vancouver, 2008), 7–10, http://doi.acm.org/10.1145/1462027.1462029 (accessed 25 June 2013).

Kuhn, Virginia, 'The YouTube gaze: Permission to Create?', *Enculturation* 7 (2010), http://enculturation.gmu.edu/the-youtube-gaze (accessed 25 June 2013).

—, 'The Rhetoric of Remix', *TWC* 9 (2012), doi:10.3983/twc.2012.0358 (accessed 25 June 2013).

Lamb, Brian, 'Dr Mashup; or, Why Educators Should Learn to Stop Worrying and Love the Remix', *EDUCAUSE* 42.4 (2007): 13–24.

Lange, Patricia G., 'Videos of Affinity', in *The YouTube Reader*, 70–88.

Lanham, Richard A., *The Economics of Attention: Style and Substance in the Age of Information* (Chicago, 2007).

Lanier, Douglas, *Shakespeare and Modern Popular Culture* (Oxford, 2002).

—, 'Film Spin-offs and Citations', in *Shakespeares after Shakespeare* (2007), 132–7.

—, 'Recent Shakespeare Adaptation and the Mutations of Cultural Capital', *SSt* 38 (2010): 104–13.

—, 'Post-Textual Shakespeare', *SS* 64 (2011): 145–62.

Lehmann, Courtney, *Shakespeare Remains: Theatre to Film, Early Modern to Postmodern* (Ithaca, NY, 2002).

Lehmann, Courtney and Lisa Starks, eds, *Spectacular Shakespeare: Critical Theory and Popular Cinema* (Madison, NJ, 2002).

Lessig, Lawrence, *Remix: Making Art and Commerce Thrive in the Hybrid Economy* (London, 2008). Available at http://www.scribd.com/doc/47089238/Remix (accessed 25 June 2013).

Li, Stephanie, *Signifying without Specifying: Racial Discourse in the Age of Obama* (New Brunswick, NJ, 2012).

Lister, Martin et al., *New Media: A Critical Introduction* (London, 2009).

Loomba, Ania, *Shakespeare, Race, and Colonialism* (Oxford, 2002).

Lovink, G., *Networks Without a Cause* (London, 2011).

MacDonald, Joyce Green, 'Black Ram, White Ewe: Shakespeare, Race, and Women', in *A Feminist Companion to Shakespeare*, ed. Dympna Callaghan (Oxford, 2000), 188–207.

MacDonald, Russ, 'Planned Obsolescence or Working at the Words', in *Teaching Shakespeare: Passing it On*, 25–42.

Manovich, Lev, *The Language of New Media* (Cambridge, MA, 2001).

Marks, Elise, 'Othello/me: Racial Drag and the Pleasures of Boundary-Crossing with *Othello*', *Comparative Drama* 35.1 (2001): 101–23.

Marotti, Arthur, *Manuscript, Print and the English Renaissance Lyric* (Cornell, NY, 1995).

Marshall, Louise and Will Slocombe, 'From Passive to Active Voices: Technology, Community, and Literary Studies', in *Teaching Literature at a Distance: Open, Online and Blended Learning*, ed. Takis Kayalis and Anastasia Natsina (London, 2010), 99–112.

Maslen, R. W., *Shakespeare and Comedy* (London, 2006).

Massai, Sonia, 'Defining Local Shakespeares', in *World-Wide Shakespeares*, 3–11.

Masten, Jeffrey, 'More or Less Queer', in *Shakesqueer*, 309–18.

Mayer, Richard E., 'Applying the Science of Learning: Evidence-Based Principles for the Design of Multimedia Instruction', *American Psychologist* (2008): 760–9.

McLuhan, Marshall, *Understanding Media* (London, 1964).

McLuskie, Katherine, 'The Patriarchal Bard: Feminist Criticism and Shakespeare: *King Lear* and *Measure for Measure*', in *Political Shakespeare: Essays in Cultural Materialism*, ed. Jonathan Dollimore and Alan Sinfield (Manchester, 1994), 88–108.

—, 'Dancing and Thinking: Teaching "Shakespeare" in the Twenty-
    First Century', in *Teaching Shakespeare: Passing it On* (2009),
    121–41.

Menon, Madhavi, 'Introduction: Queer Shakes', in *Shakesqueer*,
    1–27.

Mercer, Kobena, 'Busy in the Ruins of Wretched Phantasia', in
    *Mirage: Enigmas of Race, Difference and Desire* (London,
    1995), 14–55.

Merchant, Guy, 'Unravelling the Social Network: Theory and
    Research', *Learning, Media and Technology* 37.1 (2012): 4–19.

Miller, Toby, 'Cybertarians of the World Unite: You Have Nothing
    to Lose but Your Tubes', in *The YouTube Reader*, 424–40.

Mitra, Barbara, Jenny Lewin Jones, Heather Barrett and Stella
    Williamson, 'The Use of Video to enable Deep Learning',
    *Research in Post-Compulsory Education* 15.4 (2010): 405–14.

Monk, Nicholas, Carol Rutter and Jonathan Neelands, *Open Space
    Learning* (London, 2011).

Morrison, Toni, 'Home', in *The House that Race Built*, ed.
    Wahneema Lubiano (New York, 1998), 3–12.

Munro, Lucy, 'Shakespeare and the Uses of the Past: Critical
    Approaches and Current Debates', *Shakespeare* 7.1 (2011): 102–25.

Murray, Janet H., *Hamlet on the Holodeck: The Future of
    Narrative in Cyberspace* (Cambridge, MA, 1997).

Naji, Jeneen, 'Interactive Poetry: New Content for New
    Technologies', in *Managing Media Economy, Media Content
    and Technology in the Age of Digital Convergence*, ed. Zvezdan
    Vukanovic and Paulo Faustino (Lisbon, 2011), 471–96.

Nakamura, Lisa, *Cybertypes: Race, Ethnicity and Identity on the
    Internet* (London, 2001).

—,*Digitizing Race: Visual Cultures of the Internet* (Minneapolis,
    2008).

Neill, Michael, 'Unproper Beds: Race, Adultery, and the Hideous in
    *Othello*', *SQ* 40 (1989): 383–412.

—, 'Postcolonial Shakespeare? Writing away from the Centre', in
    *Postcolonial Shakespeares* (1998), 164–85.

Newman, Karen, '"And Wash the Ethiop White": Femininity
    and the Monstrous in *Othello*', in *Essaying Shakespeare*
    (Minneapolis, 2009), 37–58.

Noronha, Emelia, 'The Poetics of "Videopoetry" and Video Blogs',
    2012 International Conference on Language, Medias and

Culture, *IPEDR* 33 (2012): 109–13, www.ipedr.com/vol33/
vol33–ICLMC2012–Contents.pdf (accessed 25 June 2013).

Novy, Marianne, *Engaging with Shakespeare: Responses of George
Eliot and Other Women Novelists* (Iowa City, 1998).

—, *Transforming Shakespeare: Contemporary Women's Re-Visions
in Literature and Performance* (New York, 1999).

Nowatzki, Robert, 'Paddy Jumps Jim Crow: Irish-Americans and
Blackface Minstrelsy', *Éire-Ireland* 41.3/4 (2007): 162–84.

*O*, dir. Time Blake Nelson (Lionsgate, 2001).

Oblinger, Diana G. and James L. Oblinger, eds, *Educating the Net
Generation* (Washington, DC, 2005).

O'Dair, Sharon, '"Pretty Much How the Internet Works"; Or,
Aiding and Abetting the Deprofessionalization of Shakespeare
Studies', *SS* 64 (2011): 83–96.

Olive, Sarah, 'Shakespeare and Lady Gaga', *Alluvium*, 1.1 (2012),
http://www.alluvium-journal.org/2012/06/01/shakespeare-and-
lady-gaga–2/ (accessed 25 June 2013).

O'Neill, Fionnuala, 'Review of Shakespeare's *Coriolanus* (adapted
for film and directed by Ralph Fiennes)', *Shakespeare* 8.4
(2012): 456–60.

O'Neill, Stephen, 'Uploading *Hamlet*: Agency, Convergence and
YouTube Shakespeare', *Anglistica* 15.2 (2011): 63–75, http://
www.anglistica.unior.it/content/uploading-hamlet-agency-
convergence-and-youtube-shakespeare (accessed 25 June
2013).

O'Rourke, James, 'Racism and Homophobia in *The Merchant of
Venice*', *ELH* 70 (2003): 375–97.

Osborne, Laurie, 'Clip Art: Theorizing the Shakespeare Film Clip',
*SQ* 53.2 (2002): 227–40.

Osche, Roger, 'Digital Shakespeare: Integrating Texts and
Technology', in *For all Time? Critical Issues in Teaching
Shakespeare*, ed. Peter Skrebels and Sieta van de Hoeven (Kent
Town, 2002), 44–54.

*Othello*, dir. Stuart Burge (Eagle Films, 1965).

*Othello*, dir. Oliver Parker (Castle Rock, 1995).

Pao, Angela, *No Safe Spaces: Re-casting Race, Ethnicity, and
Nationality in American Theatre* (Ann Arbor, MI, 2011).

Patterson, Don, 'Shakespeare's *Sonnets*', *Guardian*, 16 October
2010, http://www.guardian.co.uk/books/2010/oct/16/
shakespeare-sonnets-don-paterson (accessed 25 June 2013).

Pechter, Edward, '"Too Much Violence": Murdering Wives in *Othello*', in *Othello*, Norton Critical Edition, ed. Edward Pechter (New York, 2004), 366–87.

Peters, Kathrin and Andrea Seier, 'Home Dance: Mediacy and Aesthetics of the Self on YouTube', in *YouTube Reader*, 187–203.

Pfister, Manfred and Jürgen Gutsch, eds, *William Shakespeare's 'Sonnets' for the First Time Globally Reprinted: A Quatercentenary Anthology 1609–2009*, with a DVD (Dozwil, Switzerland, 2009).

Phelan, Peggy, *Unmarked: the Politics of Performance* (London and New York, 1993).

Pipher, Mary, *Reviving Ophelia: Saving the Selves of Adolescent Girls* (New York, 1994).

Prensky, Marc, 'Digital Natives, Digital Immigrants', *On the Horizon* 9.5 (2001), http://www.marcprensky.com/writing/ (accessed 25 June 2013).

Prescott, Paul, 'Shakespeare and Popular Culture', in *New Cambridge Companion to Shakespeare*, 269–85.

*Prince of the Himalays*, dir. Sherwood Hu (Shanghai Film Studios, 2006).

Purcell, Stephen, *Popular Shakespeare: Simulation and Subversion on the Modern Stage* (Basingstoke, 2009).

*Renaissance Man*, dir. Penny Marshall (Touchstone, 1994).

Rhodes, Neil and Jonathan Sawday, eds, *The Renaissance Computer: Knowledge Technology in the First Age of Print* (London, 2000).

Richmond Macrae, Hugh, 'The Audience's Role in *Othello*', in *Othello: New Critical Essays*, ed. Philip C. Kolin (New York, 2002).

Roberts, Josephine A., '"Thou maist have thy Will": The Sonnets of Shakespeare and his Stepsisters', *SQ* 47.4 (1996): 412–15.

Romanska, Magda, 'NercOphelia: Death, Femininity and the Making of Modern Aesthetics', *Performance Research* 10.3 (2005): 35–53.

*Romeo + Juliet*, dir. Baz Luhrmann (Twentieth Century Fox, 1996).

Rosmarin, Adena, 'Hermeneutics versus Erotics: Shakespeare's *Sonnets* and Interpretative History', *PMLA* 100 (1985): 20–37.

Rowe, Katherine, '"Remember me": Technologies of Memory in Michael Almereyda's *Hamlet*', in *Shakespeare: The Movie II* (2003), 37–55.

—, 'Crowd-Sourcing Shakespeare: Screen Work and Screen Play in Second Life', *SSt* 38 (2010): 58–67, http://www.brynmawr.edu/english/Faculty_and_Staff/rowe/CrowdSourcing.html.

—, 'Shakespeare and Media History', in *New Cambridge Companion to Shakespeare* (2010), 303–25.

Rowe, Katherine and Thomas Cartelli, *New Wave Shakespeare on Screen* (London, 2007).

RSC (Royal Shakespeare Company), *Shakespeare: A Worldwide Classroom*, http://www.rsc.org.uk/education/research-case-studies/how-the-world-teaches-shakespeare/worldwide-classroom.aspx (accessed 25 June 2013).

—, *Stand Up for Shakespeare* http://www.rsc.org.uk/education/sufs/ (accessed 25 June 2013).

Rumbold, Kate, 'From "Access" to "Creativity": Shakespeare Institutions, New Media, and the Language of Cultural Value', *SQ* 63.1 (2010): 313–36.

—, 'Brand Shakespeare?', *SS* 64 (2011): 25–37.

Rutter, Carol Chillington, *Enter the Body: Women and Representation on Shakespeare's Stage* (London, 2001).

Ryan, Kiernan, *Shakespeare*, 3rd edn (Basingstoke, 2002).

Sanders, Julie, *Adaptation and Appropriation* (London, 2006).

—, *Shakespeare and Music: Afterlives and Borrowings* (Cambridge, 2007).

Schwarz, Kathyrn, 'Will in Overplus: Recasting Misogyny in Shakespeare's *Sonnets*', *ELH* 75.3 (2008): 737–66.

Sedgwick, Eve Kosofsky, *Between Men: English Literature and Male Homosocial Desire* (New York, 1985).

Selwyn, Neil, 'Faceworking: Exploring Students' Education-Related Use of Facebook', *Learning, Media And Technology*, 34.2 (2009): 157–74.

Senft, Theresa M, *Camgirls: Celebrity and Community in the Age of Social Networks* (New York, 2008).

Shakespeare, *Alls Well That End's Well*, ed. G. K. Hunter (London, 1967).

Shakespeare, *As You Like It*, ed. Juliet Dusinbere (London, 2006).

Shakespeare, *Coriolanus*, ed. Peter Holland (London, 2013).

Shakespeare, *Cymbeline*, ed. J. M. Nosworthy (London, 1969).

Shakespeare, *Hamlet*, ed. Ann Thompson and Neil Taylor (London, 2006).

Shakespeare, *Love's Labour's Lost*, ed. H. R. Woudhusyen (London, 1998).

Shakespeare, *Macbeth*, ed. Kenneth Muir (London, 1962).

Shakespeare, *Measure for Measure*, ed. J. W. Lever (London, 1965).

Shakespeare, *The Merchant of Venice*, ed. John Drakakis (London, 2010).

Shakespeare, *Othello*, ed. E. A. J. Honingman (London, 1997).

Shakespeare, *Romeo and Juliet*, ed. Rene Weis (London, 2012).

Shakespeare, *Sonnets*, ed. Katherine Duncan-Jones (London, 1997).

Shakespeare, *Titus Andronicus*, ed. Jonathan Bate (London, 1995).

Shakespeare, *Twelfth Night*, ed. Keir Elam (London, 2008).

*Shakespeare in Love*, dir. John Madden (Miramax, 1998).

Shaugnessy, Robert, ed. *The Cambridge Companion to Shakespeare and Popular Culture* (Cambridge, 2007).

Shifman, Limor, 'Anatomy of a YouTube Meme', *New Media Society* 14.2 (2011): 187–203.

Shiga, John, 'Copy-and-Persist: the Logic of Mash-Up Culture', *Critical Studies in Media Communication* 24.2 (2007): 93–114.

Shohet, Lauren, 'YouTube, Use, and the Idea of the Archive', *SQ* 38 (2010): 337–56.

Showalter, Elaine, 'Representing Ophelia: Women, Madness, and the Responsibilities of Feminist Criticism', in *Shakespeare and the Question of Theory*, ed. Geoffrey Hartman and Patricia Parker (London, 1985), 77–94.

Silverstone, Catherine, 'Shakespeare Live: Reproducing Shakespeare at the "new" Globe', *Textual Practice* 19.1 (2005): 31–50.

Simanowski, Roberto, *Digital Art and Meaning: Reading Kinetic Poetry, Text Machines, Mapping Art, and Interactive Installations* (Minneapolis, 2011).

Sinfield, Alan, *Shakespeare, Authority and Sexuality: Unfinished Business in Cultural Materialism* (London, 2006).

Skrebels, Paul, 'Shakespeare Reworked: Textual Intervention Strategies in the University Writing Classroom', in *For all Time? Critical Issues in Teaching Shakespeare*, 55–67.

Smith, Ian, 'Barbarian Errors: Performing Race in Early Modern England', *SQ* 49.2 (1998): 168–86.

Snickars, Pelle and Patrick Vonderau, eds, *The YouTube Reader* (Stockholm, 2009).

Spence, Lester K., *Stare in the Darkness: The Limits of Hip-Hop and Black Politics* (Minneapolis, 2011).

Stallybrass, Peter, 'Editing as Cultural Formation: The Sexing of Shakespeare's *Sonnets*', *MLQ* 54.1 (1993): 91–103.

Stanivuković, Goran, 'Beyond Sodomy: What is Still Queer about Early Modern Queer Studies', in *Queer Renaissance Historiography: Backward Gaze*, ed. Stephen Guy-Bray, Vin Nardizzi and Will Stockton (Farnham, Surrey, 2009), 42–65.

Stern, Tiffany, 'Teaching Shakespeare in Higher Education', in *Shakespeare in Education*, ed. Martin Blocksidge (London, 2005), 120–40.

Stockton, Will, 'Shakespeare and Queer Theory', *SQ* 63.2 (2012): 224–35.

Strangelove, Michael, *Watching YouTube: Extraordinary Videos by Ordinary People* (Toronto, 2010).

Streete, Adrian, 'The Politics of Ethical Presentism: Appropriation, Spirituality and the Case of *Antony and Cleopatra*', *Textual Practice* 22.3 (2008): 405–31.

Strehovec, Janez, 'Text as Loop/On the Digital Poetry', *Proceedings of the Fifth International Digital Arts and Culture Conference* (Melbourne, Australia, 19–23 May 2003), http://hypertext.rmit.edu.au/dac/papers/n.pdf (accessed 25 June 2013).

Sullivan, Ceri, 'The Importance of Boredom in Learning about The Early Modern', in *Teaching the Early Modern Period*, 222–4.

Tadros, Marilyn, 'A Social Media Approach to Higher Education', in *Cutting-Edge Technologies in Higher Education*, 83–106.

Tapscott, Don, *Grown Up Digital: How the Net Generation is Changing Your World* (New York, 2009).

Tarleton, Gillespie, 'The Relevance of Algorithms', http://culturedigitally.org/2012/11/the-relevance-of-algorithms/ (accessed 25 June 2013).

Taylor, Gary, *Buying Whiteness: Race, Culture, and Identity from Columbus to Hip-Hop* (New York, 2005).

Teague, Fran, 'Using Shakespeare with Memes, Remixes and Fanfic', *SS* 64 (2011): 74–82.

Thacker, David, 'The Director's Cut: Interviews with David Thacker and Darko Tresnjak', in *The Merchant of Venice*, ed. Jonathan Bate and Eric Rasmussen (Basingstoke, 2010), 140–56.

Thew, Neil, *Teaching Shakespeare: A Survey of the Undergraduate Level in Higher Education*, The Higher Education Academy (London, 2006).

Thompson, Ayanna, *Passing Strange: Shakespeare, Race and Contemporary America* (Oxford, 2011).

—, 'To Notice or Not To Notice: Shakespeare, Black Actors, and Performance', *Borrowers and Lenders* 4.1 (2008), http://www.borrowers.uga.edu/7157/toc (accessed 25 June 2013).

Toffoletti, Kim, *Cyborgs and Barbie Dolls: Feminism, Popular Culture and the Posthuman Body* (London, 2007).

Toner, Terri L. and Caroline Lego Munoz, 'Facebook and Education: A Classroom Connection', in *Cutting-Edge Technologies in Higher Education*, 33–57.

Traub, Valerie, 'Sex without Issue: Sodomy, Reproduction, and Signification in Shakespeare's *Sonnets*', in *Shakespeare's 'Sonnets': Critical Essays*, 431–54.

Urla, Jacqueline and Alan C. Swedlund, 'The Anthropometry of Barbie: Unsettling Ideals of the Feminine Body in Popular Culture', in *A Reader in Promoting Public Health: Challenges and Controversy*, ed. Jenny Douglas et al. (London, 2007), 123–32.

Vaidhyanathan, Siva, *The Googlization of Everything* (Berkeley, 2011)

van Dijck, Jose, '"You" as in YouTube: Defining User Agency in Social Media', in *Managing Media Economy, Media Content and Technology in the Age of Digital Convergence*, ed. Zvezdan Vukanovic and Paulo Faustino (Lisbon, 2011), 291–318.

Vaughan, Virginia Mason, 'Review of Ayanna Thompson, *Passing Strange*', *SQ* 63.2 (2012): 244–6.

Wasko, Janet and Mary Erickson, 'The Political Economy of YouTube', in *The YouTube Reader*, 372–86.

Wegenstein, Bernadette, *Getting Under the Skin: The Body and Media Theory* (Cambridge, MA, 2006).

Wesch, Michael, 'An Anthropological Introduction to YouTube', http://www.youtube.com/watch?v=TPAO-lZ4_hU&feature=player_embedded (accessed 25 June 2013).

Wetmore, Kevin J., 'Big Willie Style: Staging HipHop Shakespeare and Being Down with the Bard', in *Alternative Shakespeares*, Vol. 3, ed. Diana E. Henderson (London, 2008), 147–69.

Whintrop Young, Geoffrey, 'Hardware/Software/ Wetware', in *Critical Terms for Media Studies*, 186–98.

Winnubust, Shannon, 'Is the Mirror Racist? Interrogating the Space of Whiteness', *Philosophy Social Criticism* 30 (2004): 25–50.

Wise, Tim, *Colorblind: The Rise of Post-Racial Politics and the Retreat from Racial Equality* (San Francisco, 2010).

Wray, Ramona, 'Communicating Differences: Gender, Feminism, and Queer Studies in the Changing Shakespeare Curriculum', in *Teaching Shakespeare: Passing It On*, 142–59.

Yates, Julian, 'More Life: Shakespeare's Sonnet Machines', in Menon, *Shakesqueer*, 332–42.

*Yes Sir, Mr Bones*, dir. Ron Ormond (Spartan, 1951).

Young, Alan R., 'Ophelia and Popular Culture', http://www.opheliapopularculture.com/ (accessed 25 June 2013).

Younge, Gary, 'Who thinks about the consquences of online racism?', *Guardian*, 12 July 2012, http://www.guardian.co.uk/commentisfree/2012/jul/12/consequences-of-online-racism (accessed 25 June 2013).

YouTube, *Gen V Research Men 18–34 The On-Demand Video Consumer* (May 2012), http://www.youtube.com/yt/advertise/research.html (accessed 25 June 2013).

—, Terms, http://www.youtube.com/t/terms (accessed 25 June 2013).

Zhou, Renjie, Samamon Khemmarat and Lixin Gao, 'The Impact of YouTube Recommendation System on Video Views', *Proceedings of the 10th ACM SIGCOMM Conference on Internet Measurement* (Melbourne, 2010), 404–10.

Ziegler, Susan G., 'The (mis)education of Generation M', *Learning, Media and Technology* 32.1 (2007): 69–81.

# INDEX